SWORD MASTER

GOD OF WAR

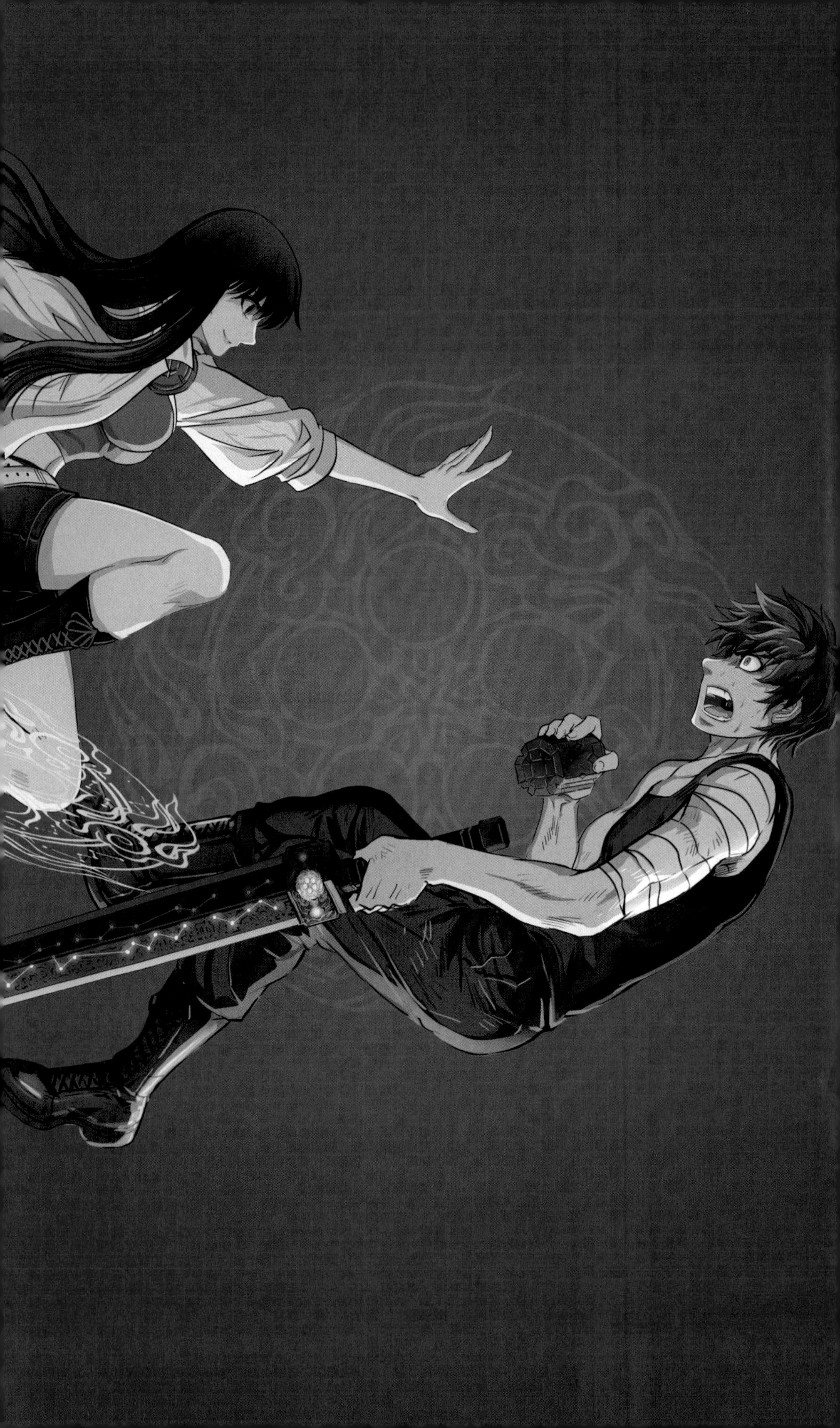

SWORD MASTER
GOD OF WAR

SHUIZHU
WRITER

GUNJI
ARTIST

AMY CHU
ADAPTATION

VC's **TRAVIS LANHAM**
LETTERER

GUNJI
COVER ART

MARTIN BIRO & **TOM GRONEMAN**
ASSISTANT EDITORS

MARK PANICCIA
EDITOR

SPECIAL THANKS TO
WINNI WOO, YIFAN JIANG & **ALEXANDER CHANG**

COLLECTION EDITOR JENNIFER GRÜNWALD
ASSISTANT EDITOR DANIEL KIRCHHOFFER
ASSISTANT MANAGING EDITOR MAIA LOY
ASSISTANT MANAGING EDITOR LISA MONTALBANO
VP PRODUCTION & SPECIAL PROJECTS JEFF YOUNGQUIST
BOOK DESIGNER STACIE ZUCKER WITH ADAM DEL RE
SVP PRINT, SALES & MARKETING DAVID GABRIEL
EDITOR IN CHIEF C.B. CEBULSKI

SWORD MASTER VOL. 2: GOD OF WAR. Contains material originally published in magazine form as SWORD MASTER (2019) #7-12. First printing 2020. ISBN 978-1-302-91949-8. Published by MARVEL WORLDWIDE, INC., a subsidiary of MARVEL ENTERTAINMENT, LLC. OFFICE OF PUBLICATION: 1290 Avenue of the Americas, New York, NY 10104. © 2020 MARVEL No similarity between any of the names, characters, persons, and/or institutions in this magazine with those of any living or dead person or institution is intended, and any such similarity which may exist is purely coincidental. **Printed in Canada.** KEVIN FEIGE, Chief Creative Officer; DAN BUCKLEY, President, Marvel Entertainment; JOE QUESADA, EVP & Creative Director; DAVID BOGART, Associate Publisher & SVP of Talent Affairs; TOM BREVOORT, VP, Executive Editor; NICK LOWE, Executive Editor, VP of Content, Digital Publishing; DAVID GABRIEL, VP of Print & Digital Publishing; JEFF YOUNGQUIST, VP of Production & Special Projects; ALEX MORALES, Director of Publishing Operations; DAN EDINGTON, Managing Editor; RICKEY PURDIN, Director of Talent Relations; JENNIFER GRÜNWALD, Senior Editor, Special Projects; SUSAN CRESPI, Production Manager; STAN LEE, Chairman Emeritus. For information regarding advertising in Marvel Comics or on Marvel.com, please contact Vit DeBellis, Custom Solutions & Integrated Advertising Manager, at vdebellis@marvel.com. For Marvel subscription inquiries, please call 888-511-5480. **Manufactured between 11/27/2020 and 12/29/2020 by SOLISCO PRINTERS, SCOTT, QC, CANADA.**

10 9 8 7 6 5 4 3 2 1

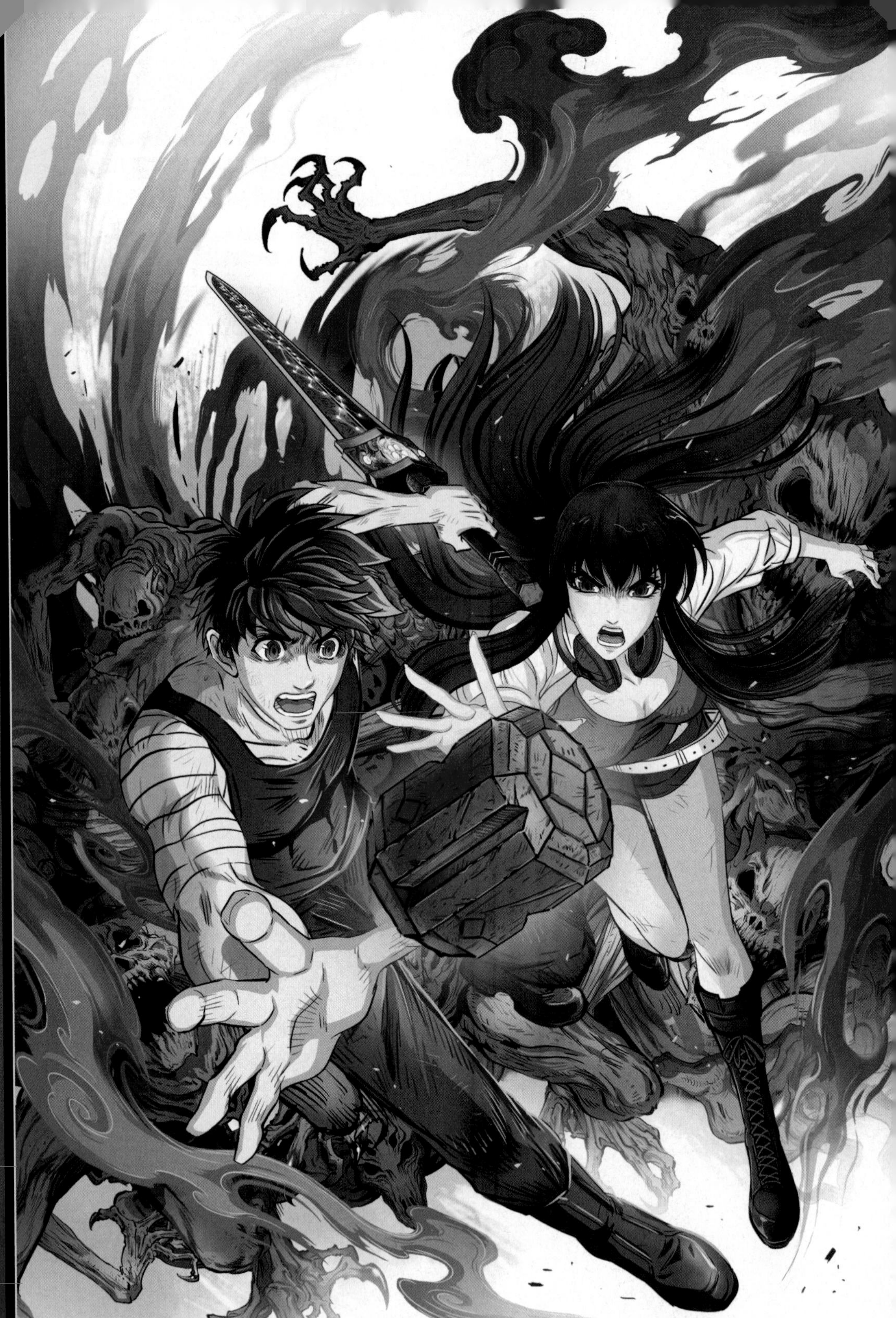

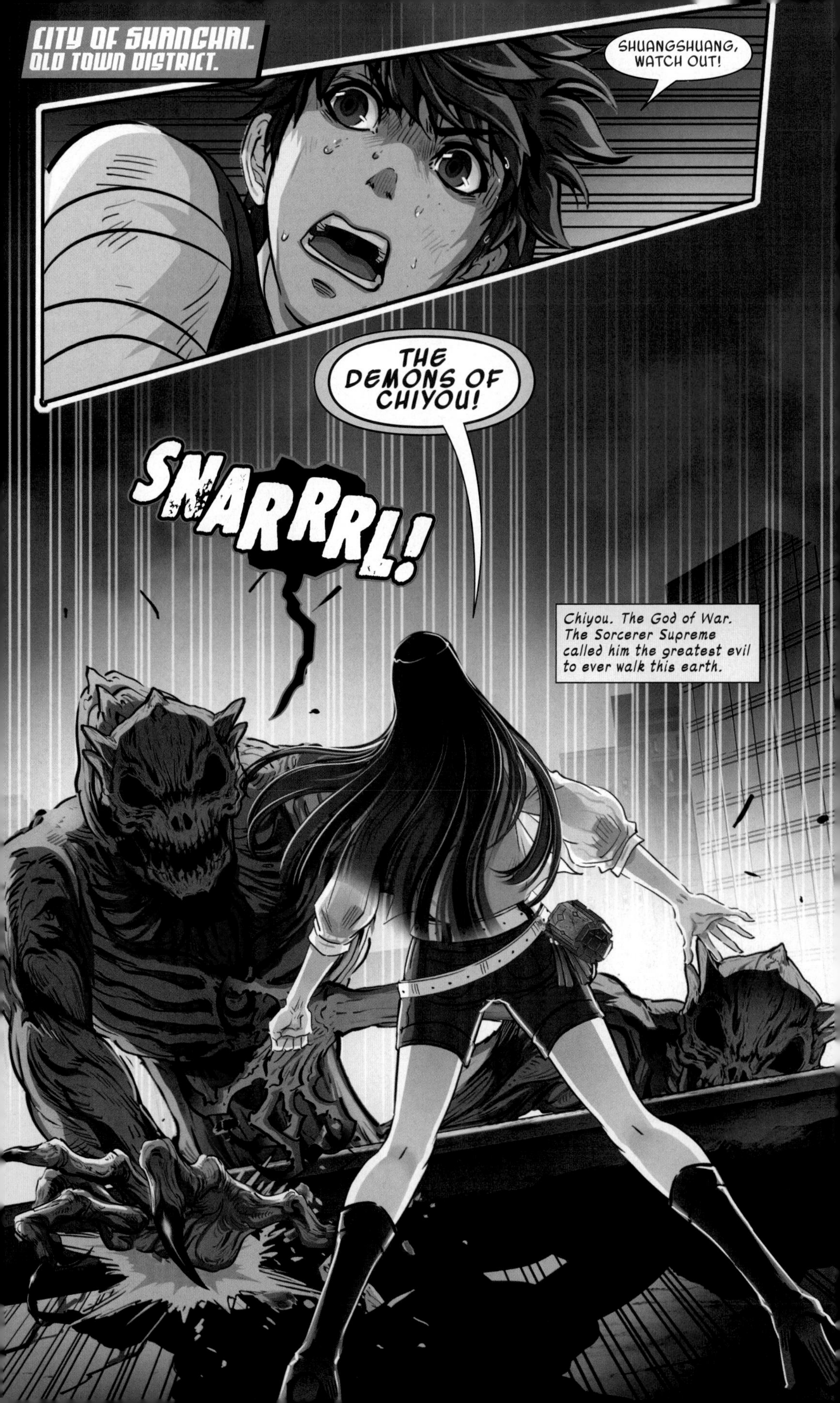
CITY OF SHANGHAI.
OLD TOWN DISTRICT.
SHUANGSHUANG, WATCH OUT!
THE DEMONS OF CHIYOU!
SNARRRL!
Chiyou. The God of War. The Sorcerer Supreme called him the greatest evil to ever walk this earth.

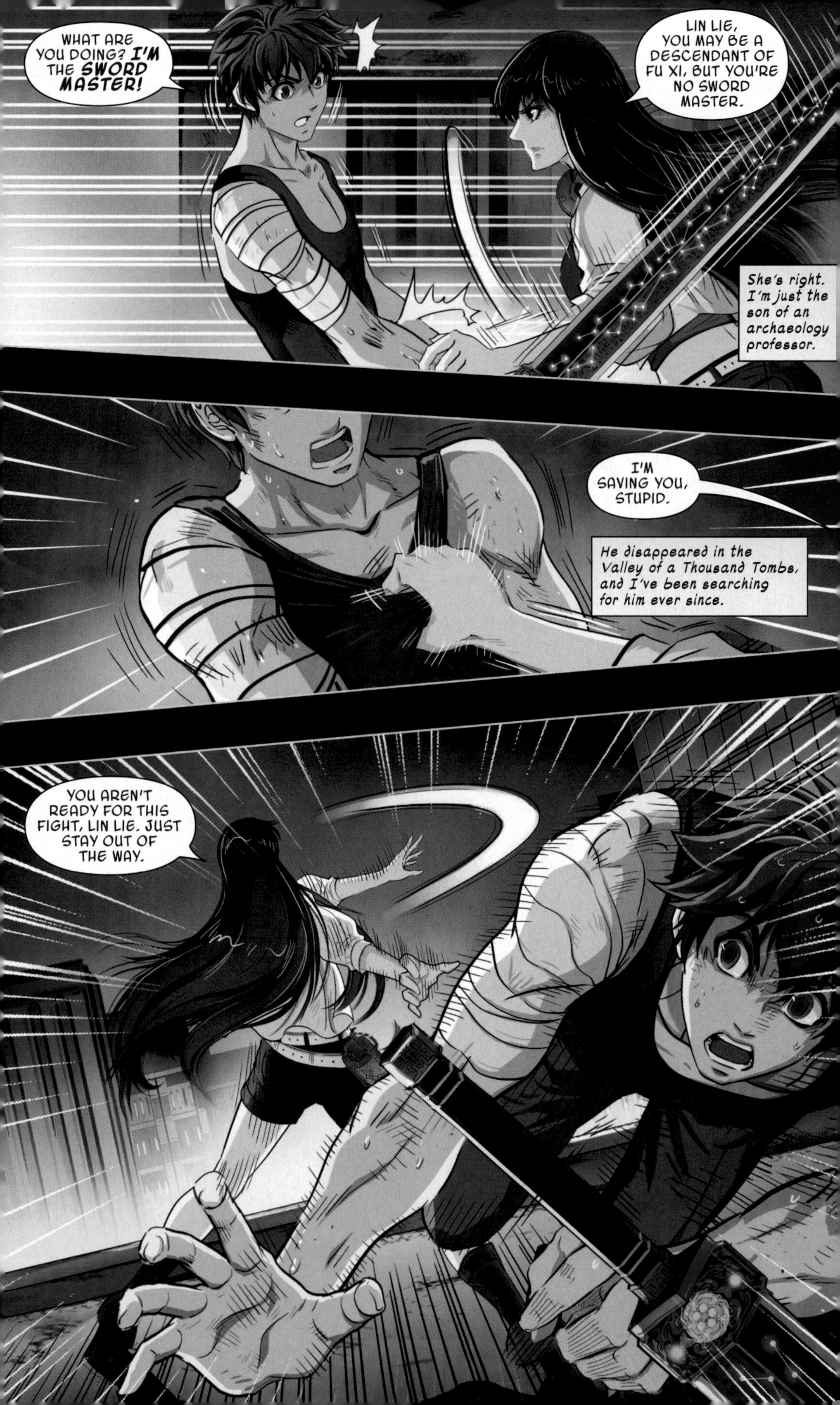

WHAT ARE YOU DOING? I'M THE SWORD MASTER!
LIN LIE, YOU MAY BE A DESCENDANT OF FU XI, BUT YOU'RE NO SWORD MASTER.
She's right. I'm just the son of an archaeology professor.
I'M SAVING YOU, STUPID.
He disappeared in the Valley of a Thousand Tombs, and I've been searching for him ever since.
YOU AREN'T READY FOR THIS FIGHT, LIN LIE. JUST STAY OUT OF THE WAY.

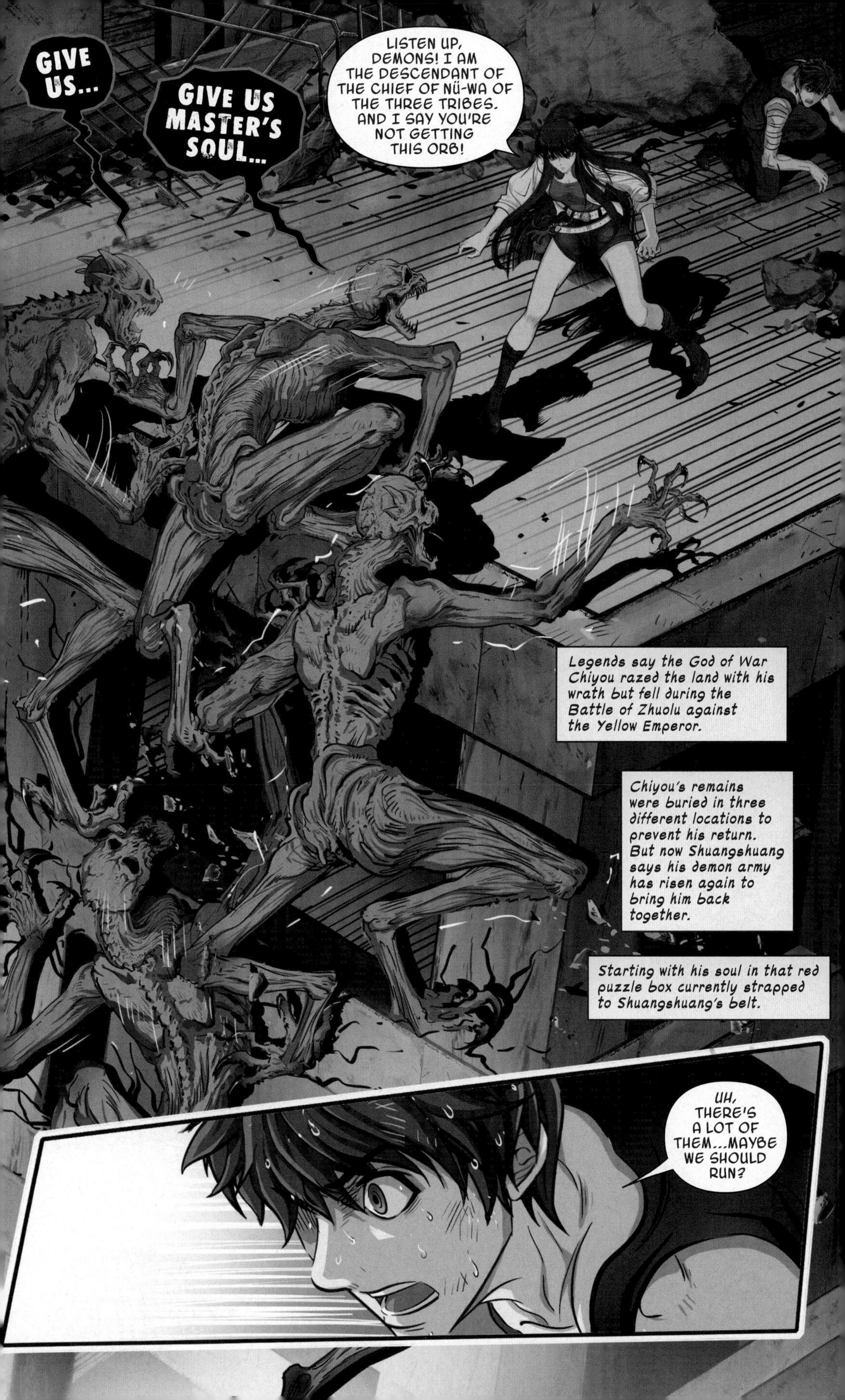
GIVE US...
GIVE US MASTER'S SOUL...
LISTEN UP, DEMONS! I AM THE DESCENDANT OF THE CHIEF OF NÜ-WA OF THE THREE TRIBES. AND I SAY YOU'RE NOT GETTING THIS ORB!
Legends say the God of War Chiyou razed the land with his wrath but fell during the Battle of Zhuolu against the Yellow Emperor.
Chiyou's remains were buried in three different locations to prevent his return. But now Shuangshuang says his demon army has risen again to bring him back together.
Starting with his soul in that red puzzle box currently strapped to Shuangshuang's belt.
UH, THERE'S A LOT OF THEM...MAYBE WE SHOULD RUN?

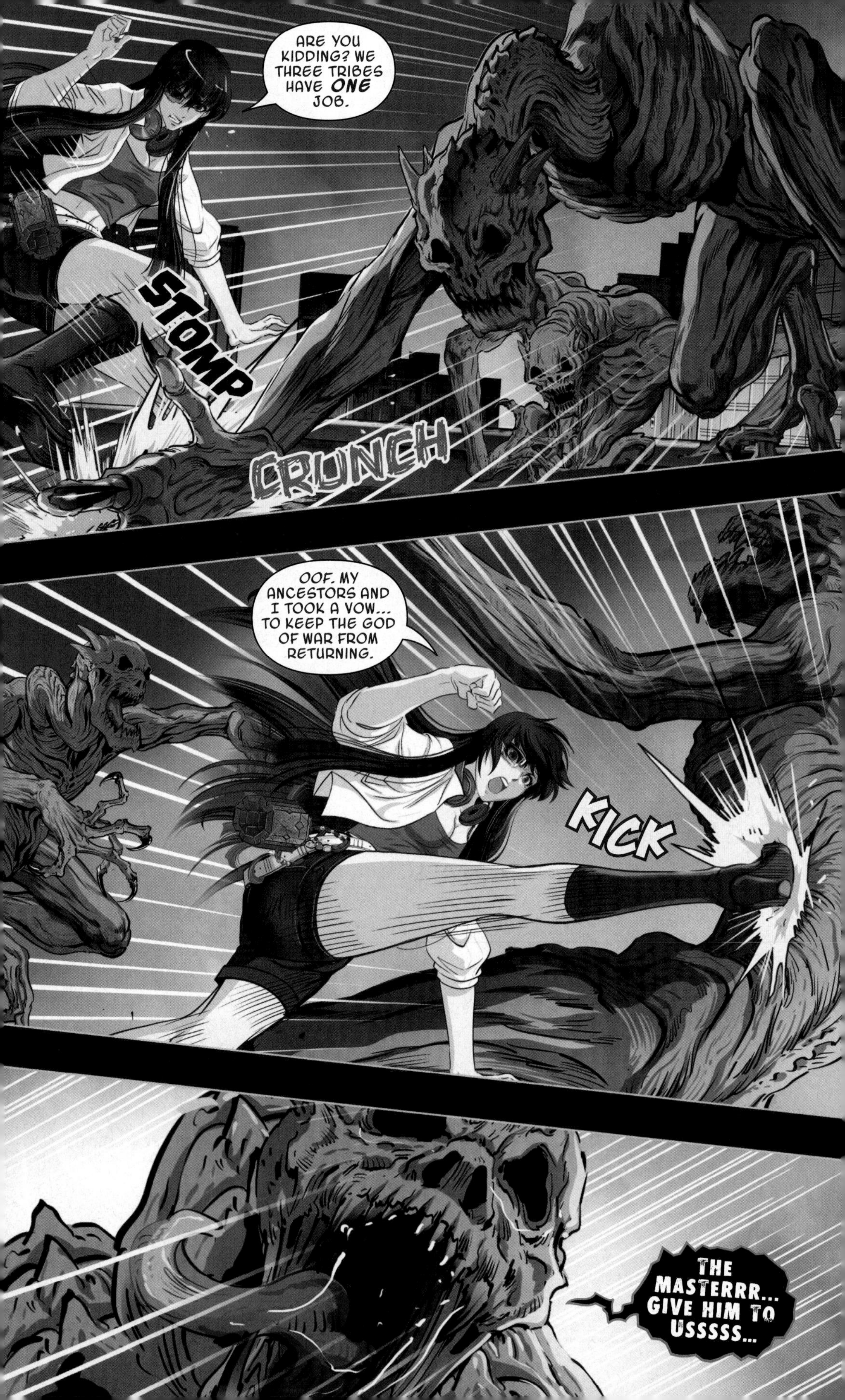
ARE YOU KIDDING? WE THREE TRIBES HAVE ONE JOB.
STOMP
CRUNCH
OOF. MY ANCESTORS AND I TOOK A VOW... TO KEEP THE GOD OF WAR FROM RETURNING.
KICK
THE MASTERRR... GIVE HIM TO USSSSS...

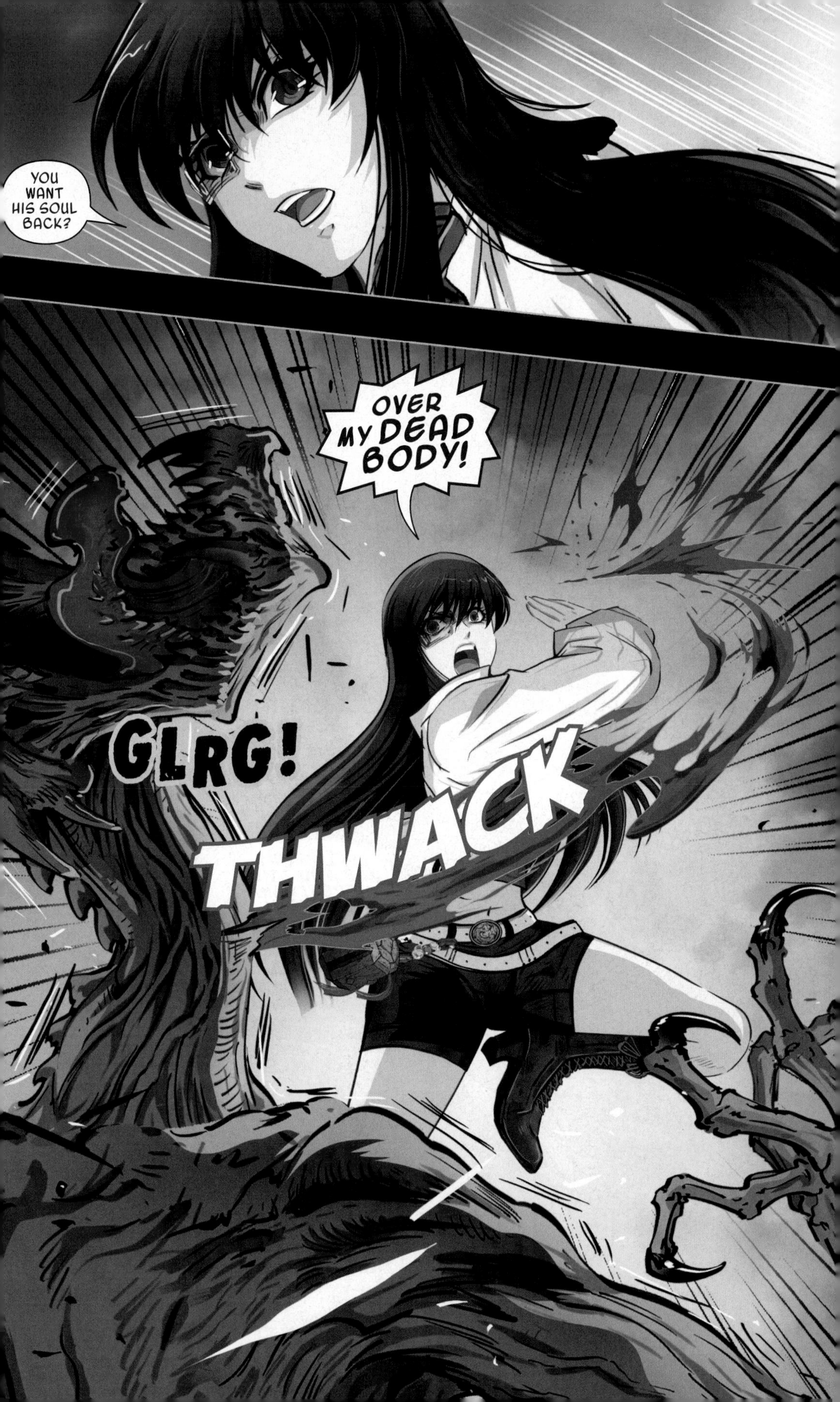
YOU WANT HIS SOUL BACK?
OVER MY DEAD BODY!
GLRG!
THWACK

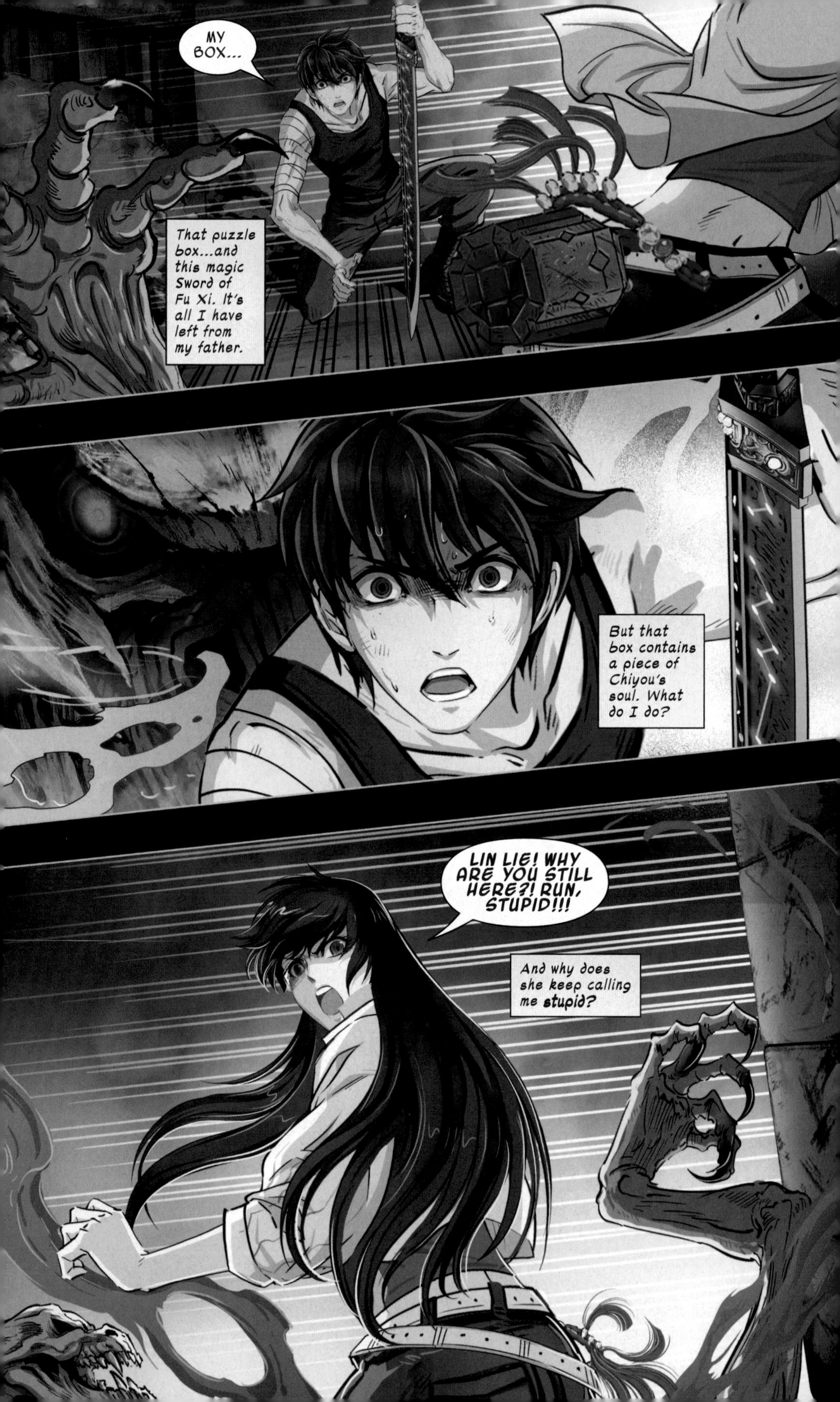
MY BOX...
That puzzle box...and this magic Sword of Fu Xi. It's all I have left from my father.
But that box contains a piece of Chiyou's soul. What do I do?
LIN LIE! WHY ARE YOU STILL HERE?! RUN, STUPID!!!
And why does she keep calling me stupid?

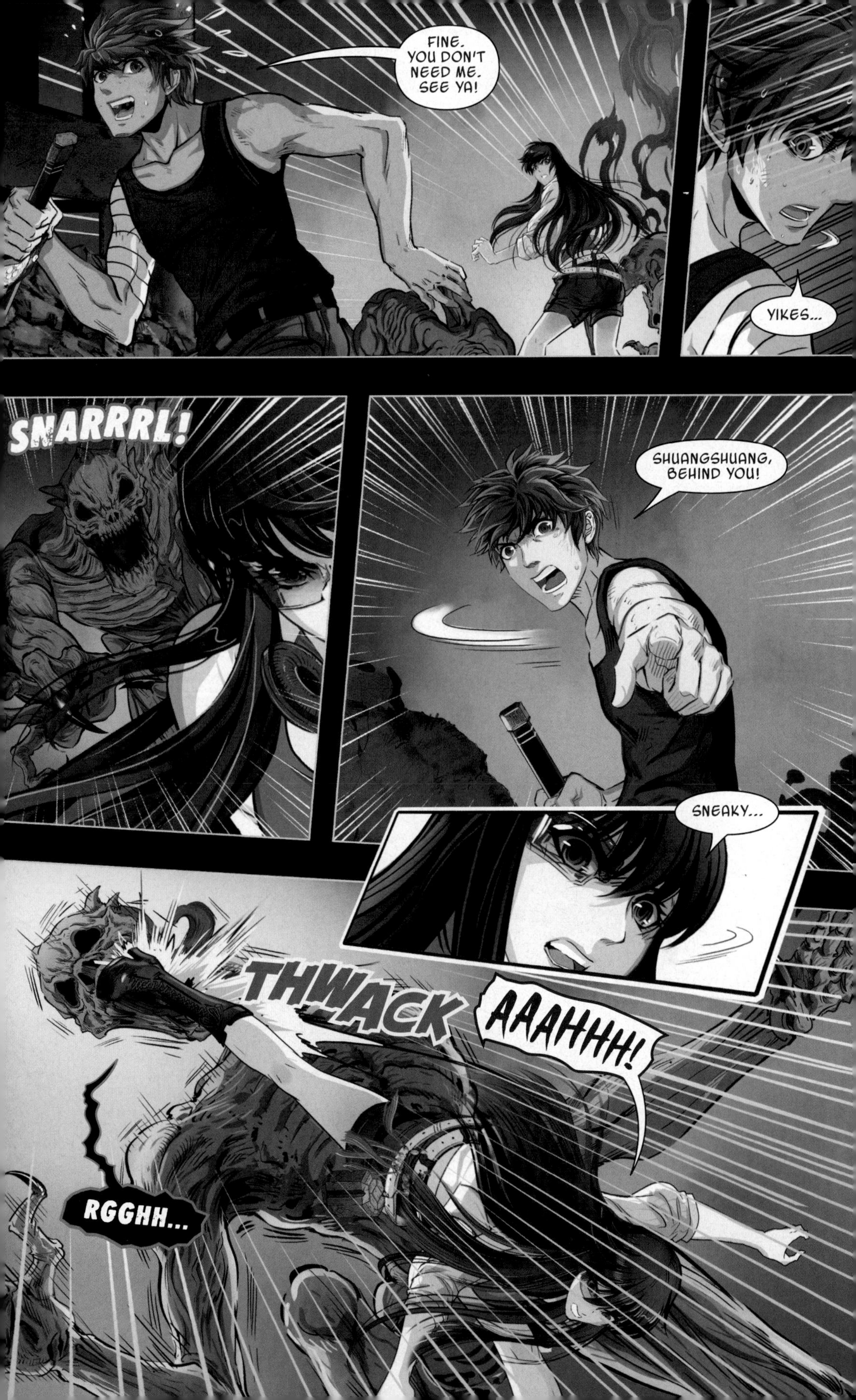
FINE. YOU DON'T NEED ME. SEE YA!
YIKES...
SNARRRL!
SHUANGSHUANG, BEHIND YOU!
SNEAKY...
THWACK
AAAHHH!
RGGHH...

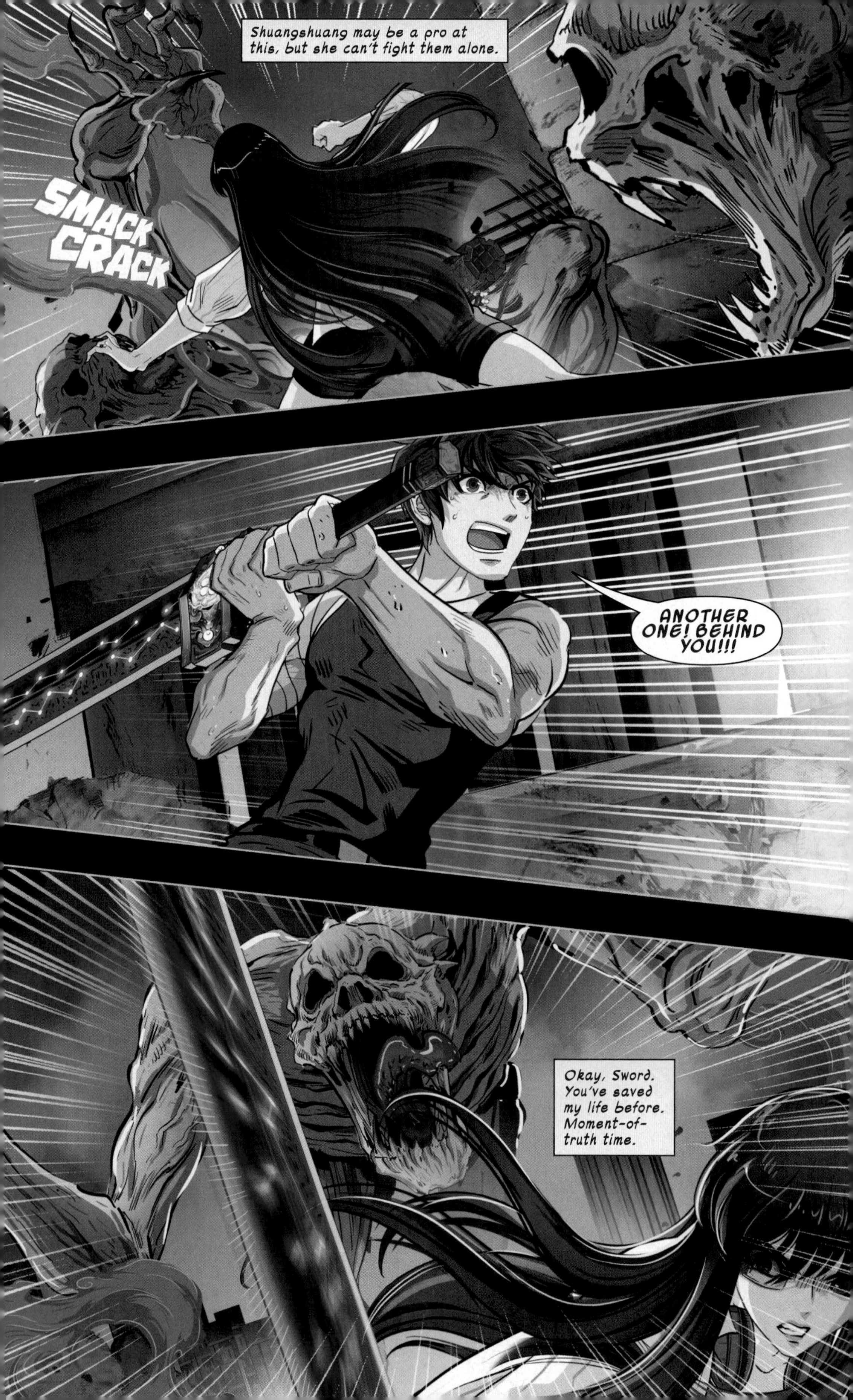
Shuangshuang may be a pro at this, but she can't fight them alone.
SMACK
CRACK
ANOTHER ONE! BEHIND YOU!!!
Okay, Sword. You've saved my life before. Moment-of-truth time.

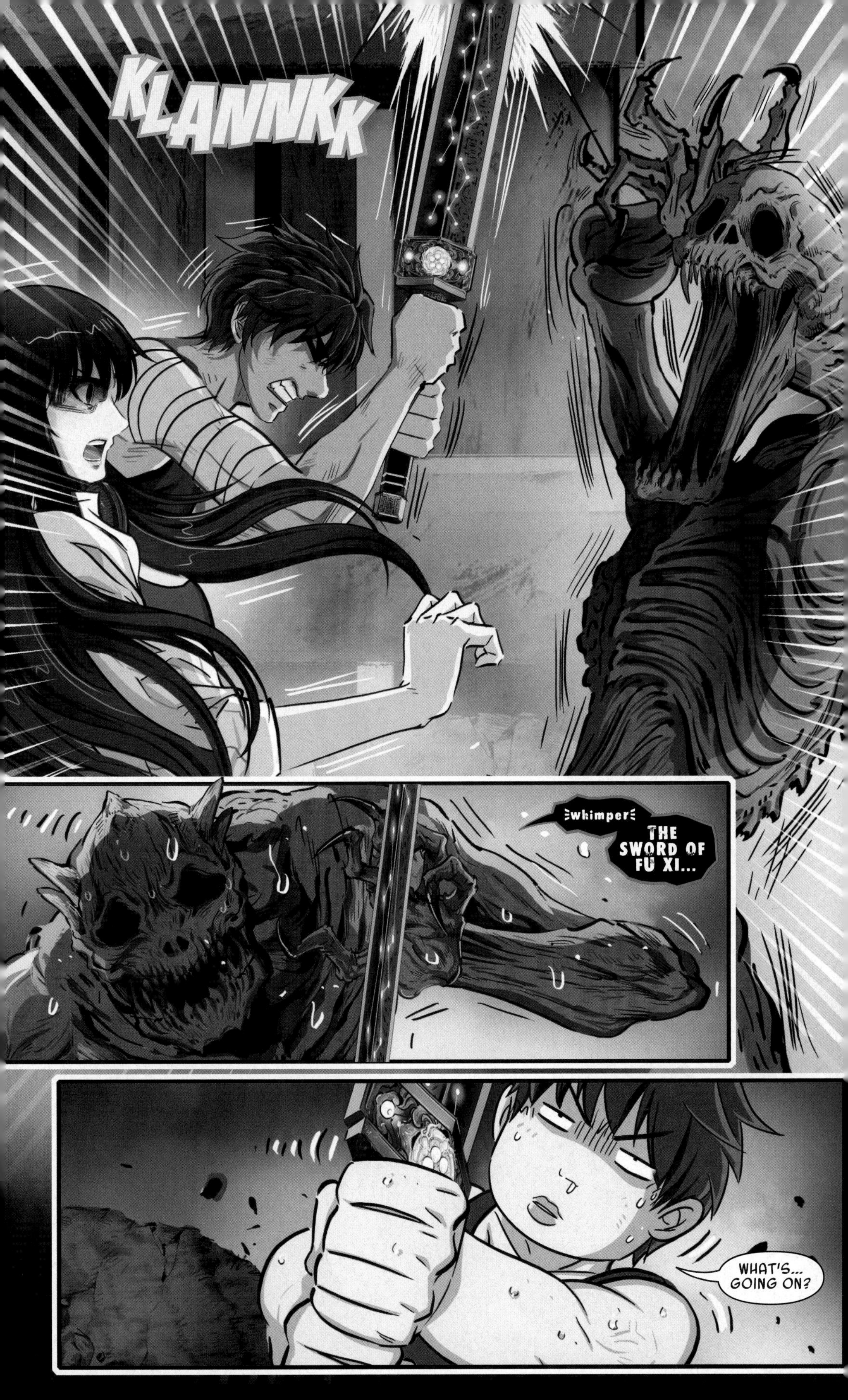
KLANNKK
whimper
THE SWORD OF FU XI...
WHAT'S... GOING ON?

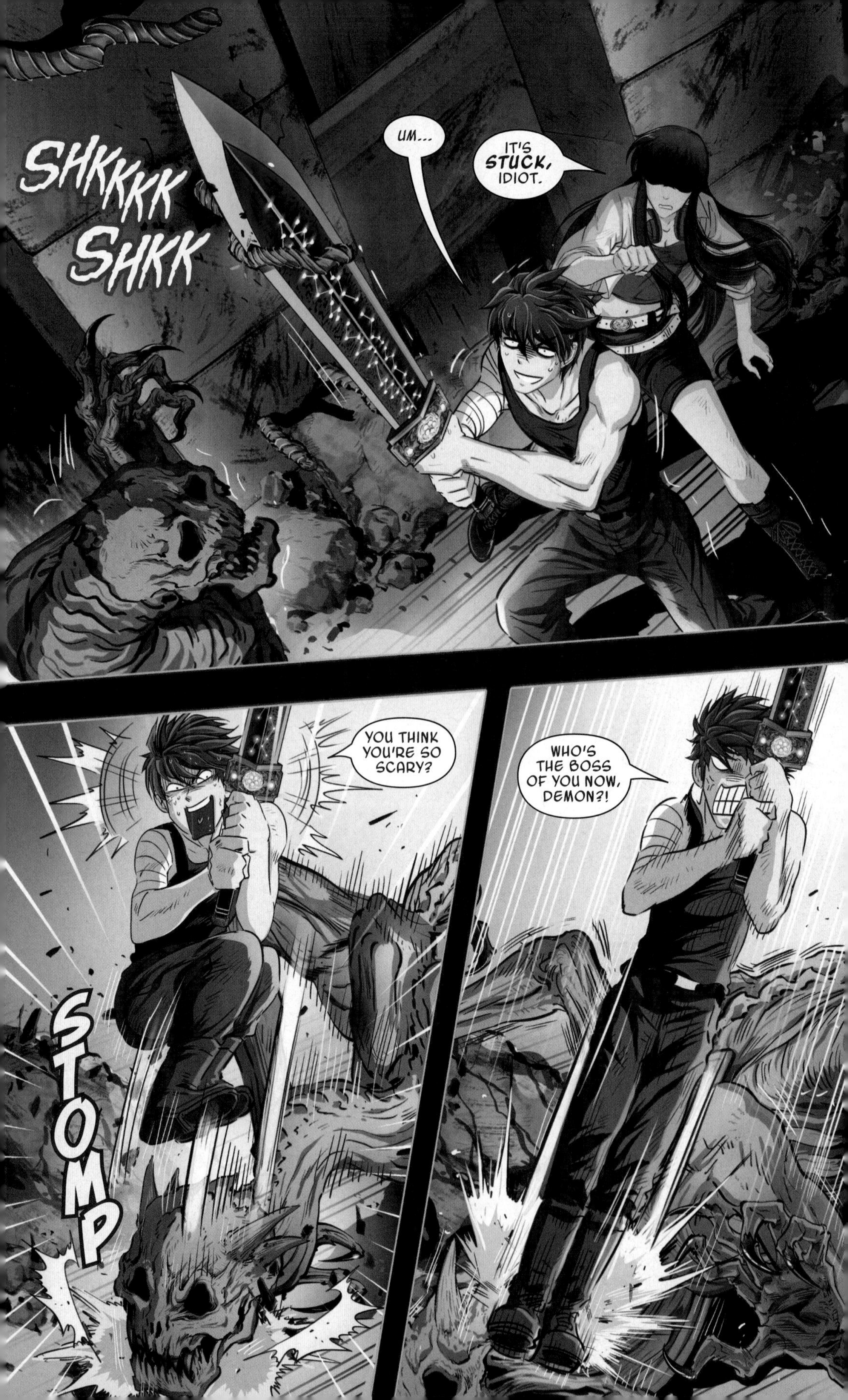
SHKKKK SHKK
UM...
IT'S STUCK, IDIOT.
YOU THINK YOU'RE SO SCARY?
STOMP
WHO'S THE BOSS OF YOU NOW, DEMON?!

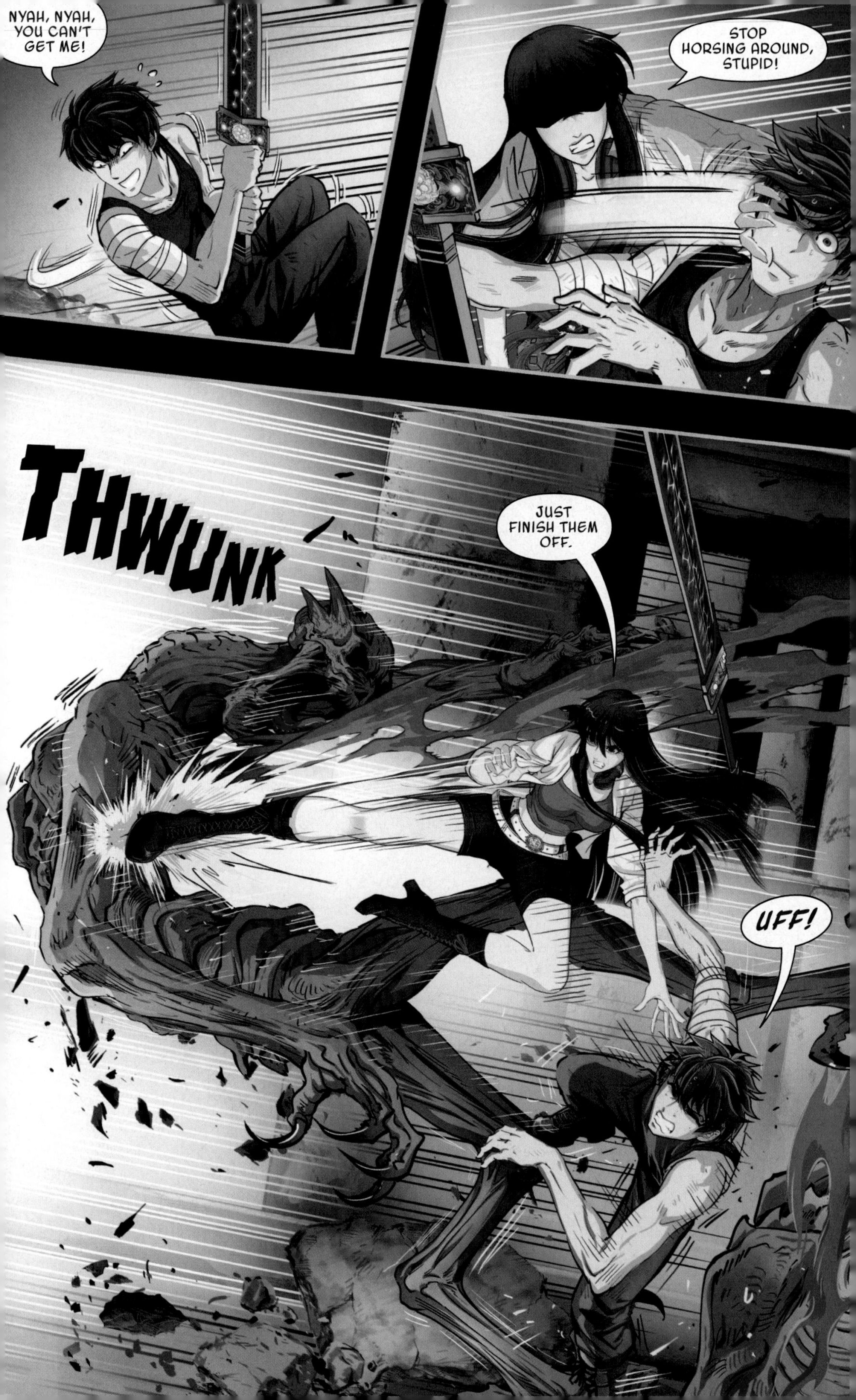

NYAH, NYAH, YOU CAN'T GET ME!
STOP HORSING AROUND, STUPID!
THWUNK
JUST FINISH THEM OFF.
UFF!

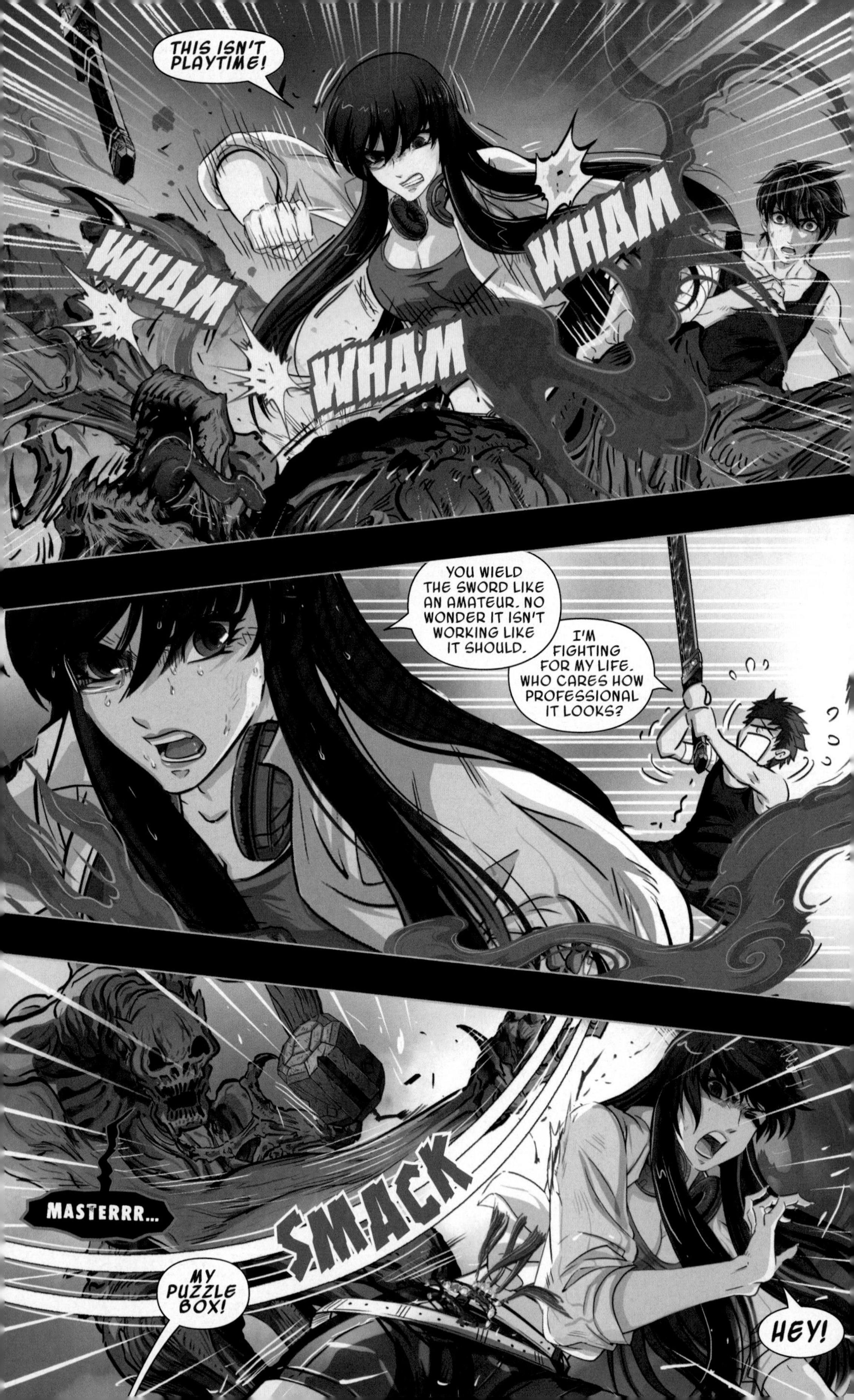
THIS ISN'T PLAYTIME!
WHAM
WHAM
WHAM
YOU WIELD THE SWORD LIKE AN AMATEUR. NO WONDER IT ISN'T WORKING LIKE IT SHOULD.
I'M FIGHTING FOR MY LIFE. WHO CARES HOW PROFESSIONAL IT LOOKS?
MASTERRR...
SMACK
MY PUZZLE BOX!
HEY!

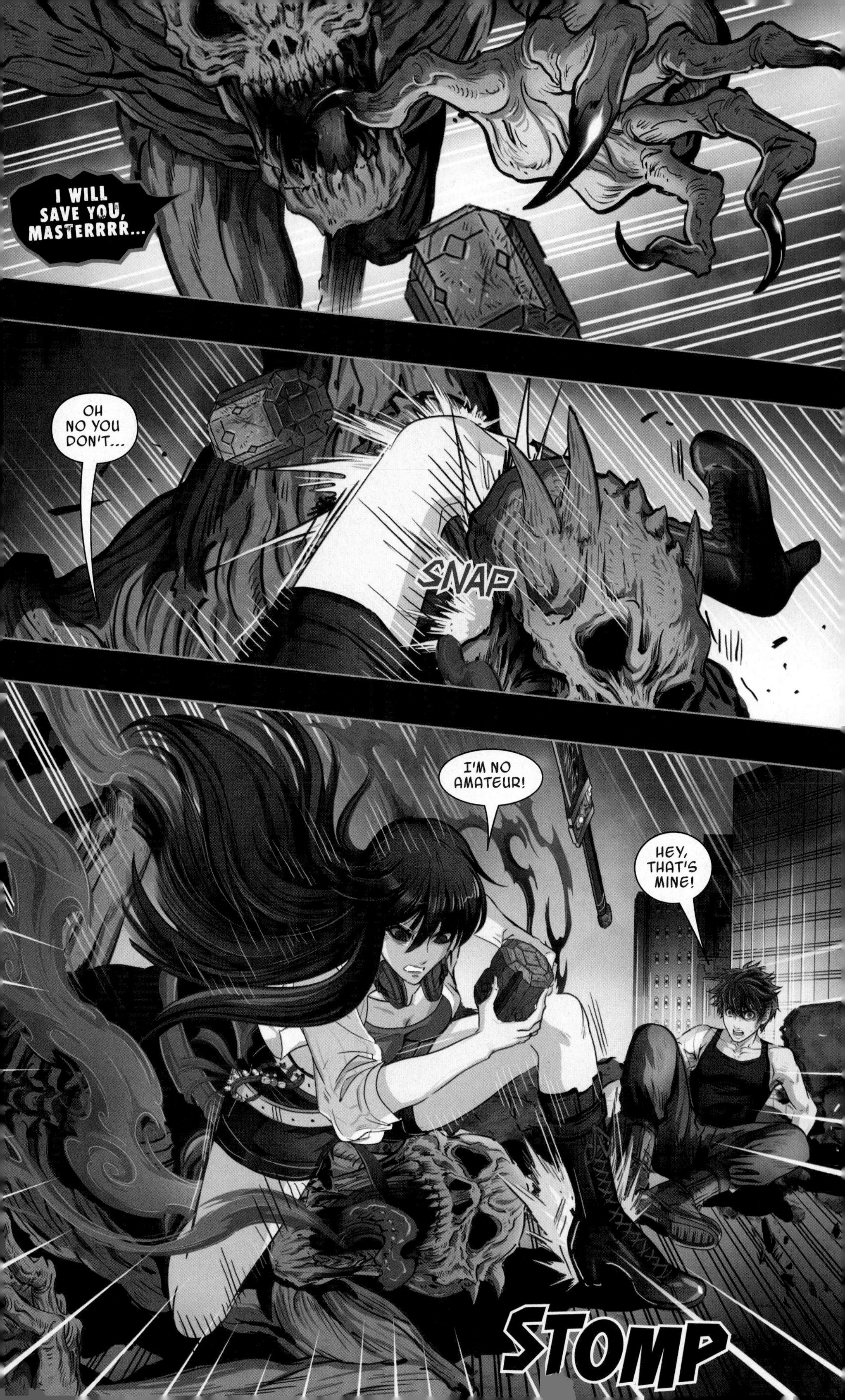
I WILL SAVE YOU, MASTERRRR...
OH NO YOU DON'T...
SNAP
I'M NO AMATEUR!
HEY, THAT'S MINE!
STOMP

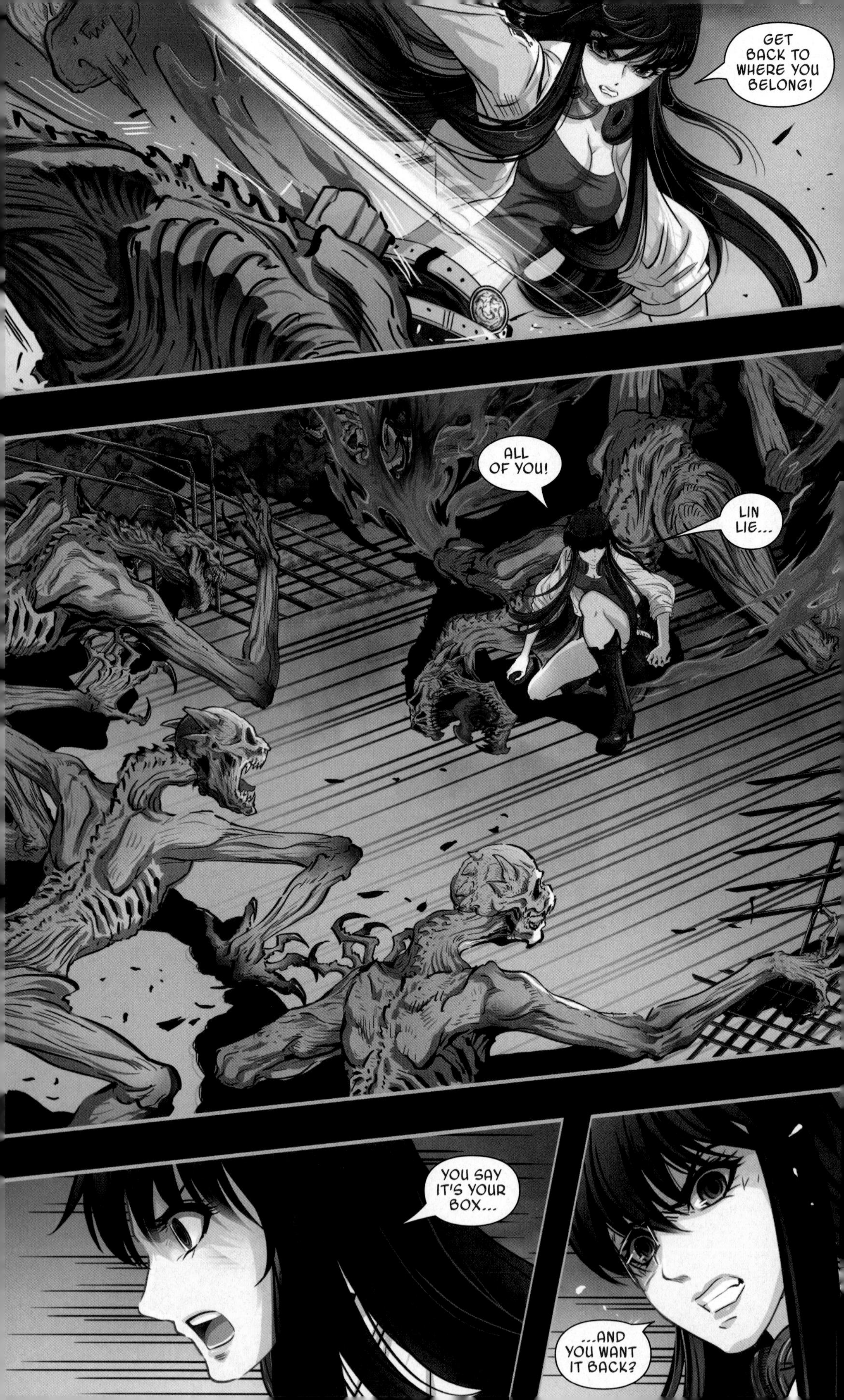
GET BACK TO WHERE YOU BELONG!
ALL OF YOU!
LIN LIE...
YOU SAY IT'S YOUR BOX...
...AND YOU WANT IT BACK?

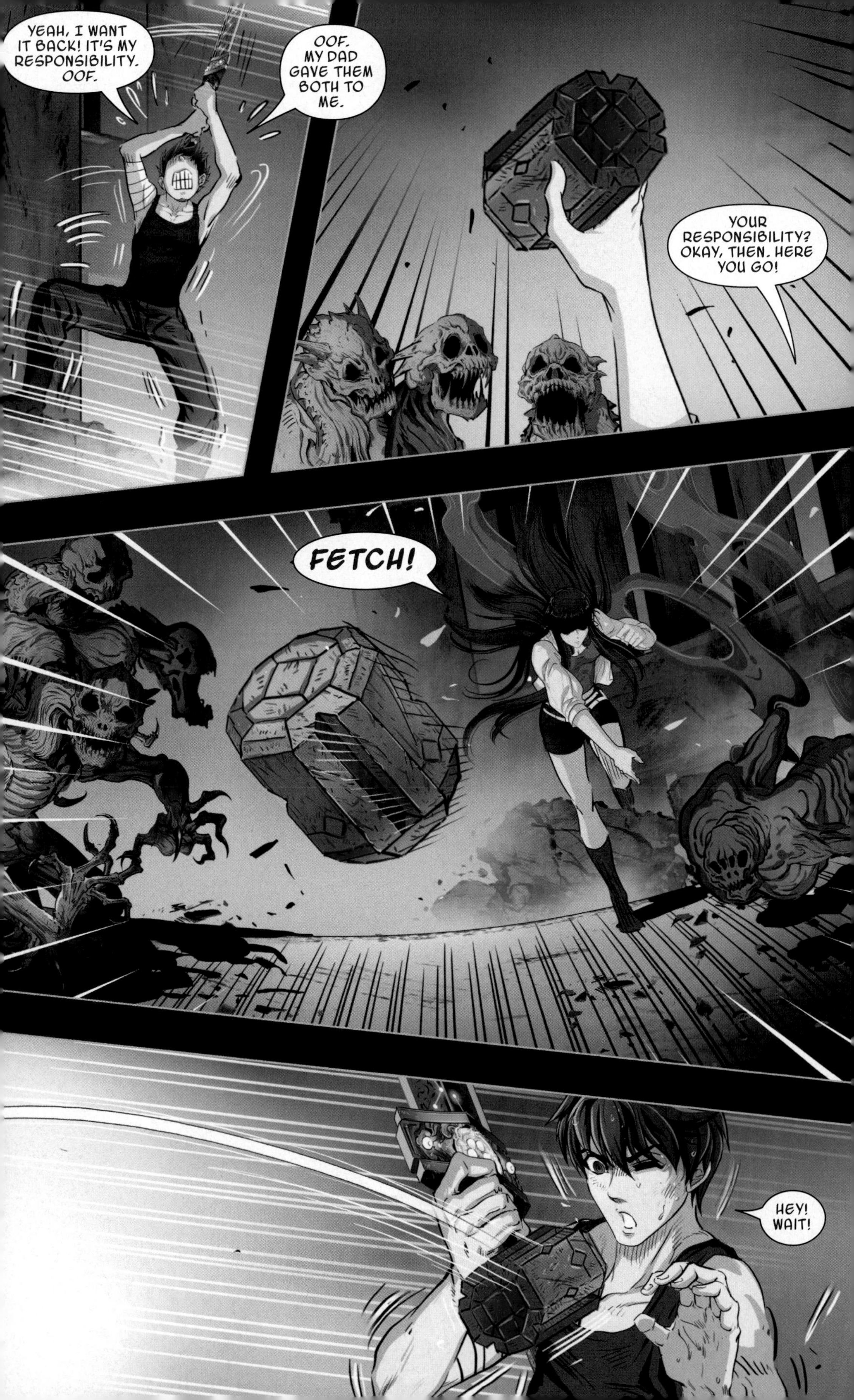
YEAH, I WANT IT BACK! IT'S MY RESPONSIBILITY. OOF.
OOF. MY DAD GAVE THEM BOTH TO ME.
YOUR RESPONSIBILITY? OKAY, THEN. HERE YOU GO!
FETCH!
HEY! WAIT!

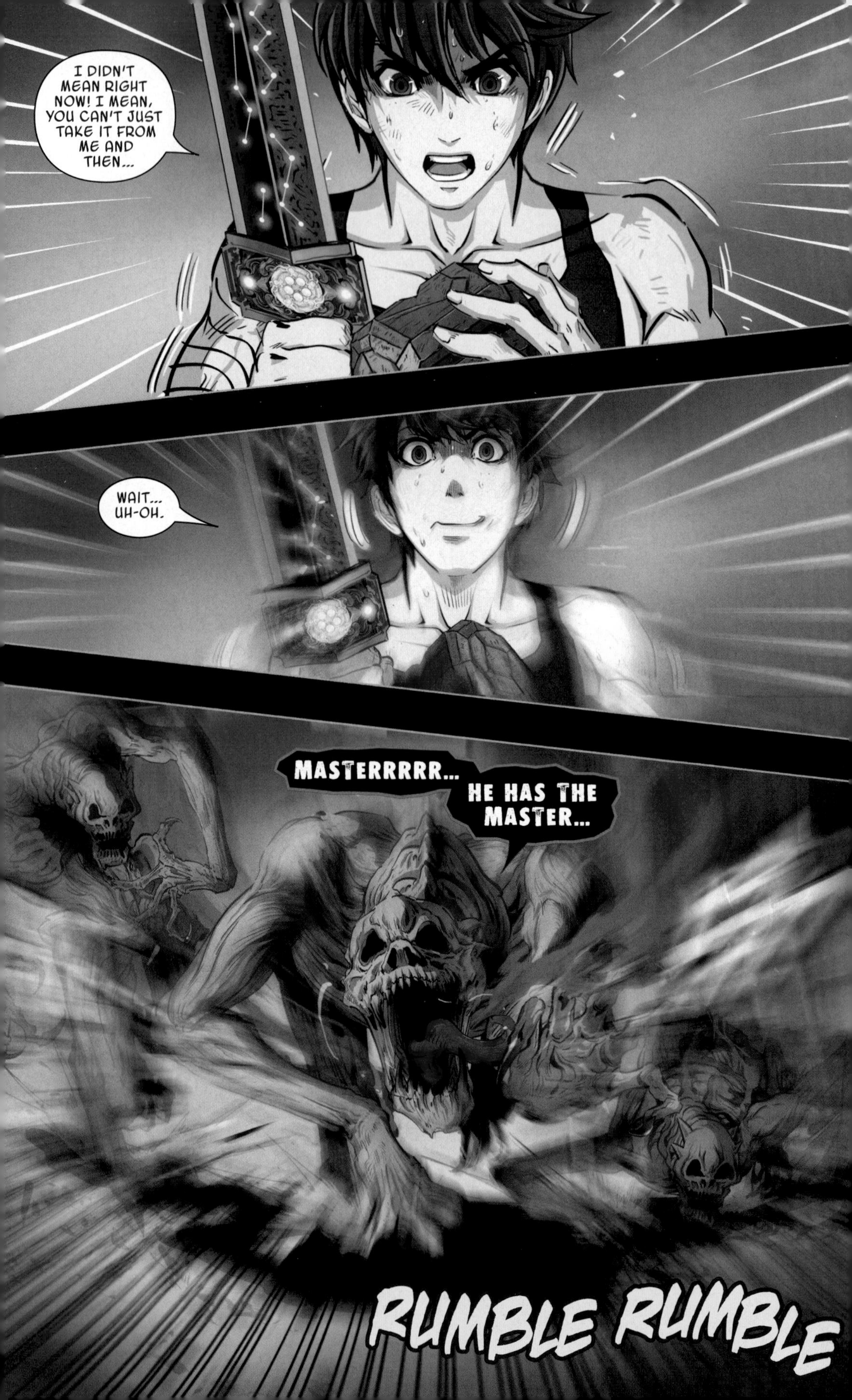
I DIDN'T MEAN RIGHT NOW! I MEAN, YOU CAN'T JUST TAKE IT FROM ME AND THEN...
WAIT... UH-OH.
MASTERRRRR...
HE HAS THE MASTER...
RUMBLE RUMBLE

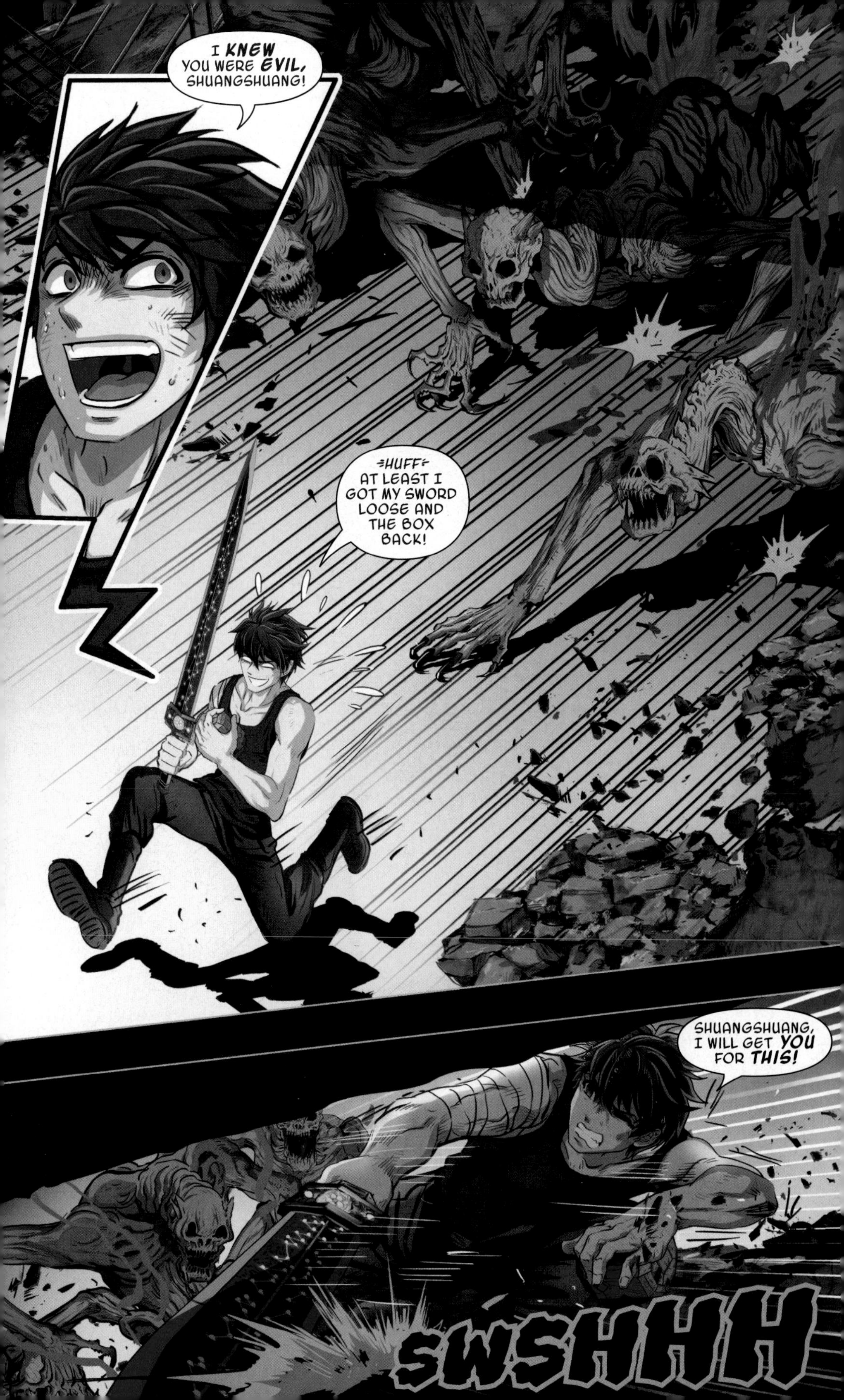
I KNEW YOU WERE EVIL, SHUANGSHUANG!
HUFF
AT LEAST I GOT MY SWORD LOOSE AND THE BOX BACK!
SHUANGSHUANG, I WILL GET YOU FOR THIS!
SWSHHH

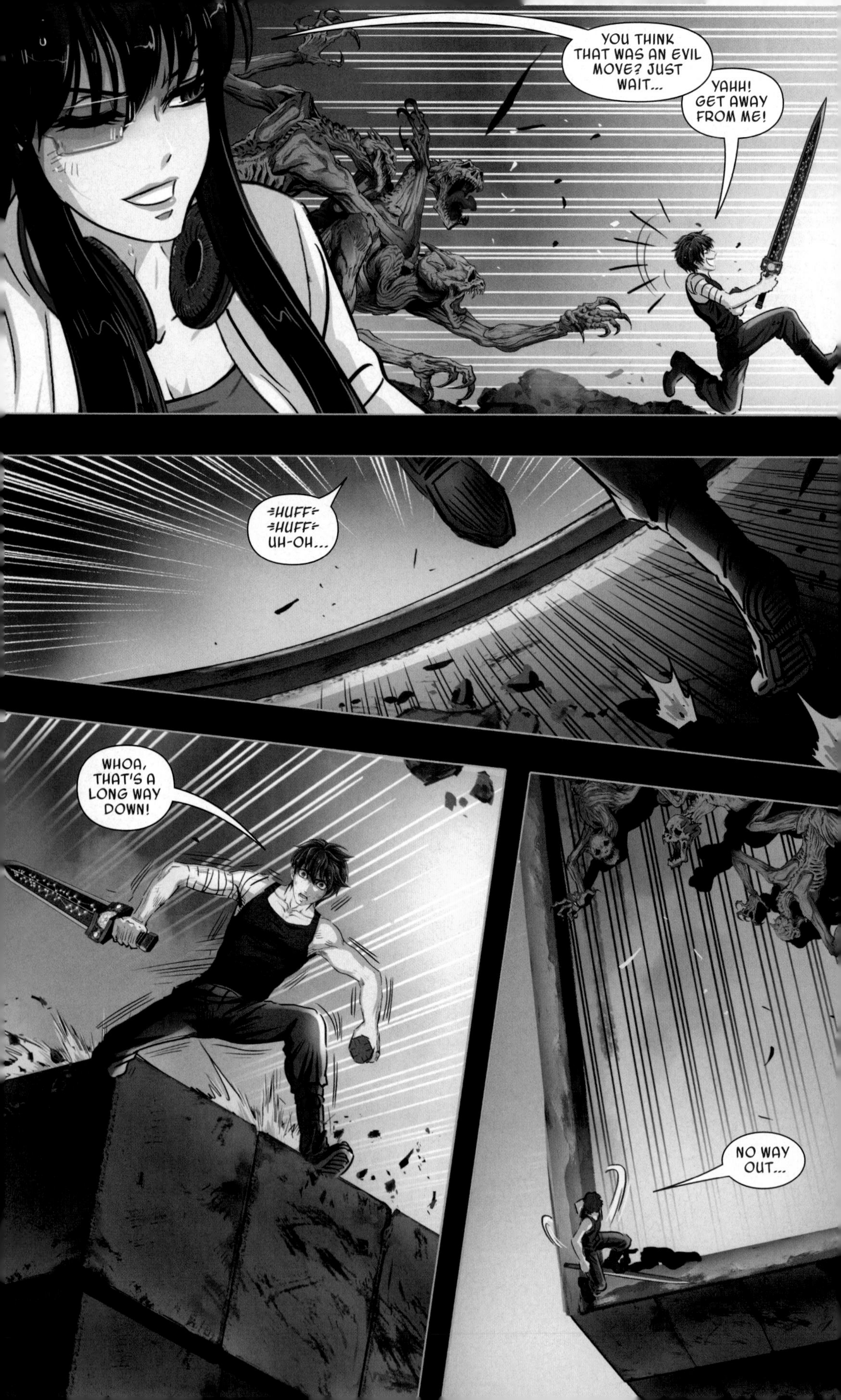
YOU THINK THAT WAS AN EVIL MOVE? JUST WAIT...
YAHH! GET AWAY FROM ME!
=HUFF= =HUFF= UH-OH...
WHOA, THAT'S A LONG WAY DOWN!
NO WAY OUT...

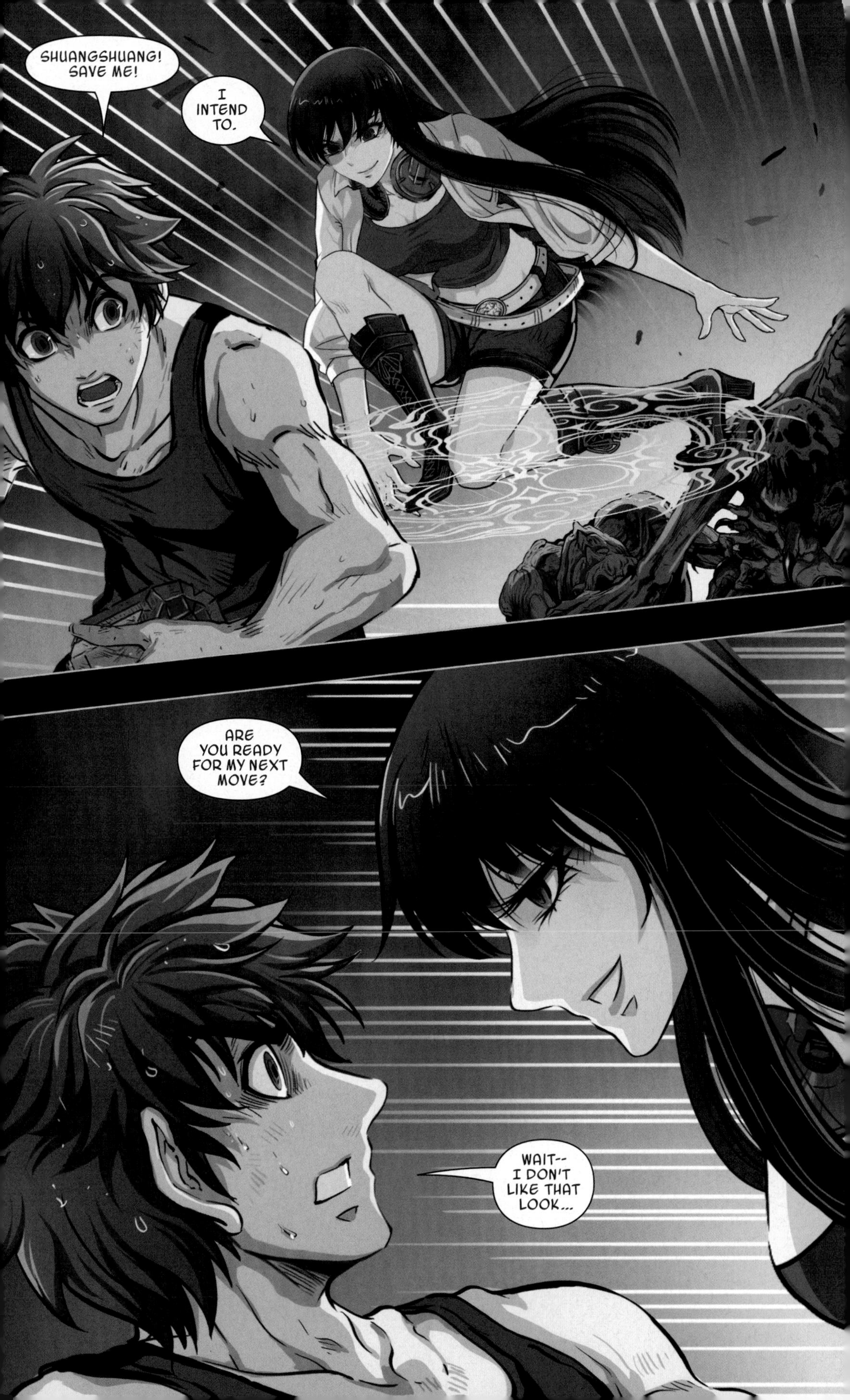
SHUANGSHUANG! SAVE ME!
I INTEND TO.
ARE YOU READY FOR MY NEXT MOVE?
WAIT-- I DON'T LIKE THAT LOOK...

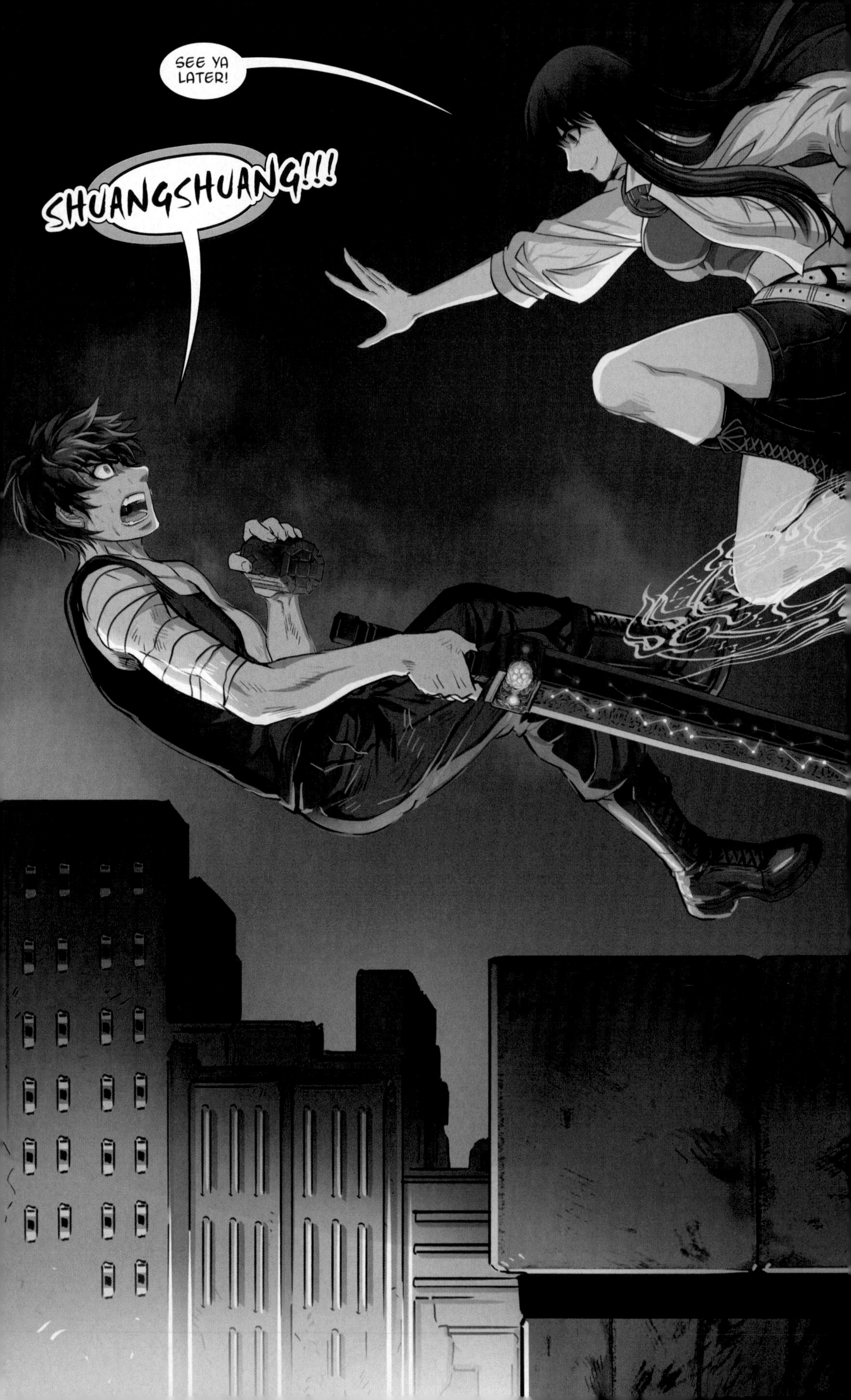
SEE YA LATER!
SHUANGSHUANG!!!

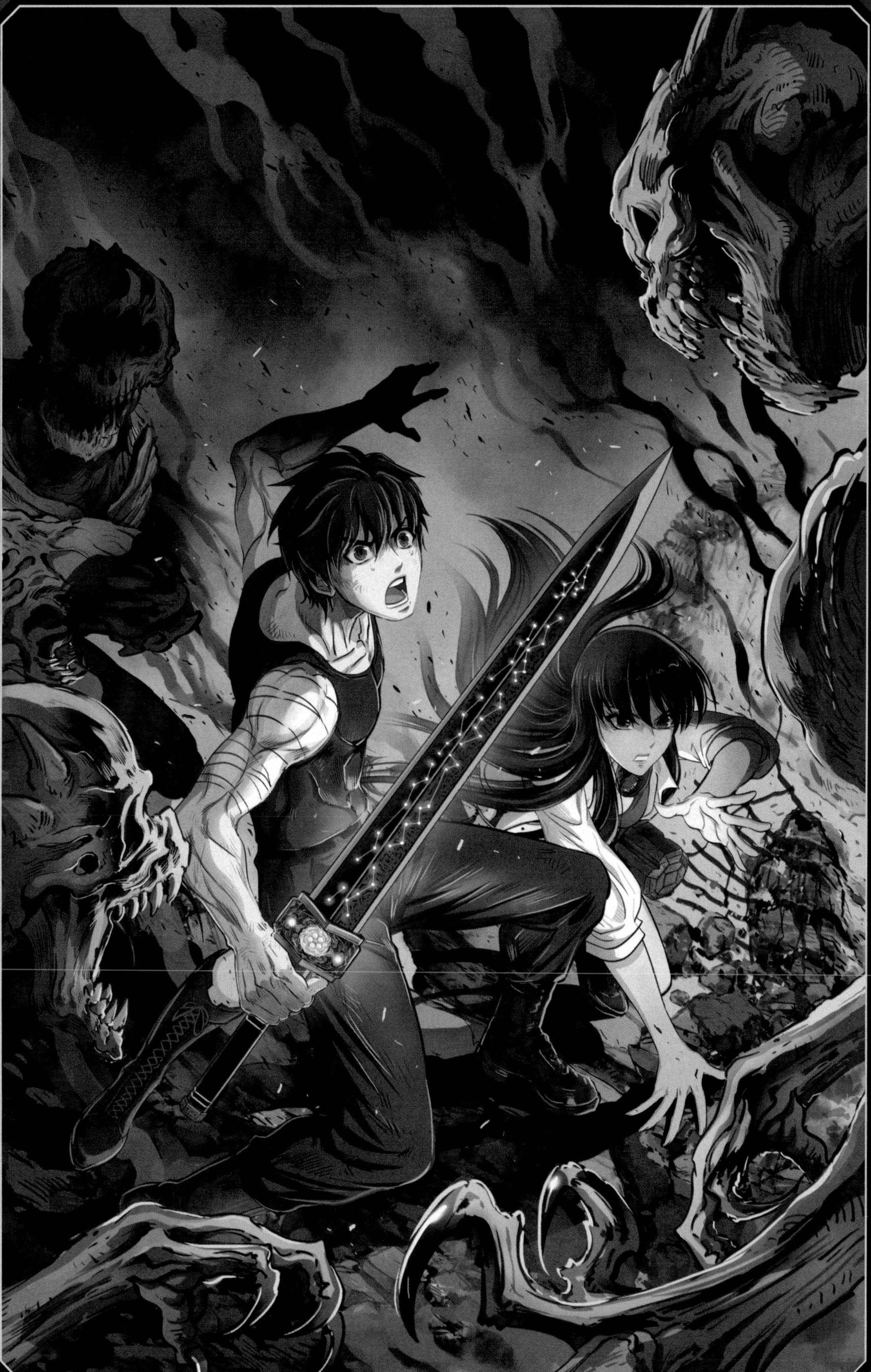

EIGHT DEMONS AT THE GATE

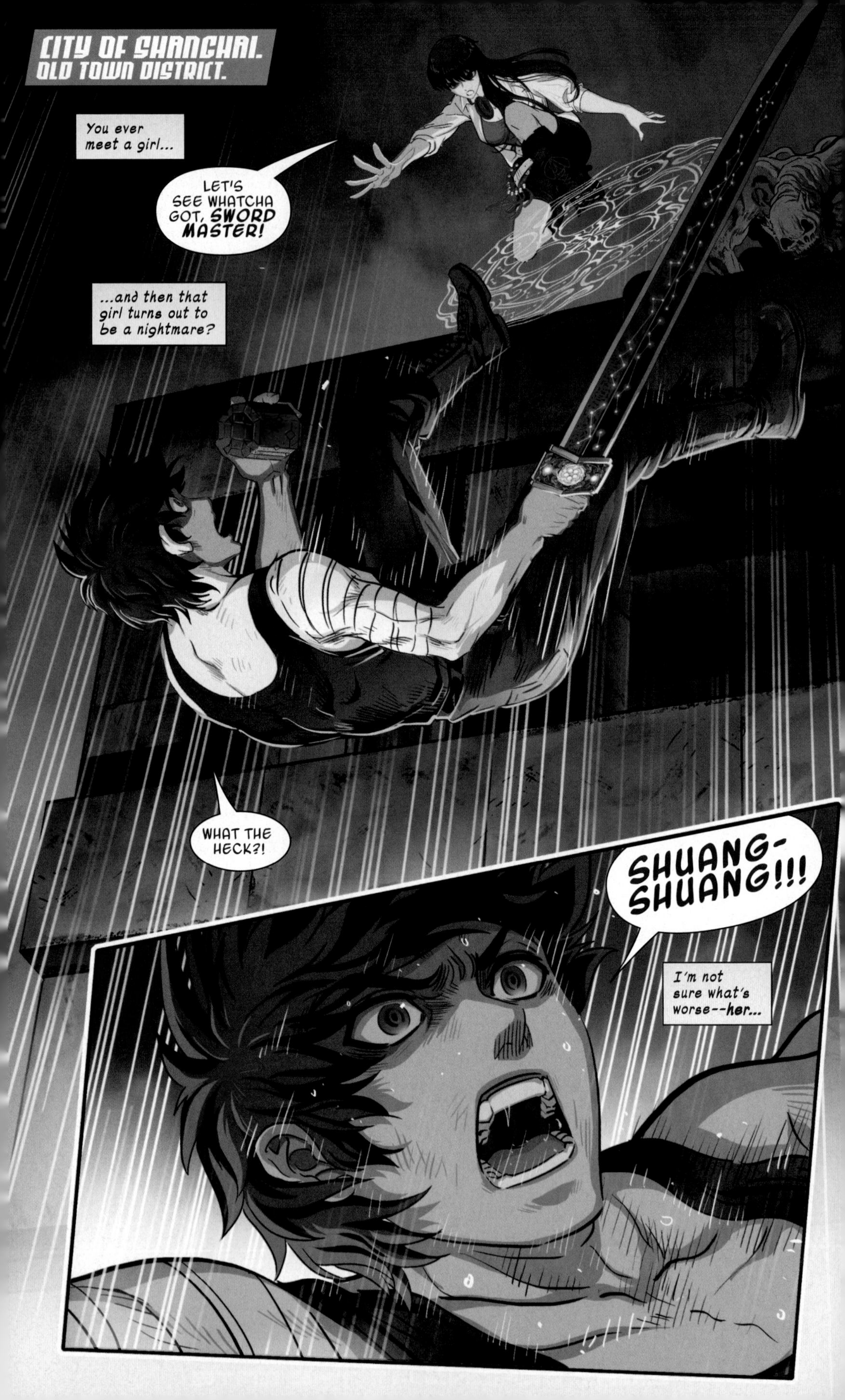
CITY OF SHANCHAI.
OLD TOWN DISTRICT.
You ever meet a girl...
LET'S SEE WHATCHA GOT, SWORD MASTER!
...and then that girl turns out to be a nightmare?
WHAT THE HECK?!
SHUANG-SHUANG!!!
I'm not sure what's worse--her...

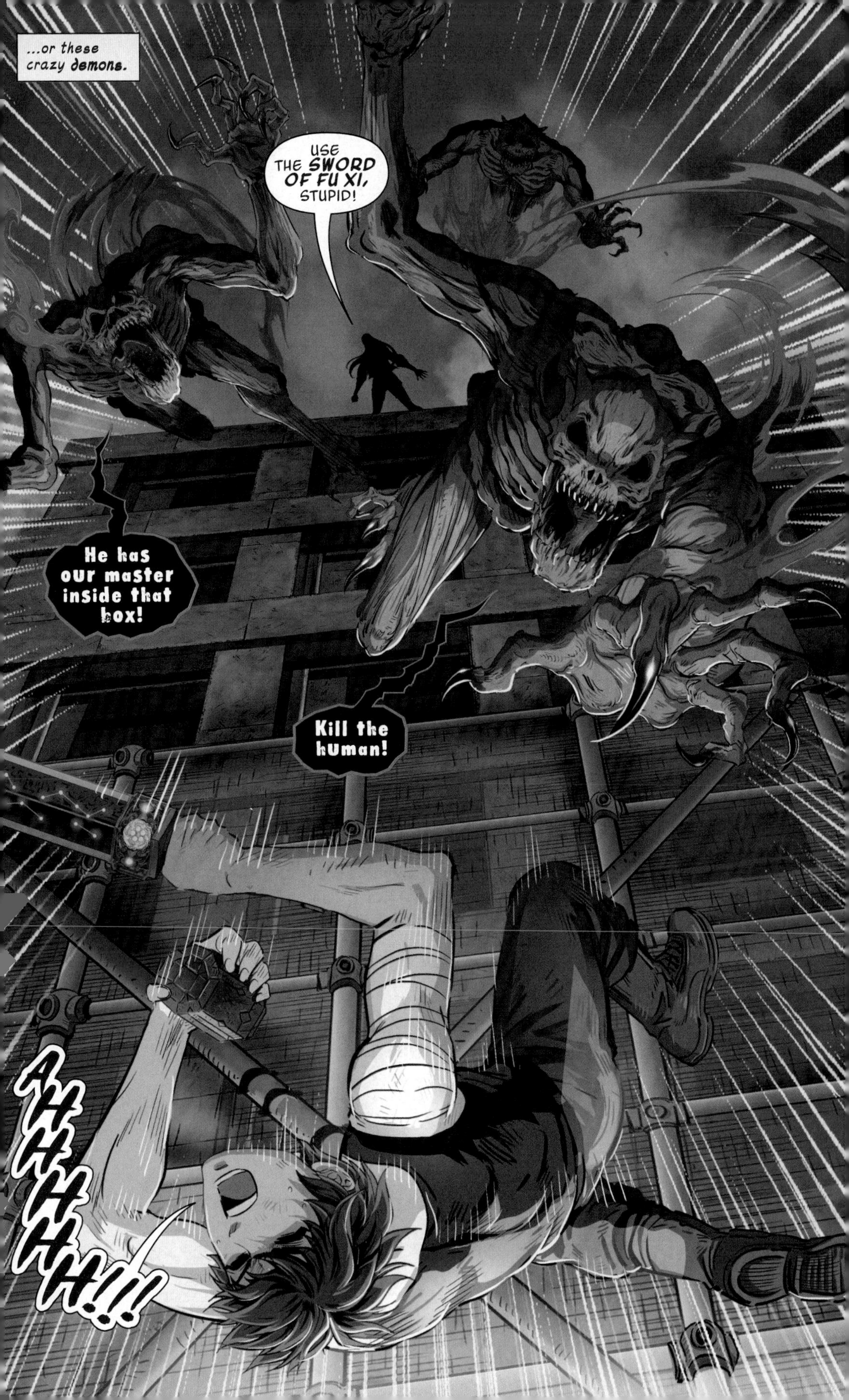
...or these crazy demons.
USE THE SWORD OF FU XI, STUPID!
He has our master inside that box!
Kill the human!
AHHHHH!!!

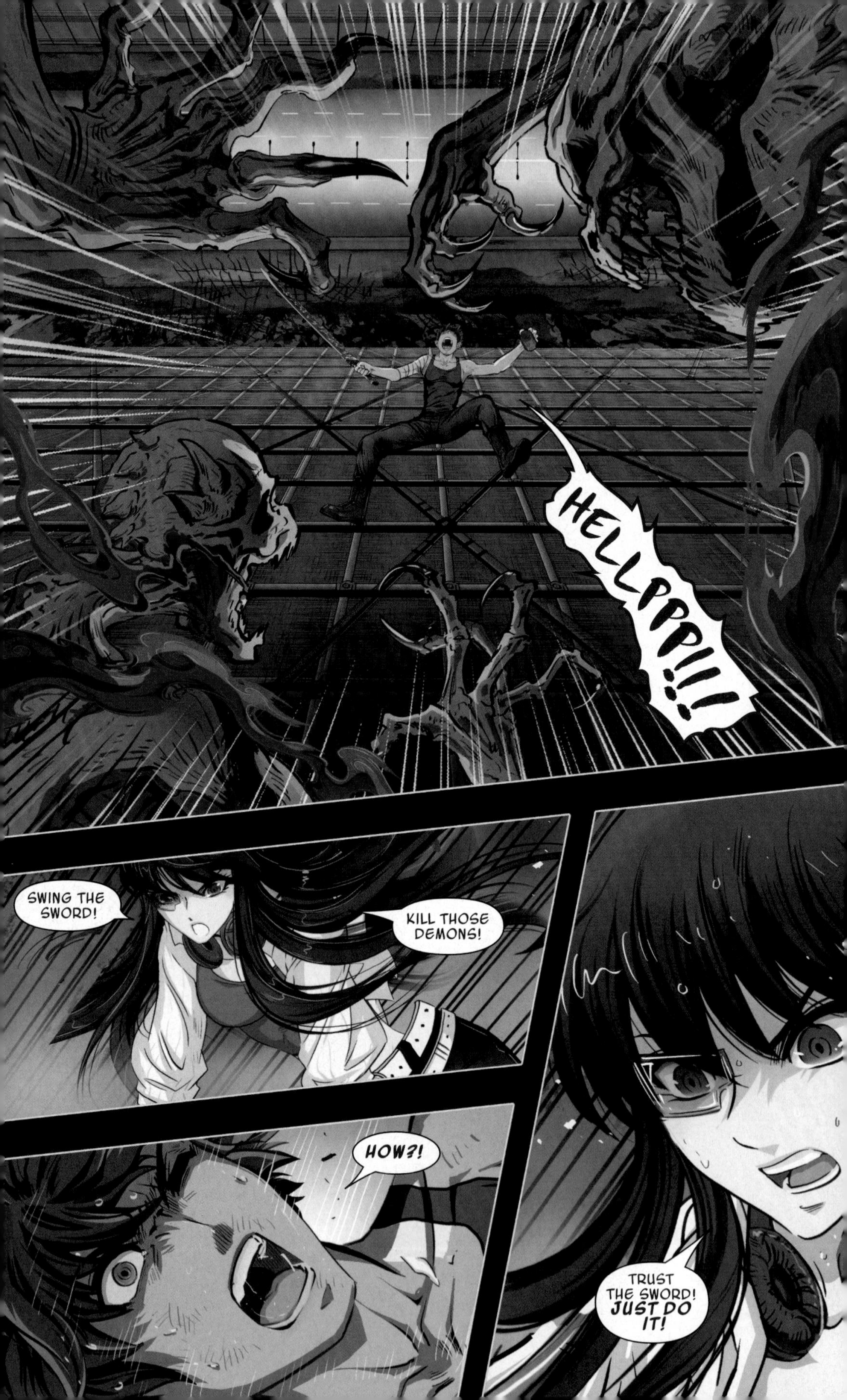
HELLPPP!!!!
SWING THE SWORD!
KILL THOSE DEMONS!
HOW?!
TRUST THE SWORD! JUST DO IT!

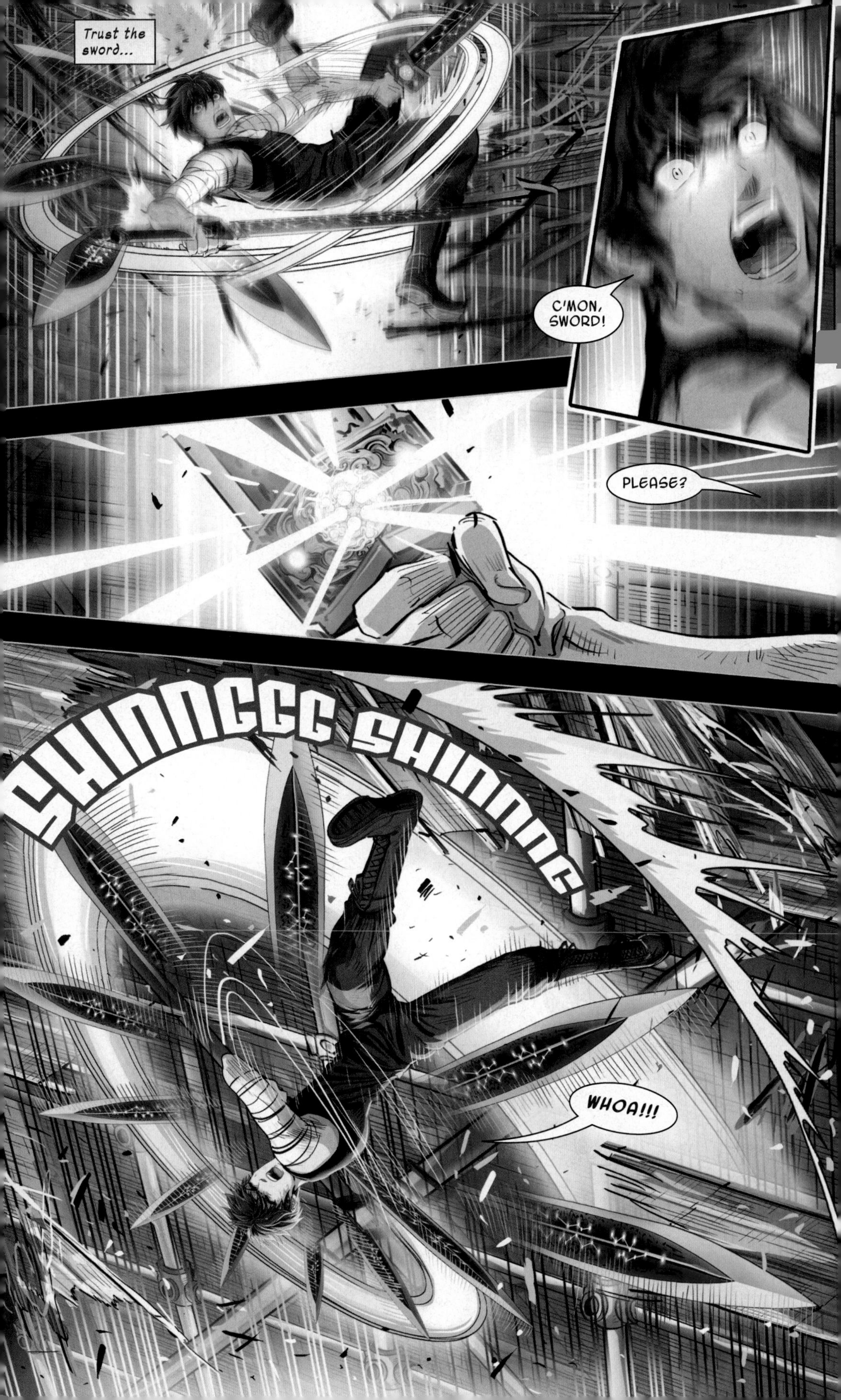
Trust the sword...
C'MON, SWORD!
PLEASE?
SHINNGGG SHINNNG
WHOA!!!

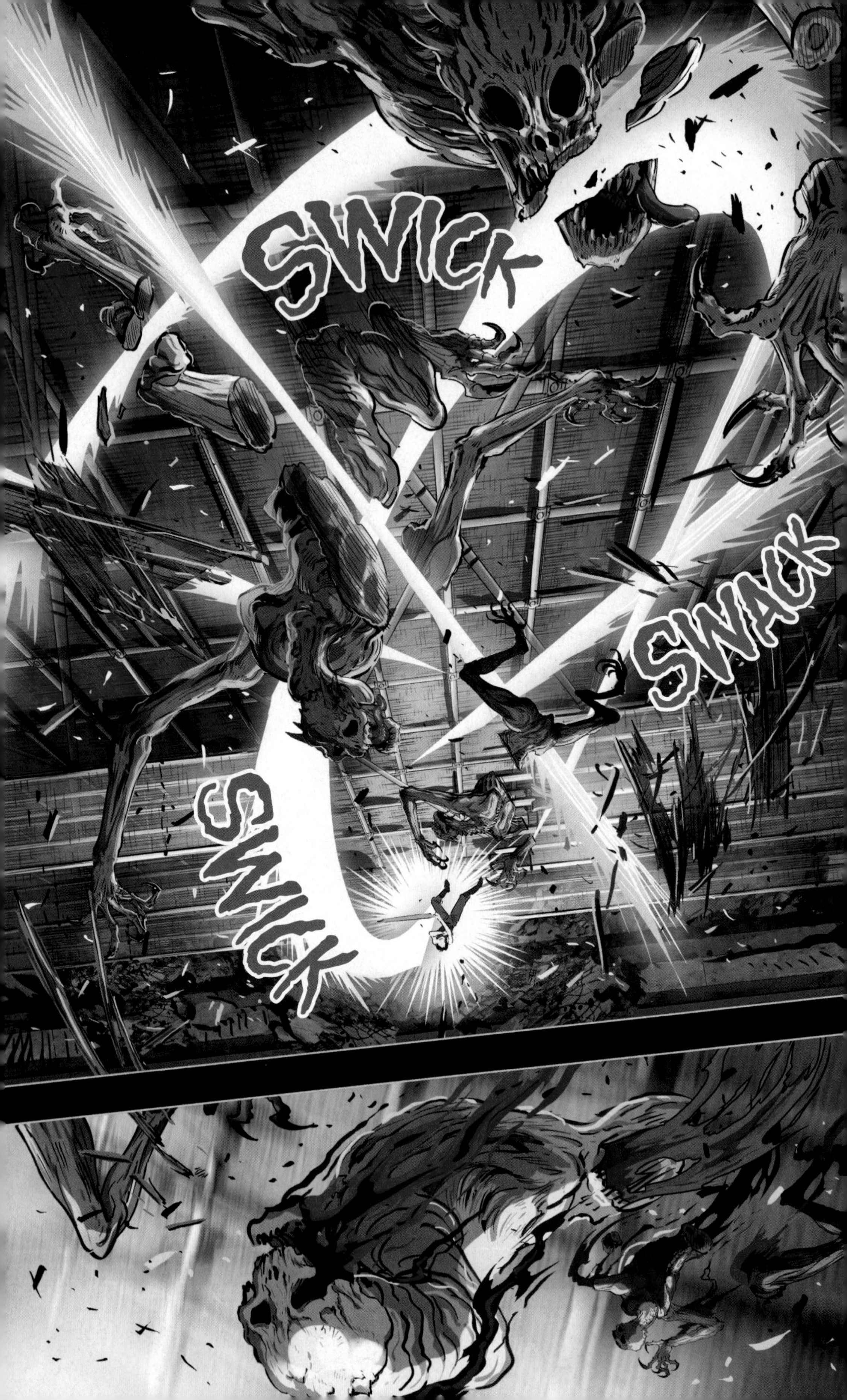
SWICK
SWACK
SWICK

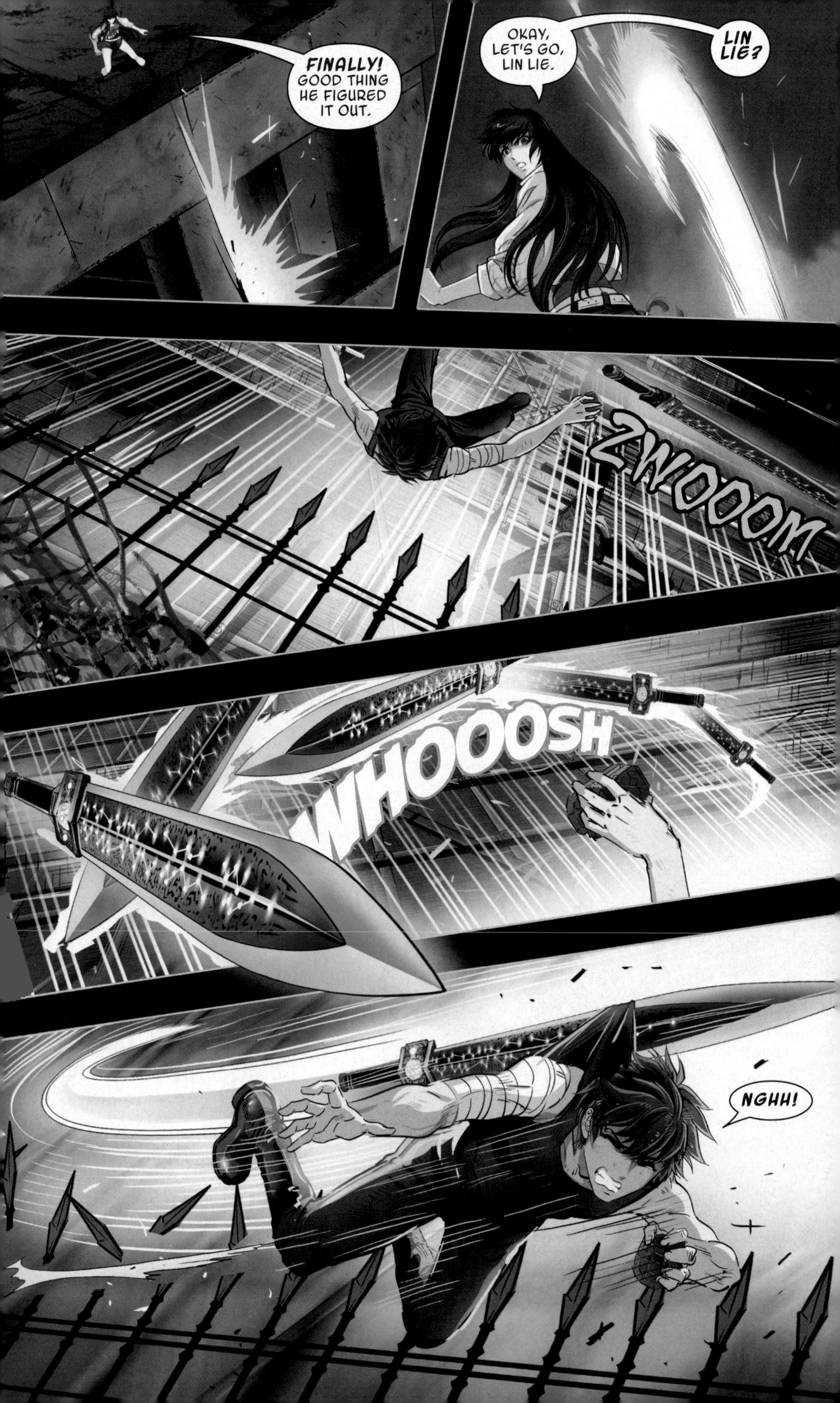
FINALLY! GOOD THING HE FIGURED IT OUT.
OKAY, LET'S GO, LIN LIE.
LIN LIE?
ZWOOOM
WHOOOSH
NGHH!

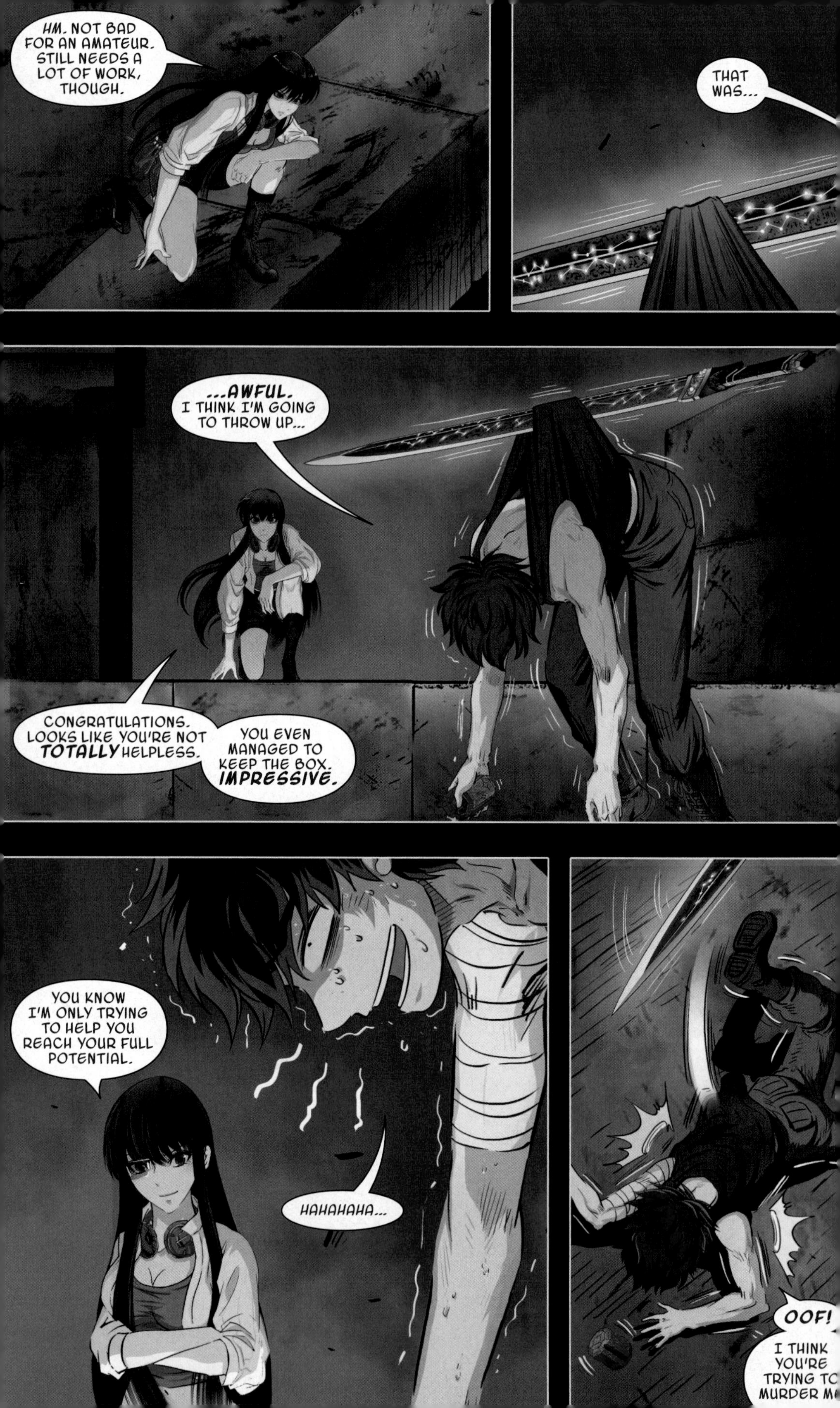
HM. NOT BAD FOR AN AMATEUR. STILL NEEDS A LOT OF WORK, THOUGH.
THAT WAS...
...AWFUL. I THINK I'M GOING TO THROW UP...
CONGRATULATIONS. LOOKS LIKE YOU'RE NOT TOTALLY HELPLESS.
YOU EVEN MANAGED TO KEEP THE BOX. IMPRESSIVE.
YOU KNOW I'M ONLY TRYING TO HELP YOU REACH YOUR FULL POTENTIAL.
HAHAHAHA...
OOF!
I THINK YOU'RE TRYING TO MURDER M

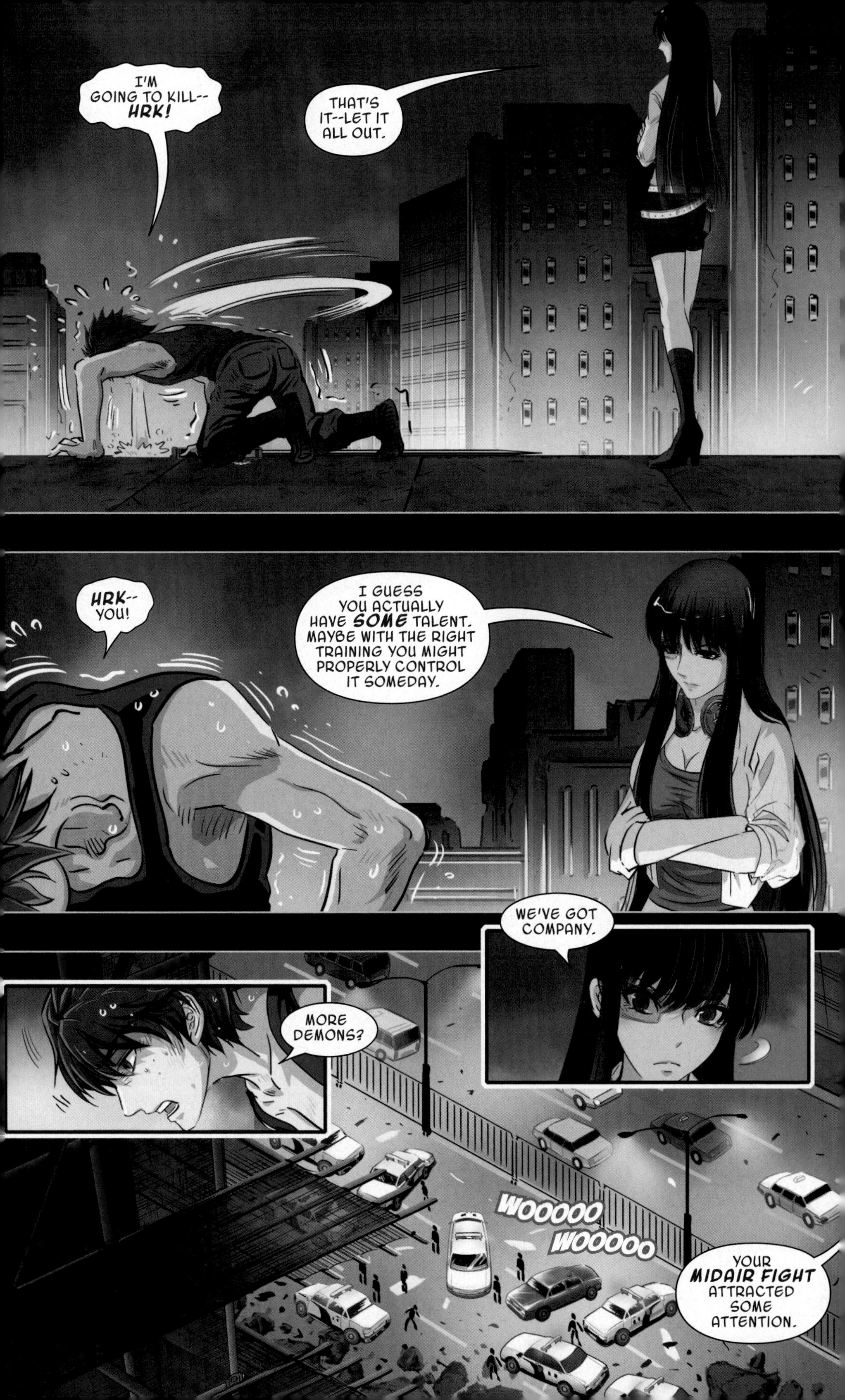

I'M GOING TO KILL-- HRK!
THAT'S IT--LET IT ALL OUT.
HRK-- YOU!
I GUESS YOU ACTUALLY HAVE SOME TALENT. MAYBE WITH THE RIGHT TRAINING YOU MIGHT PROPERLY CONTROL IT SOMEDAY.
MORE DEMONS?
WE'VE GOT COMPANY.
WOOOOO
WOOOOO
YOUR MIDAIR FIGHT ATTRACTED SOME ATTENTION.

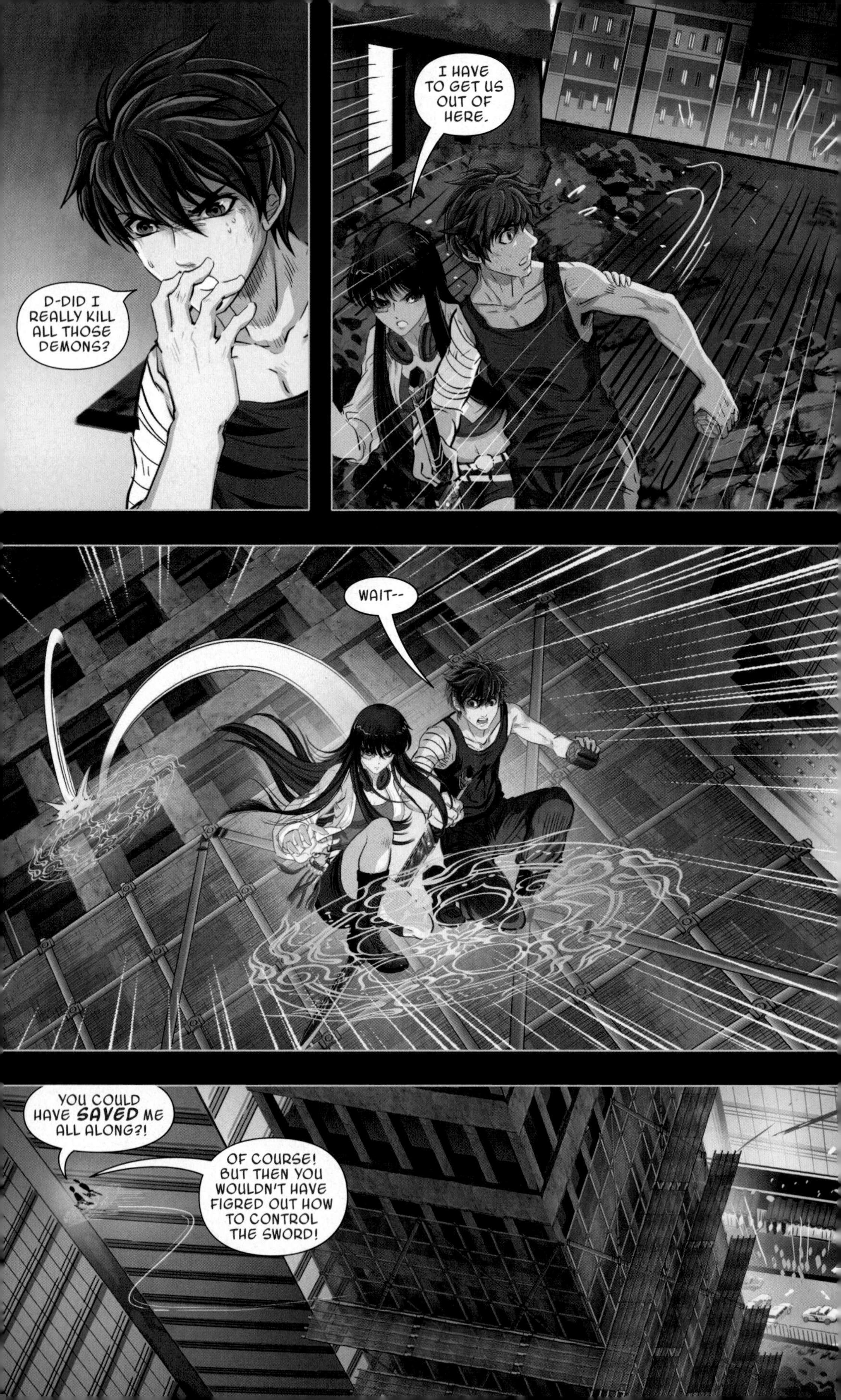
D-DID I REALLY KILL ALL THOSE DEMONS?
I HAVE TO GET US OUT OF HERE.
WAIT--
YOU COULD HAVE SAVED ME ALL ALONG?!
OF COURSE! BUT THEN YOU WOULDN'T HAVE FIGRED OUT HOW TO CONTROL THE SWORD!

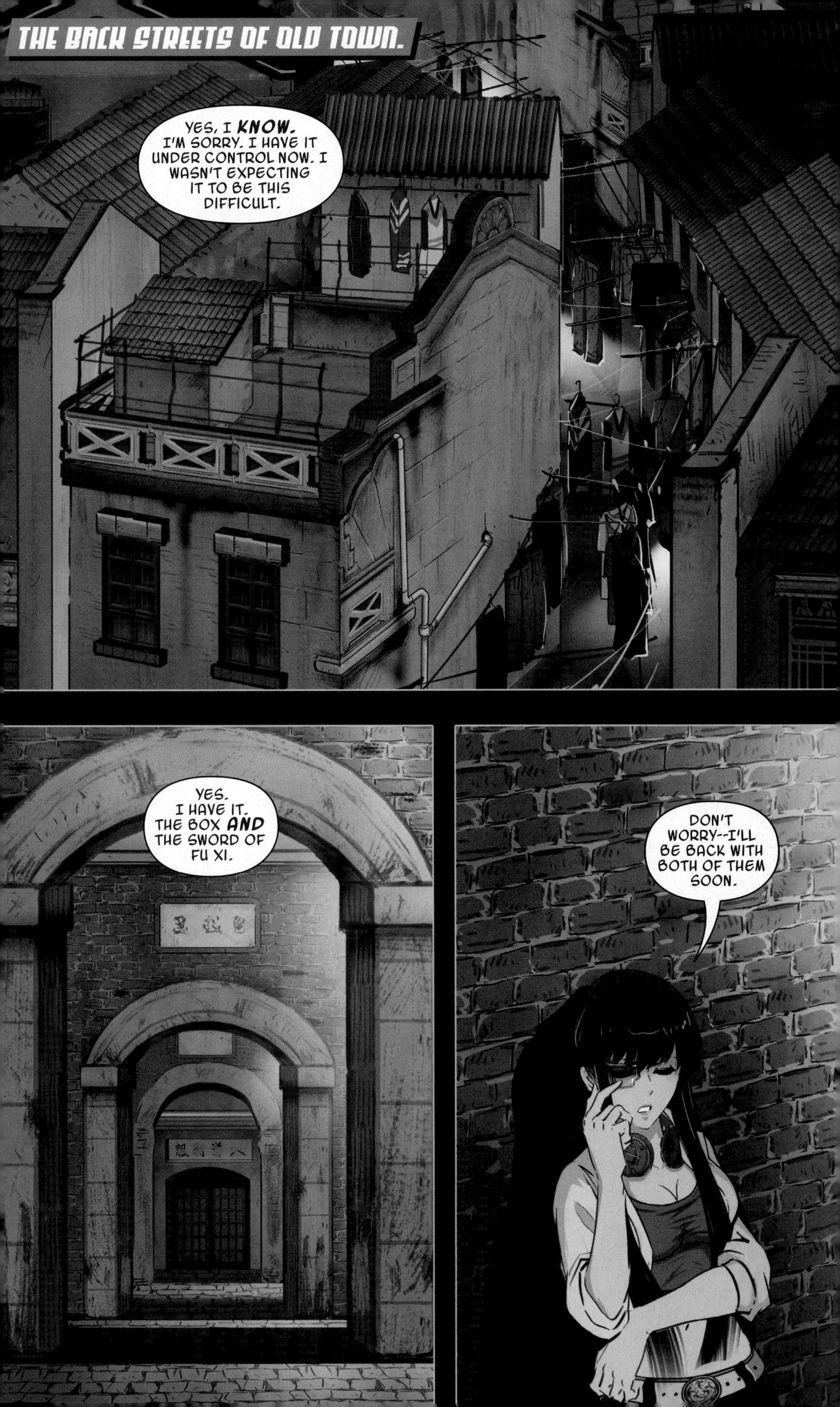
THE BACK STREETS OF OLD TOWN.
YES, I KNOW. I'M SORRY. I HAVE IT UNDER CONTROL NOW. I WASN'T EXPECTING IT TO BE THIS DIFFICULT.
YES. I HAVE IT. THE BOX AND THE SWORD OF FU XI.
DON'T WORRY--I'LL BE BACK WITH BOTH OF THEM SOON.

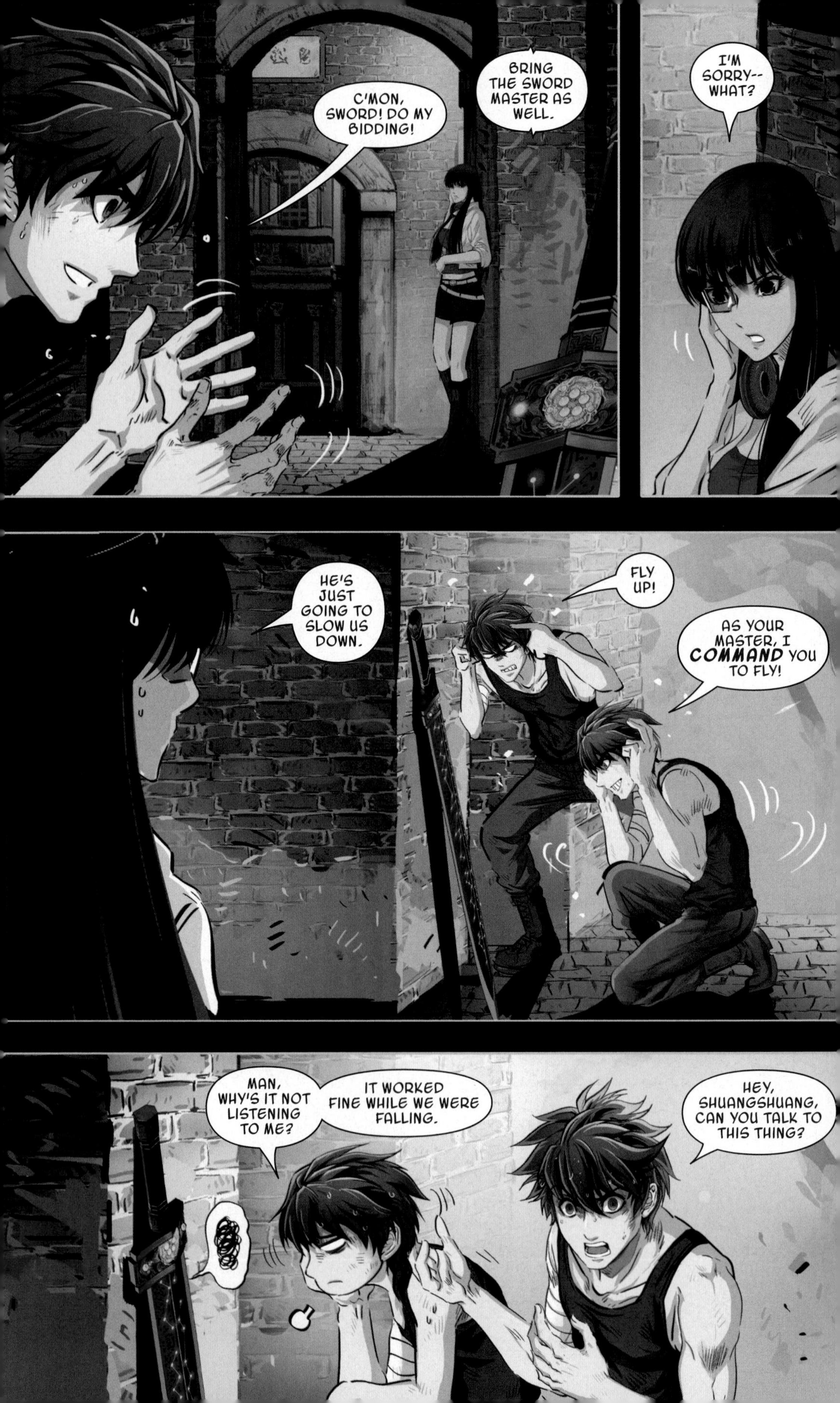
C'MON, SWORD! DO MY BIDDING!
BRING THE SWORD MASTER AS WELL.
I'M SORRY-- WHAT?
HE'S JUST GOING TO SLOW US DOWN.
FLY UP!
AS YOUR MASTER, I COMMAND YOU TO FLY!
MAN, WHY'S IT NOT LISTENING TO ME?
IT WORKED FINE WHILE WE WERE FALLING.
HEY, SHUANGSHUANG, CAN YOU TALK TO THIS THING?

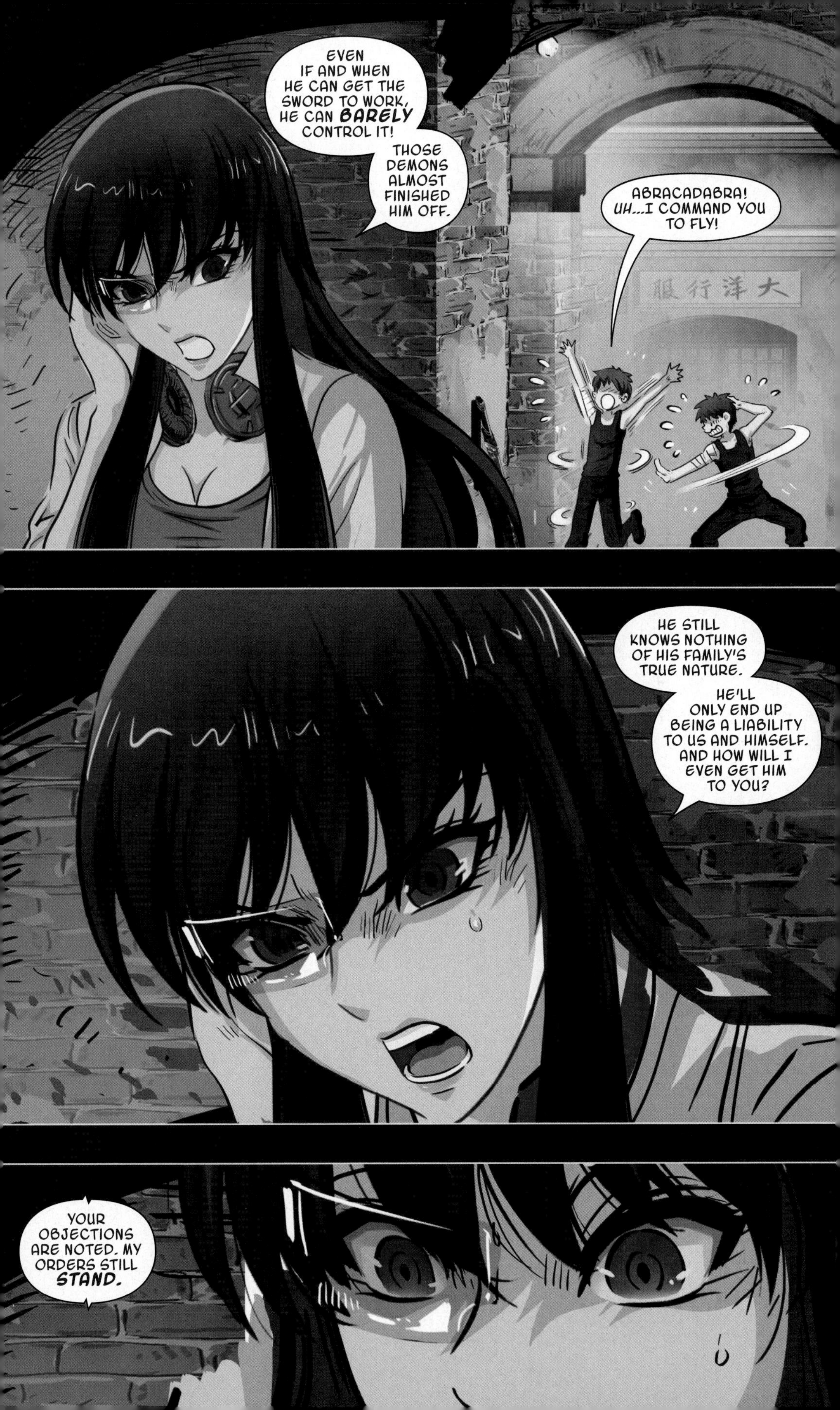
EVEN IF AND WHEN HE CAN GET THE SWORD TO WORK, HE CAN BARELY CONTROL IT!
THOSE DEMONS ALMOST FINISHED HIM OFF.
ABRACADABRA! UH...I COMMAND YOU TO FLY!
大洋行服
HE STILL KNOWS NOTHING OF HIS FAMILY'S TRUE NATURE.
HE'LL ONLY END UP BEING A LIABILITY TO US AND HIMSELF. AND HOW WILL I EVEN GET HIM TO YOU?
YOUR OBJECTIONS ARE NOTED. MY ORDERS STILL STAND.

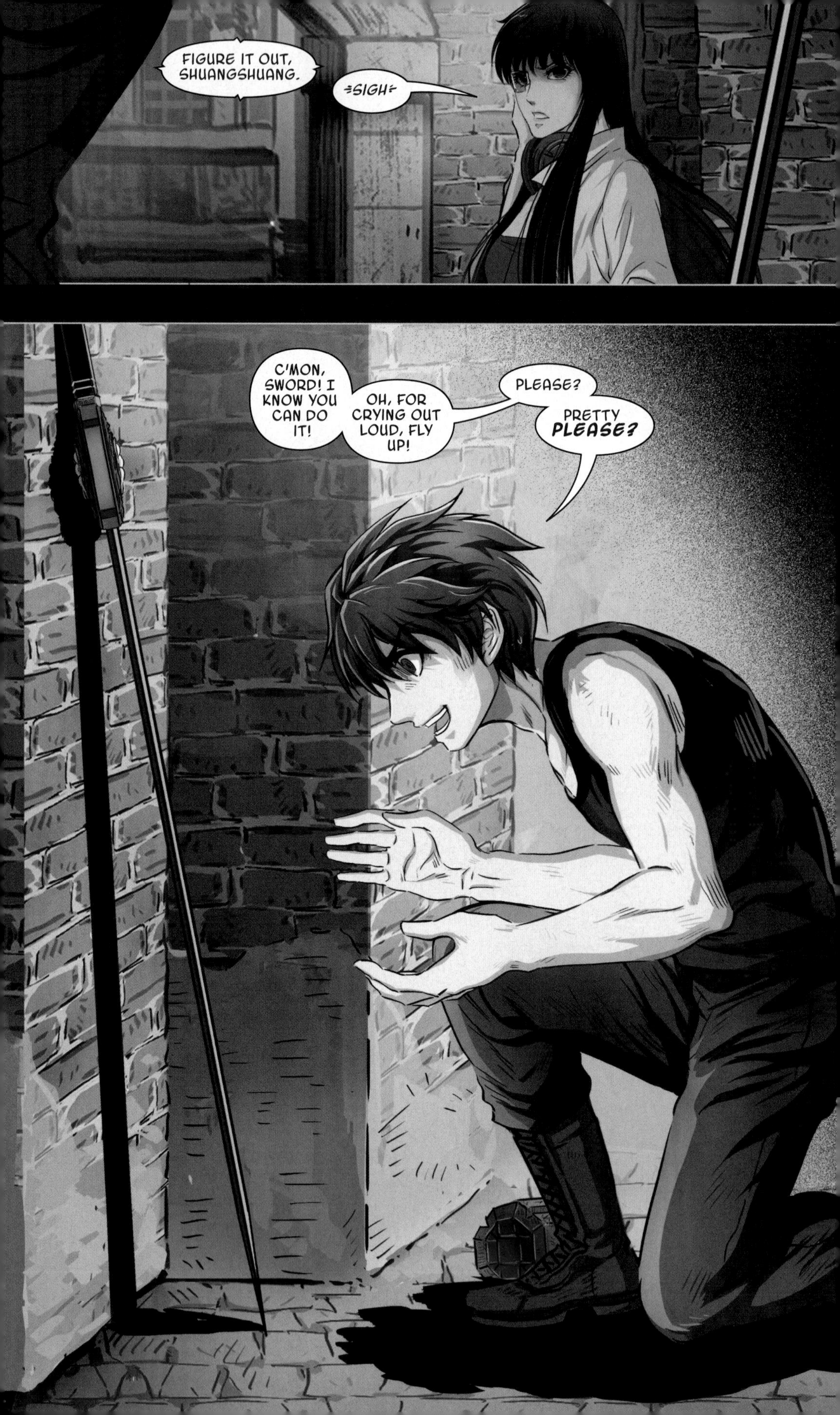
FIGURE IT OUT, SHUANGSHUANG.
=SIGH=
C'MON, SWORD! I KNOW YOU CAN DO IT!
OH, FOR CRYING OUT LOUD, FLY UP!
PLEASE?
PRETTY **PLEASE?**

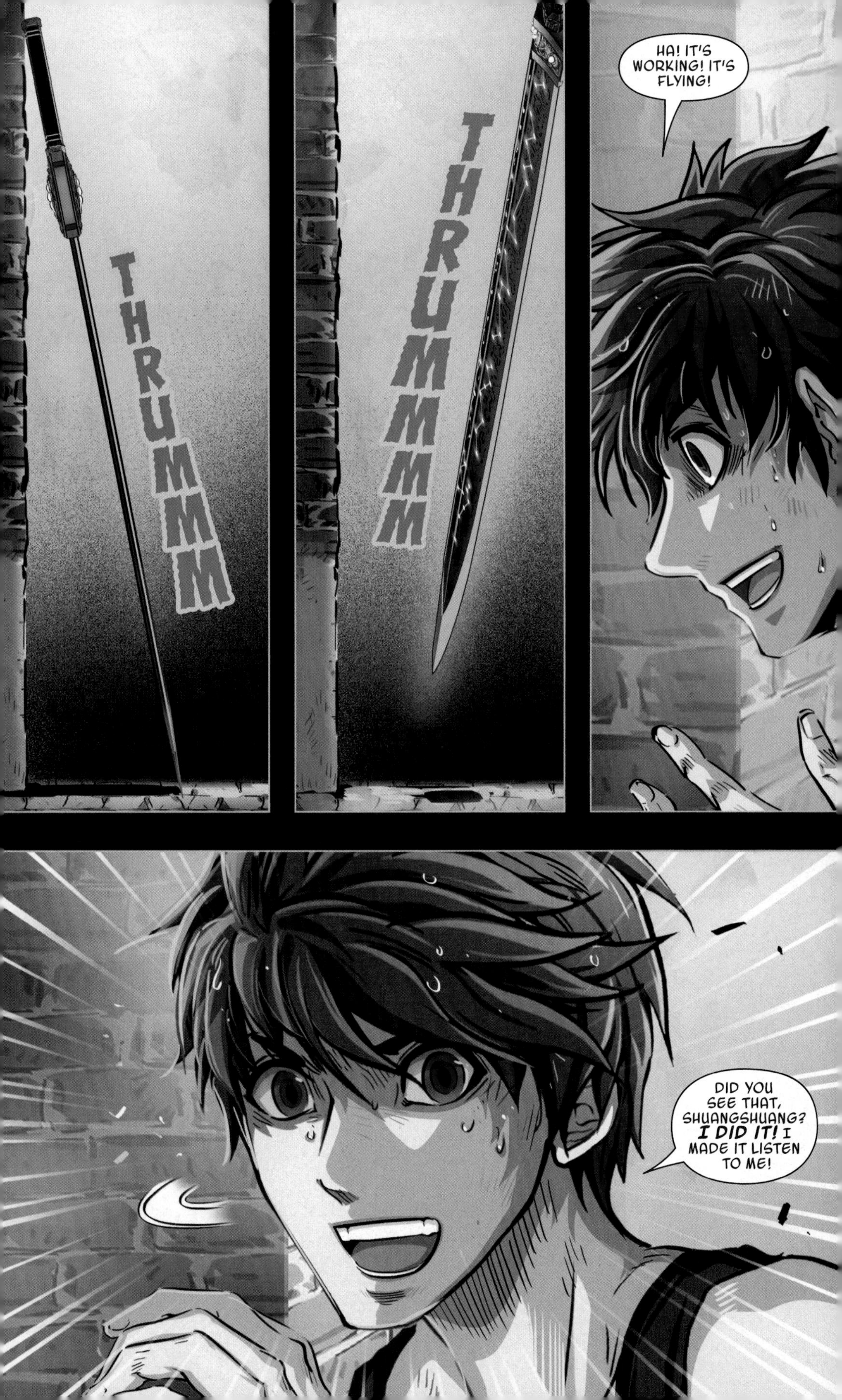
THRUMMM
THRUMMMM
HA! IT'S WORKING! IT'S FLYING!
DID YOU SEE THAT, SHUANGSHUANG? **I DID IT!** I MADE IT LISTEN TO ME!

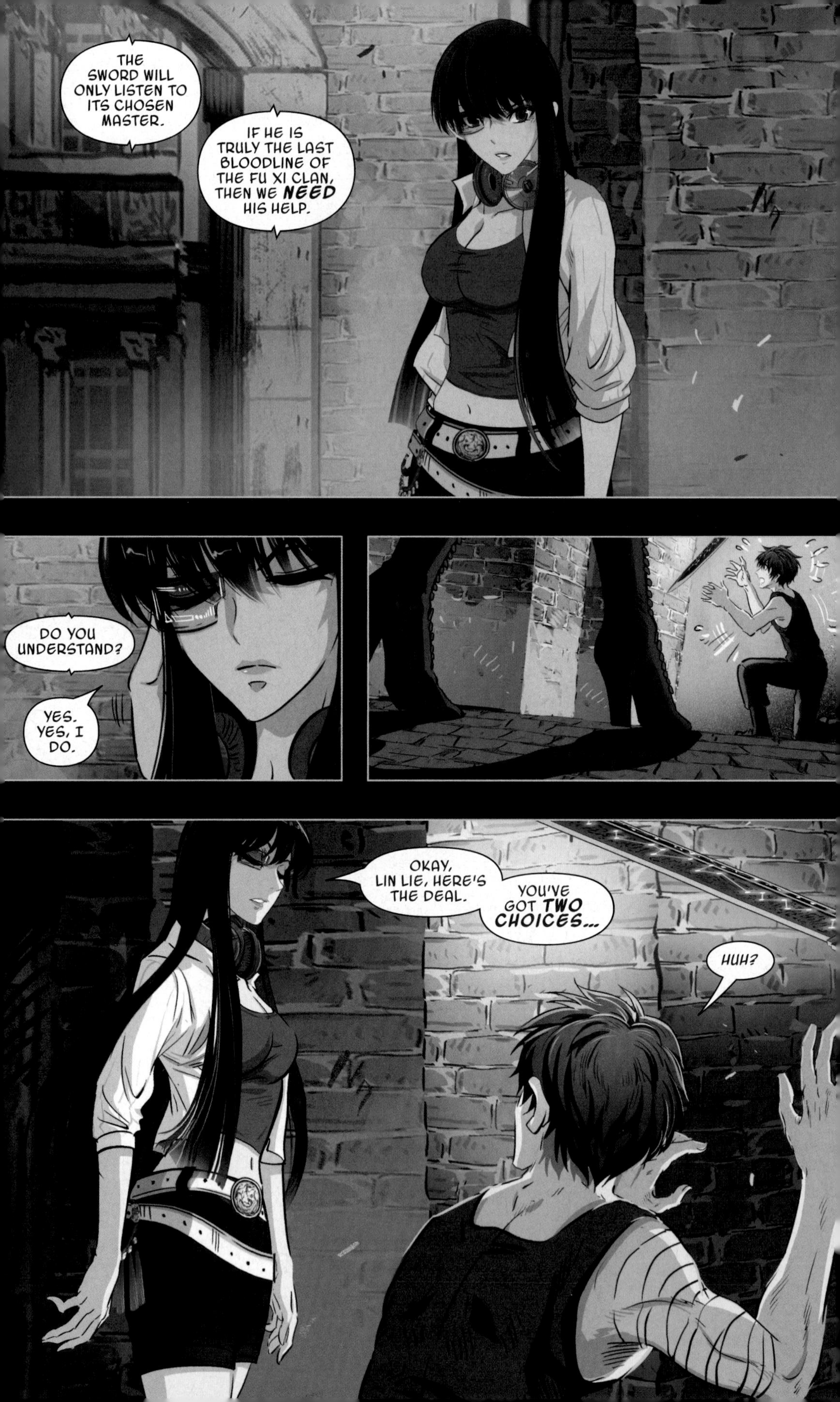
THE SWORD WILL ONLY LISTEN TO ITS CHOSEN MASTER.
IF HE IS TRULY THE LAST BLOODLINE OF THE FU XI CLAN, THEN WE **NEED** HIS HELP.
DO YOU UNDERSTAND?
YES. YES, I DO.
OKAY, LIN LIE, HERE'S THE DEAL.
YOU'VE GOT **TWO CHOICES...**
HUH?

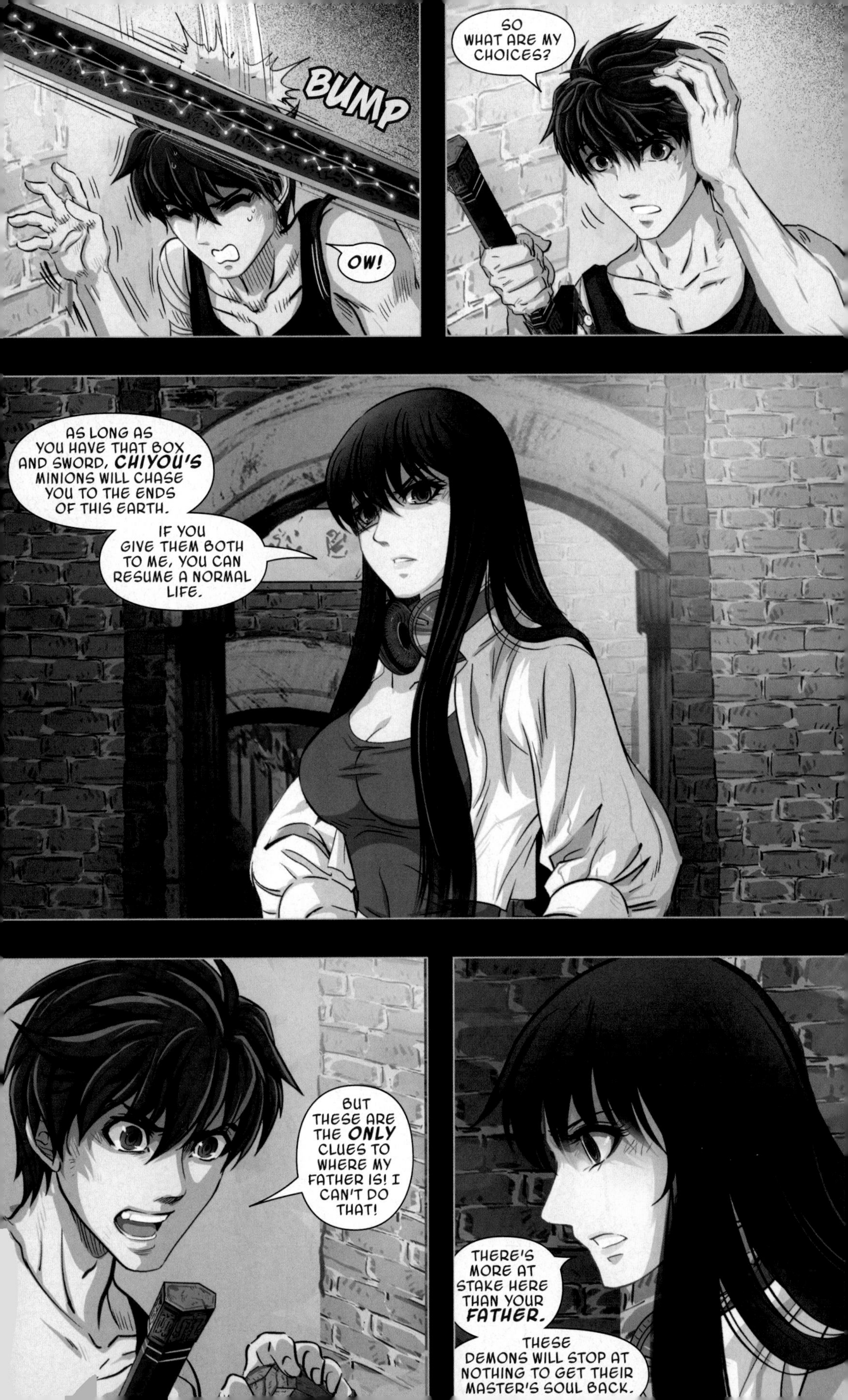
BUMP
OW!
SO WHAT ARE MY CHOICES?
AS LONG AS YOU HAVE THAT BOX AND SWORD, **CHIYOU'S** MINIONS WILL CHASE YOU TO THE ENDS OF THIS EARTH.
IF YOU GIVE THEM BOTH TO ME, YOU CAN RESUME A NORMAL LIFE.
BUT THESE ARE THE **ONLY** CLUES TO WHERE MY FATHER IS! I CAN'T DO THAT!
THERE'S MORE AT STAKE HERE THAN YOUR **FATHER.**
THESE DEMONS WILL STOP AT NOTHING TO GET THEIR MASTER'S SOUL BACK.

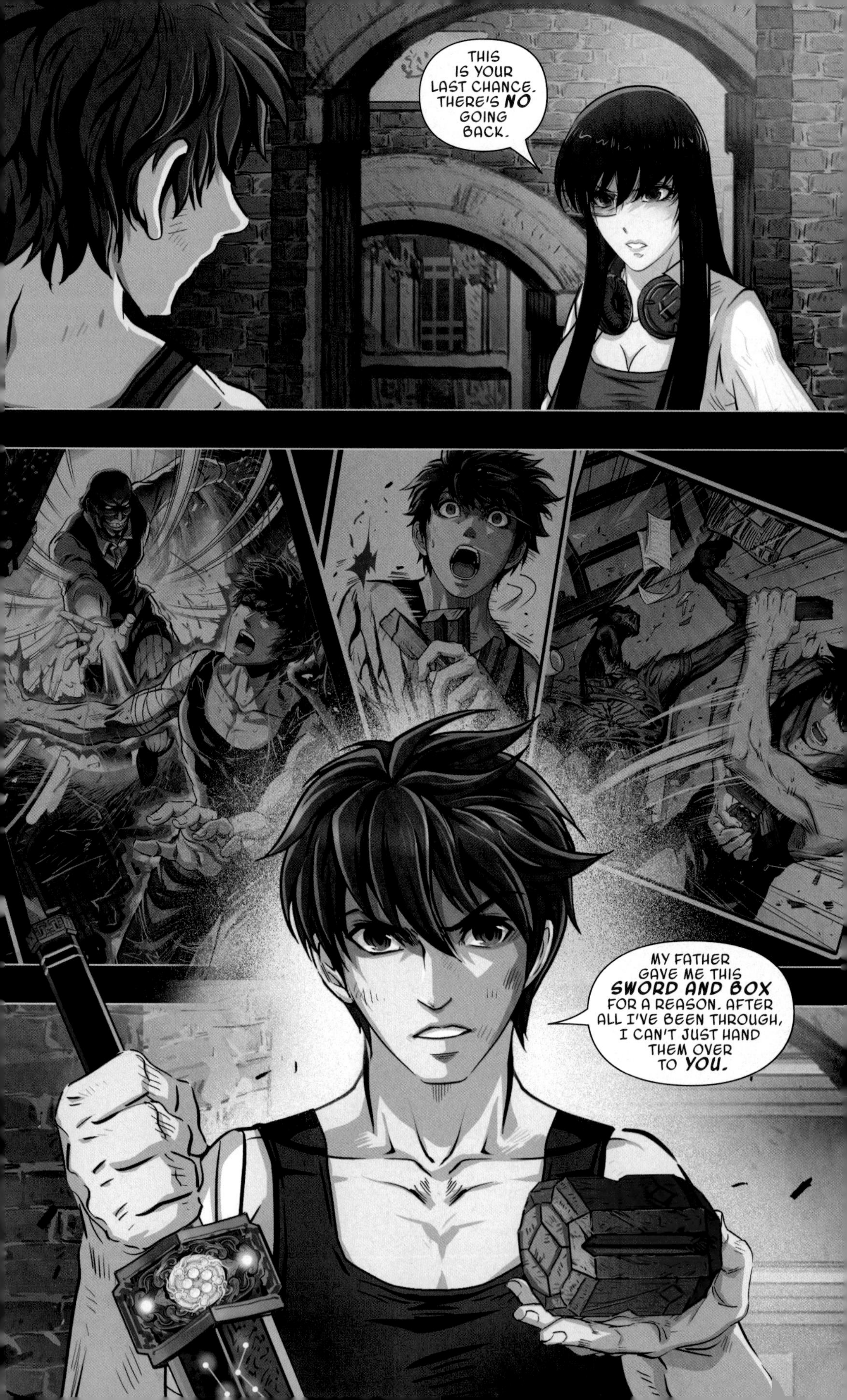
THIS IS YOUR LAST CHANCE. THERE'S NO GOING BACK.
MY FATHER GAVE ME THIS SWORD AND BOX FOR A REASON. AFTER ALL I'VE BEEN THROUGH, I CAN'T JUST HAND THEM OVER TO YOU.

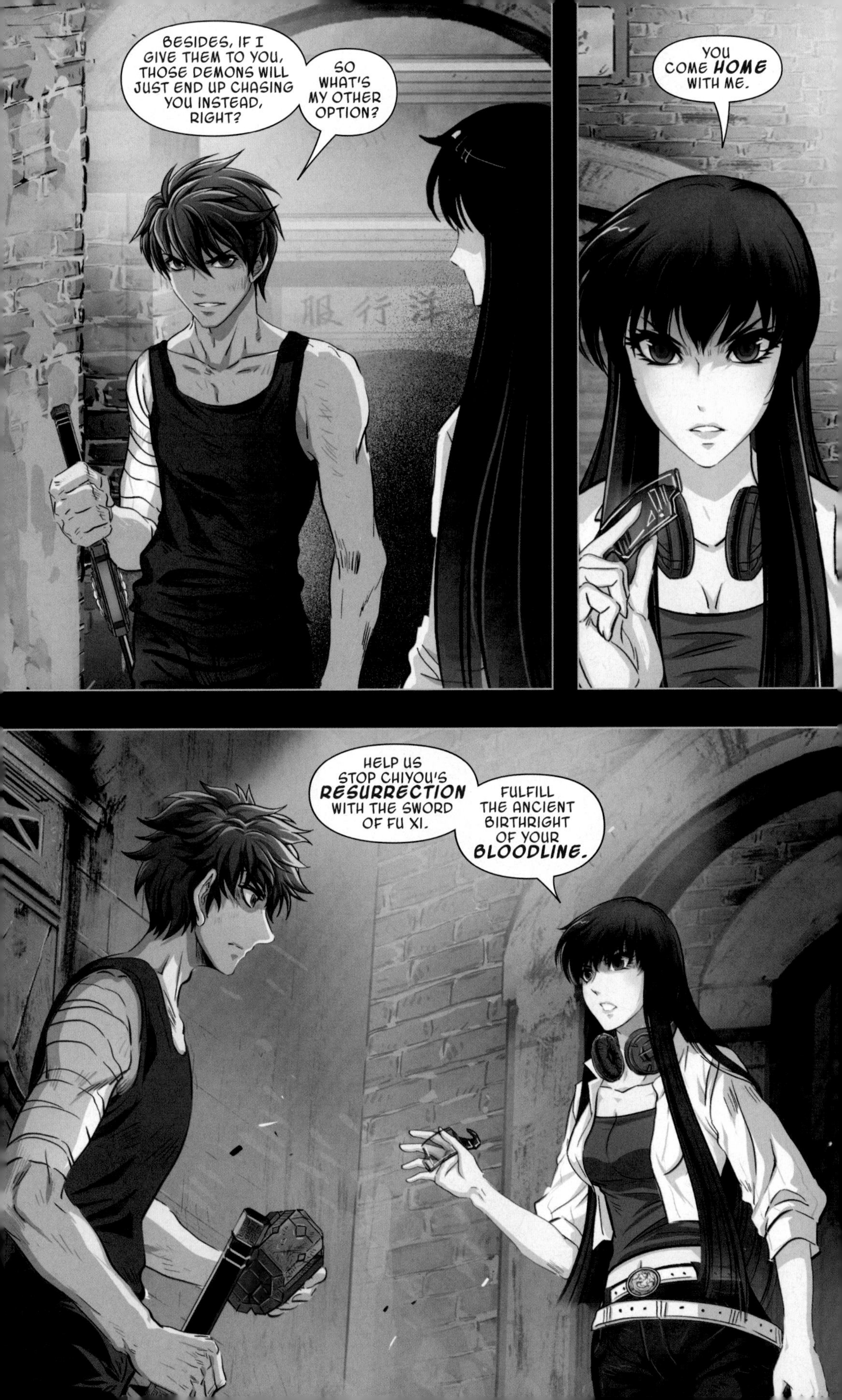
BESIDES, IF I GIVE THEM TO YOU, THOSE DEMONS WILL JUST END UP CHASING YOU INSTEAD, RIGHT?
SO WHAT'S MY OTHER OPTION?
YOU COME **HOME** WITH ME.
HELP US STOP CHIYOU'S **RESURRECTION** WITH THE SWORD OF FU XI.
FULFILL THE ANCIENT BIRTHRIGHT OF YOUR **BLOODLINE.**

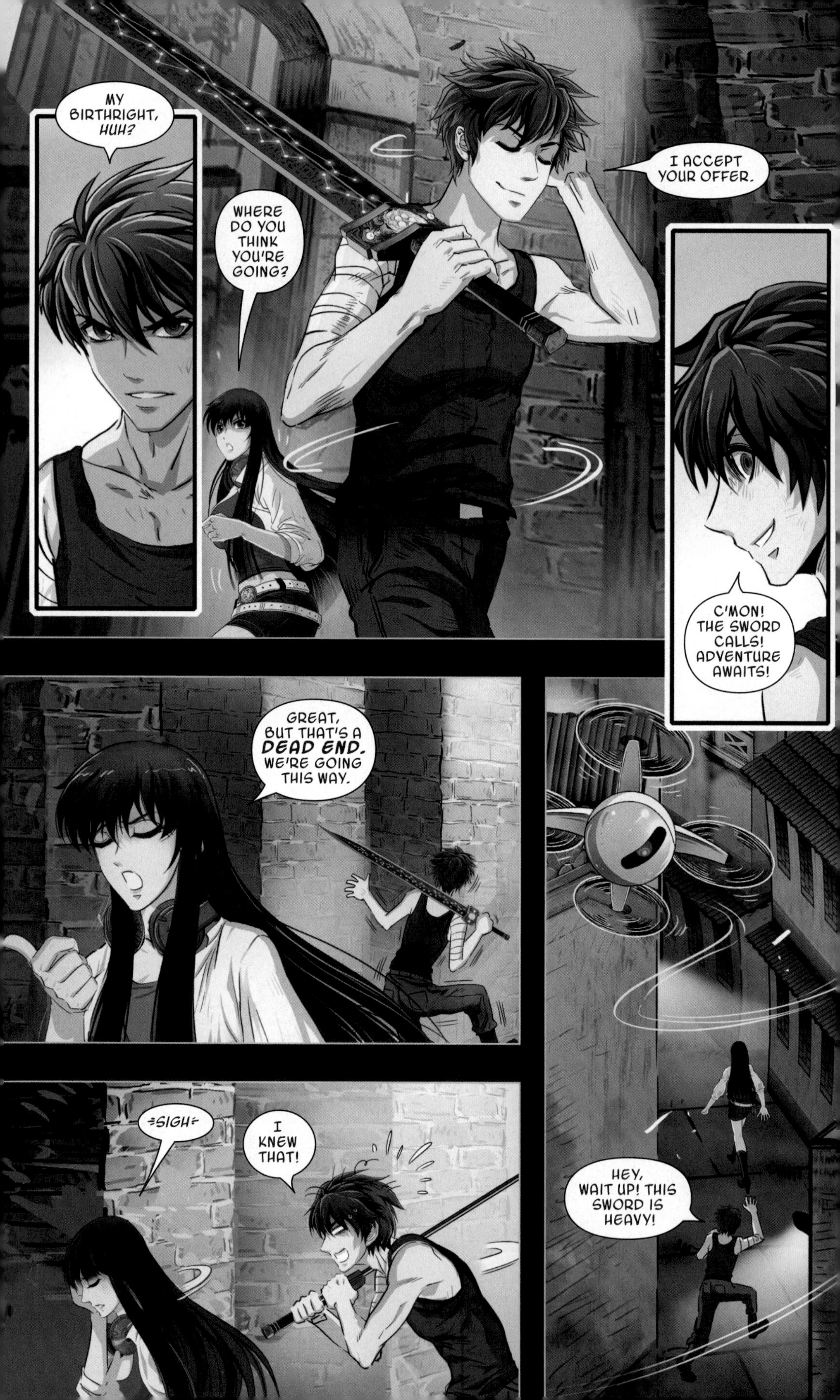

MY BIRTHRIGHT, HUH?
WHERE DO YOU THINK YOU'RE GOING?
I ACCEPT YOUR OFFER.
C'MON! THE SWORD CALLS! ADVENTURE AWAITS!
GREAT, BUT THAT'S A DEAD END. WE'RE GOING THIS WAY.
=SIGH=
I KNEW THAT!
HEY, WAIT UP! THIS SWORD IS HEAVY!

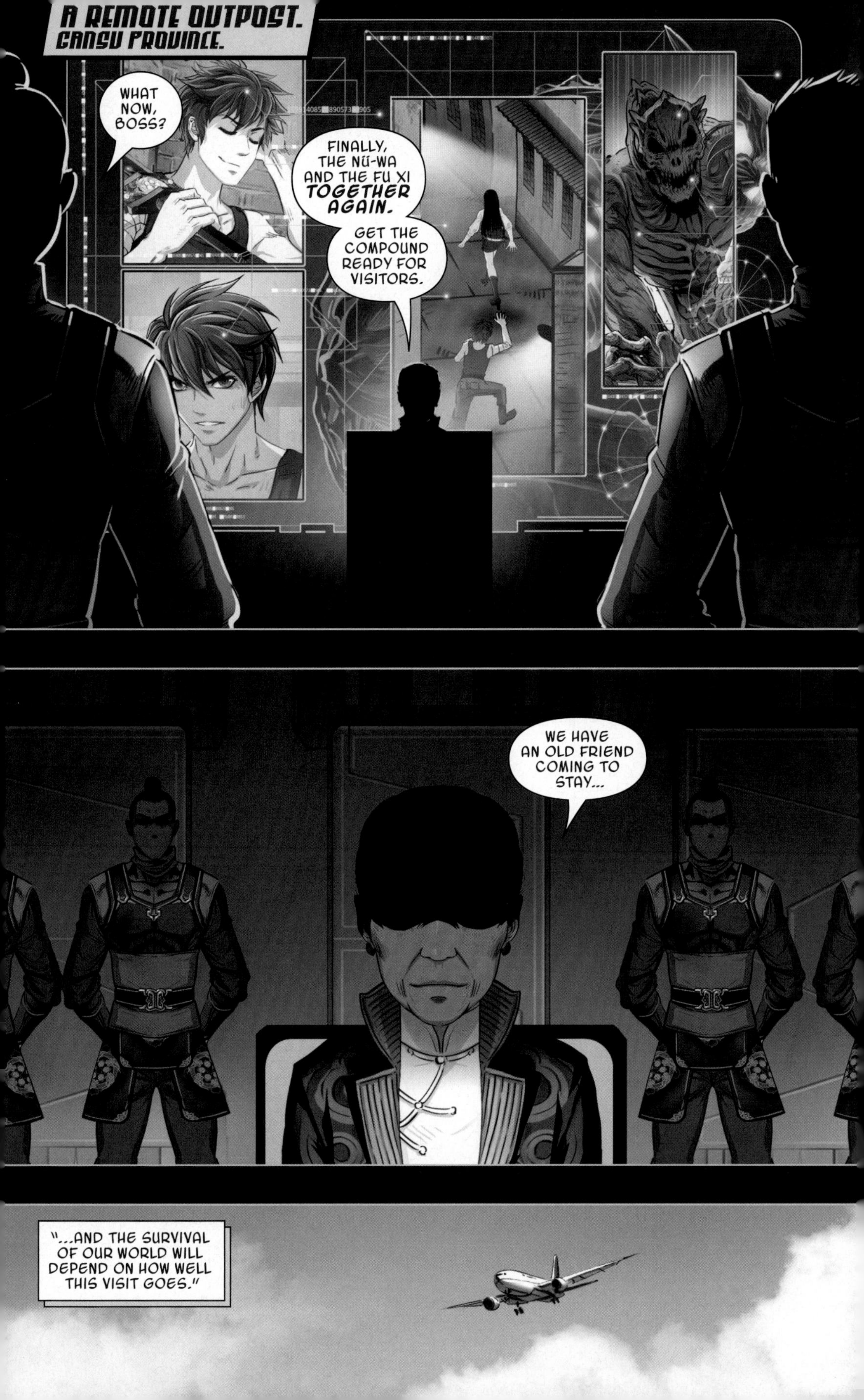
A REMOTE OUTPOST. GANSU PROVINCE.
WHAT NOW, BOSS?
FINALLY, THE NŪ-WA AND THE FU XI TOGETHER AGAIN.
GET THE COMPOUND READY FOR VISITORS.
WE HAVE AN OLD FRIEND COMING TO STAY...
"...AND THE SURVIVAL OF OUR WORLD WILL DEPEND ON HOW WELL THIS VISIT GOES."

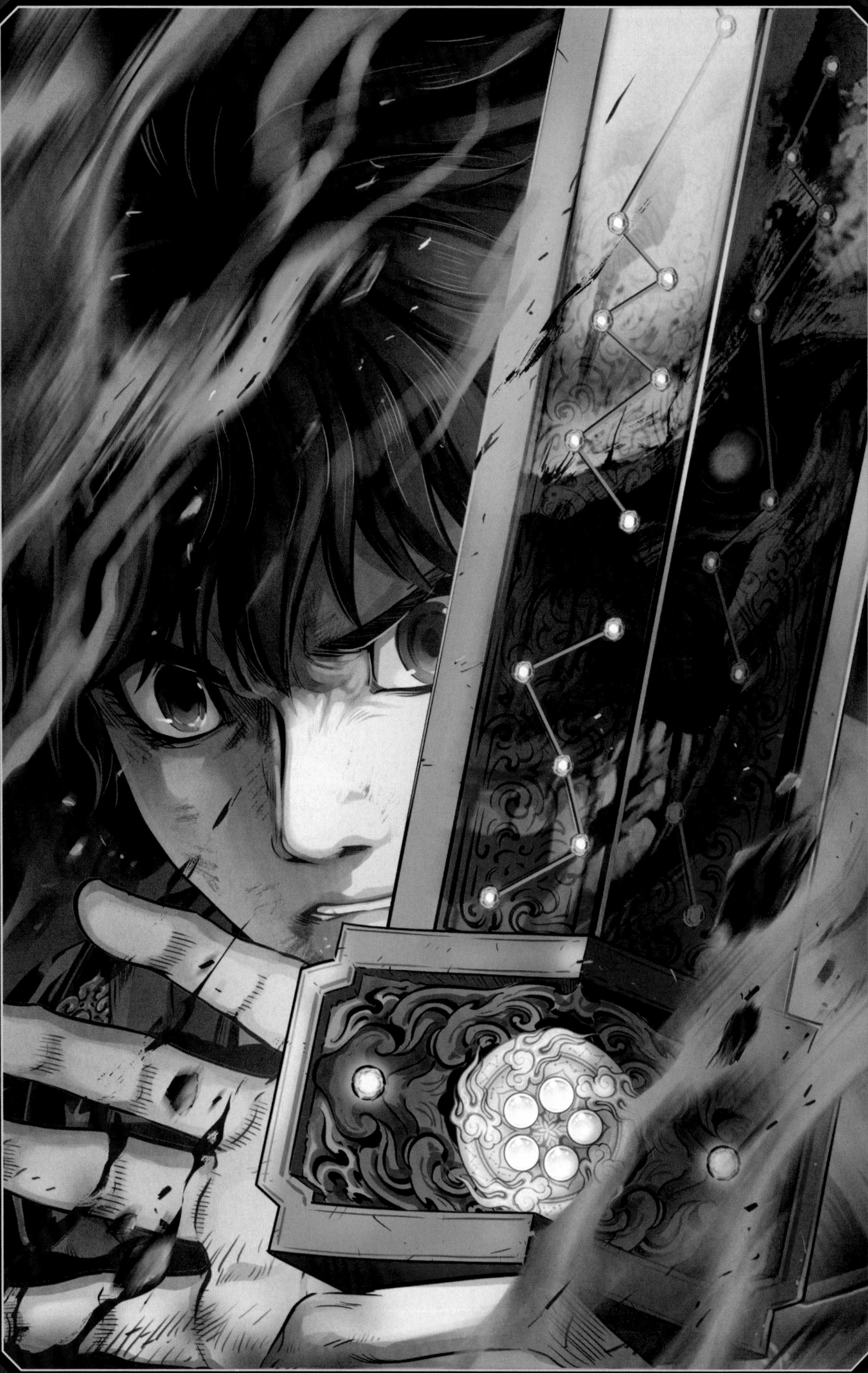

NINE FRIENDS & ENEMIES

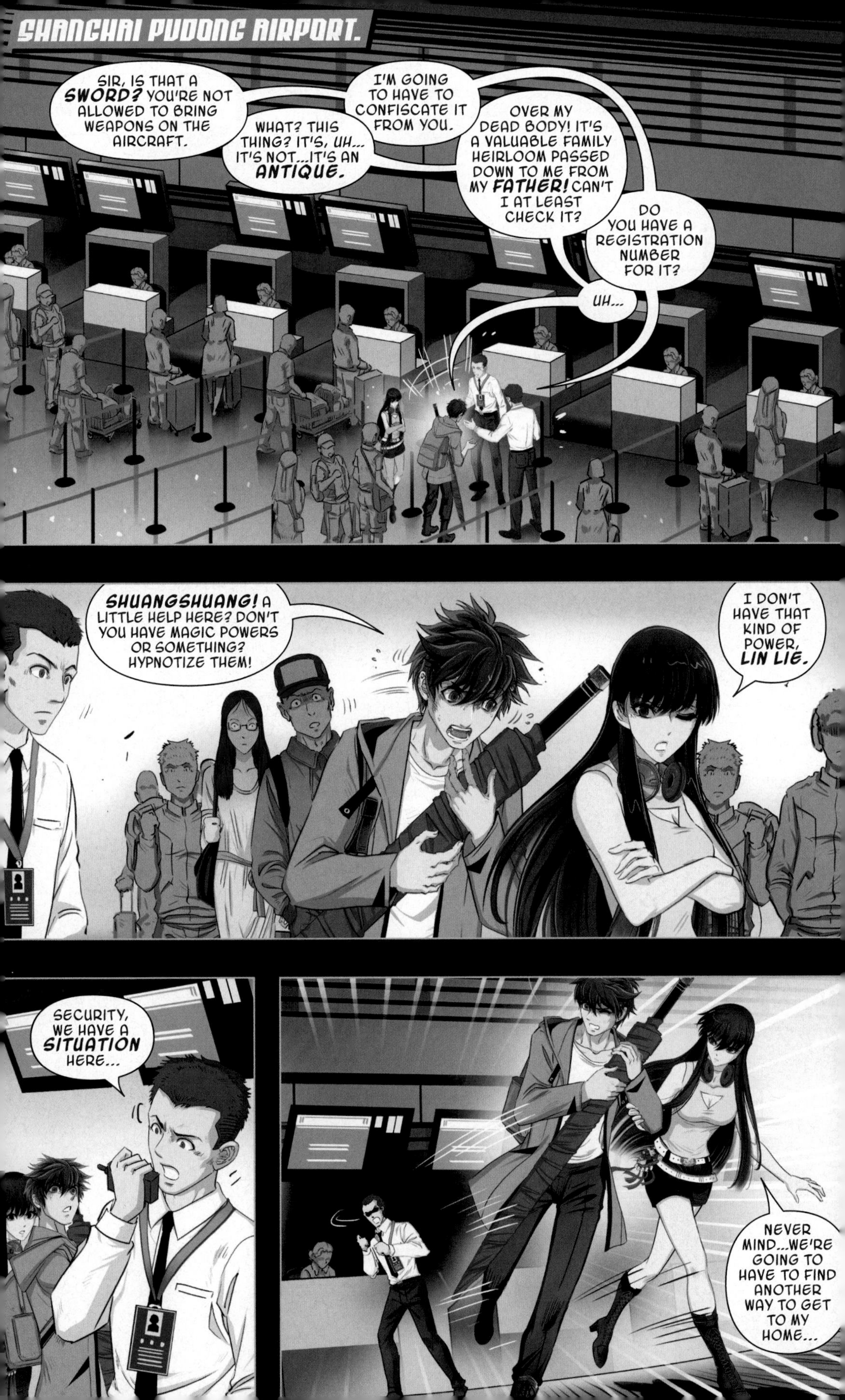
SHANGHAI PUDONG AIRPORT.
SIR, IS THAT A SWORD? YOU'RE NOT ALLOWED TO BRING WEAPONS ON THE AIRCRAFT.
WHAT? THIS THING? IT'S, UH... IT'S NOT...IT'S AN ANTIQUE.
I'M GOING TO HAVE TO CONFISCATE IT FROM YOU.
OVER MY DEAD BODY! IT'S A VALUABLE FAMILY HEIRLOOM PASSED DOWN TO ME FROM MY FATHER! CAN'T I AT LEAST CHECK IT?
DO YOU HAVE A REGISTRATION NUMBER FOR IT?
UH...
SHUANGSHUANG! A LITTLE HELP HERE? DON'T YOU HAVE MAGIC POWERS OR SOMETHING? HYPNOTIZE THEM!
I DON'T HAVE THAT KIND OF POWER, LIN LIE.
SECURITY, WE HAVE A SITUATION HERE...
NEVER MIND...WE'RE GOING TO HAVE TO FIND ANOTHER WAY TO GET TO MY HOME...

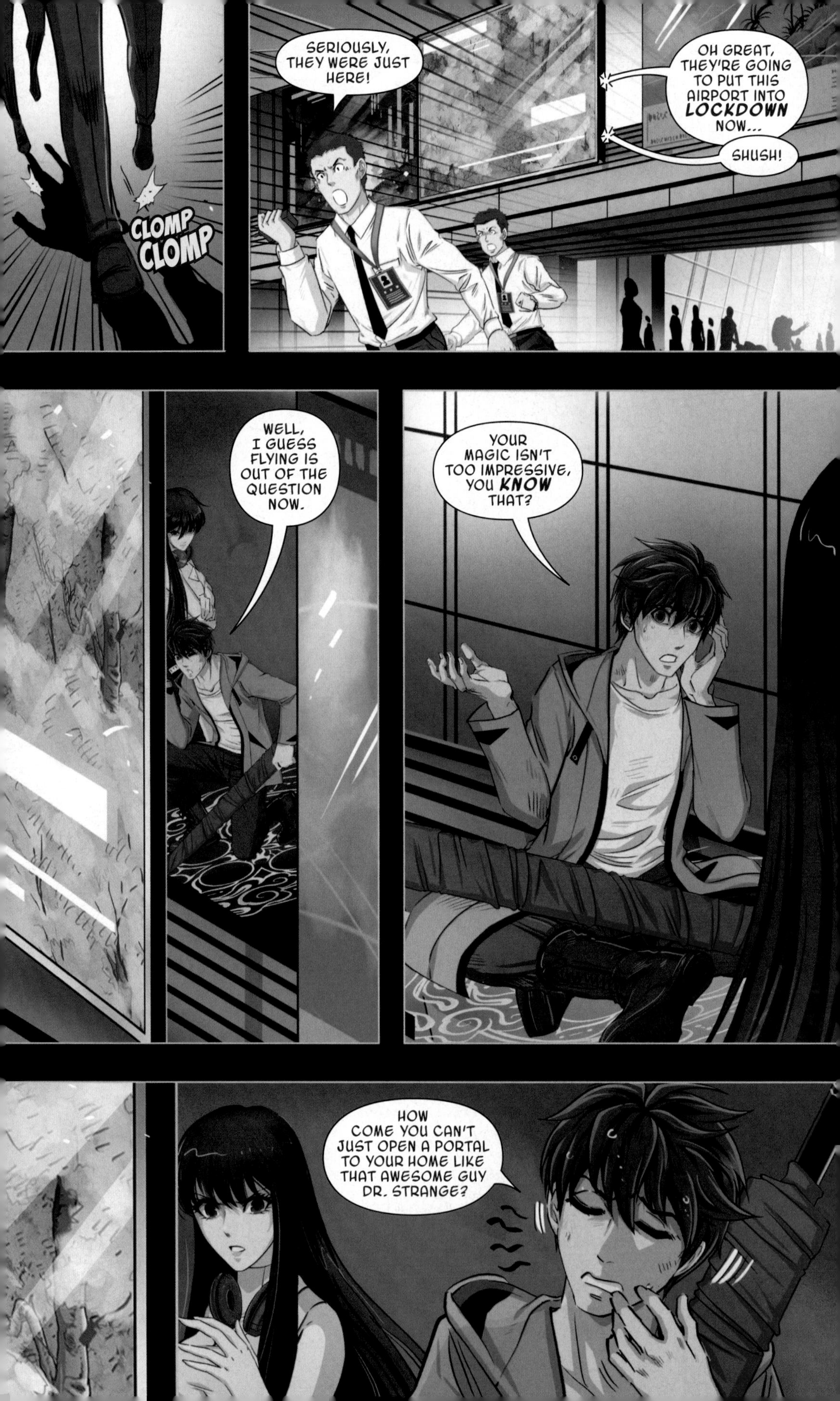
CLOMP
CLOMP
SERIOUSLY, THEY WERE JUST HERE!
OH GREAT, THEY'RE GOING TO PUT THIS AIRPORT INTO LOCKDOWN NOW...
SHUSH!
WELL, I GUESS FLYING IS OUT OF THE QUESTION NOW.
YOUR MAGIC ISN'T TOO IMPRESSIVE, YOU KNOW THAT?
HOW COME YOU CAN'T JUST OPEN A PORTAL TO YOUR HOME LIKE THAT AWESOME GUY DR. STRANGE?

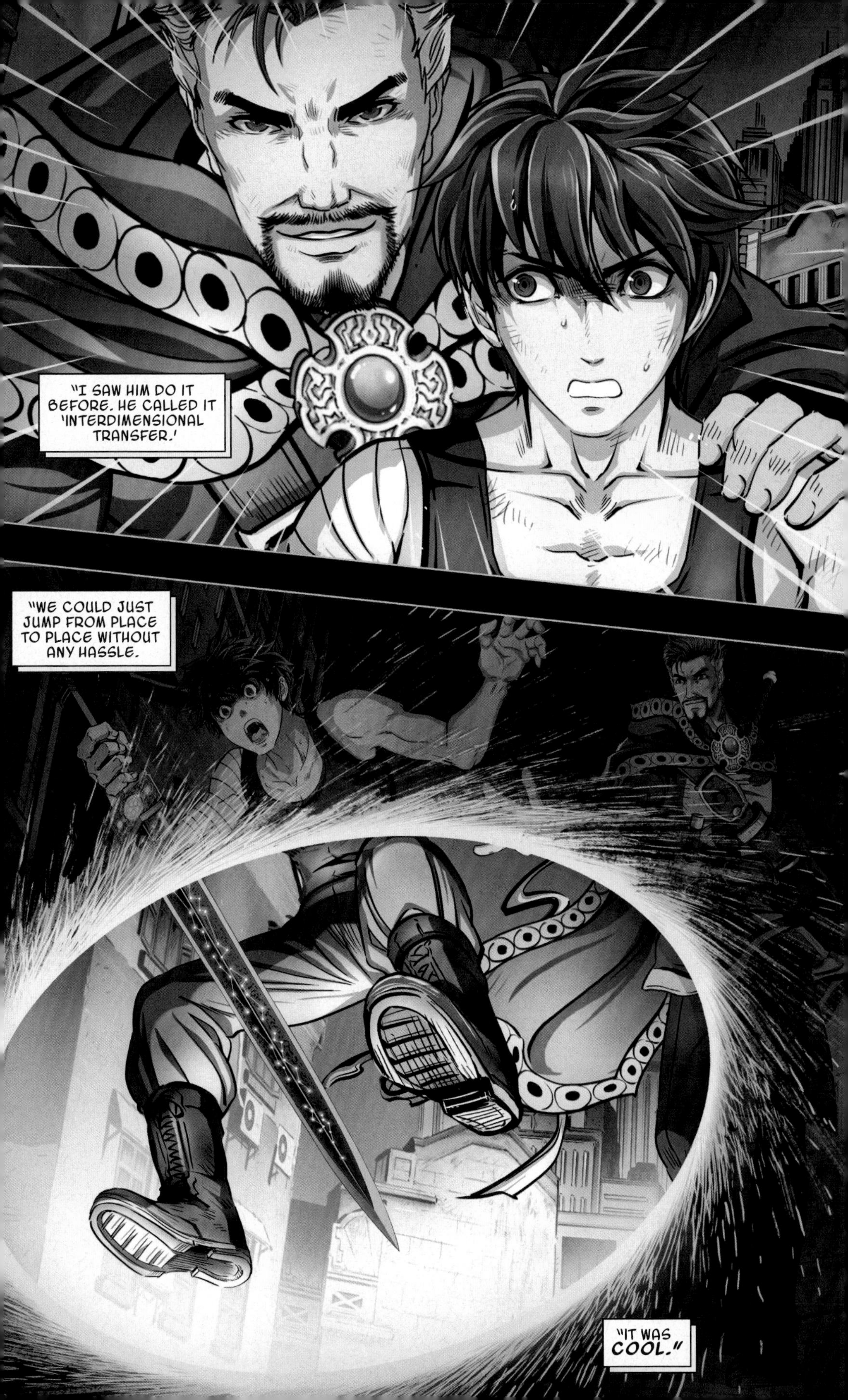
"I SAW HIM DO IT BEFORE. HE CALLED IT 'INTERDIMENSIONAL TRANSFER.'
"WE COULD JUST JUMP FROM PLACE TO PLACE WITHOUT ANY HASSLE.
"IT WAS COOL."

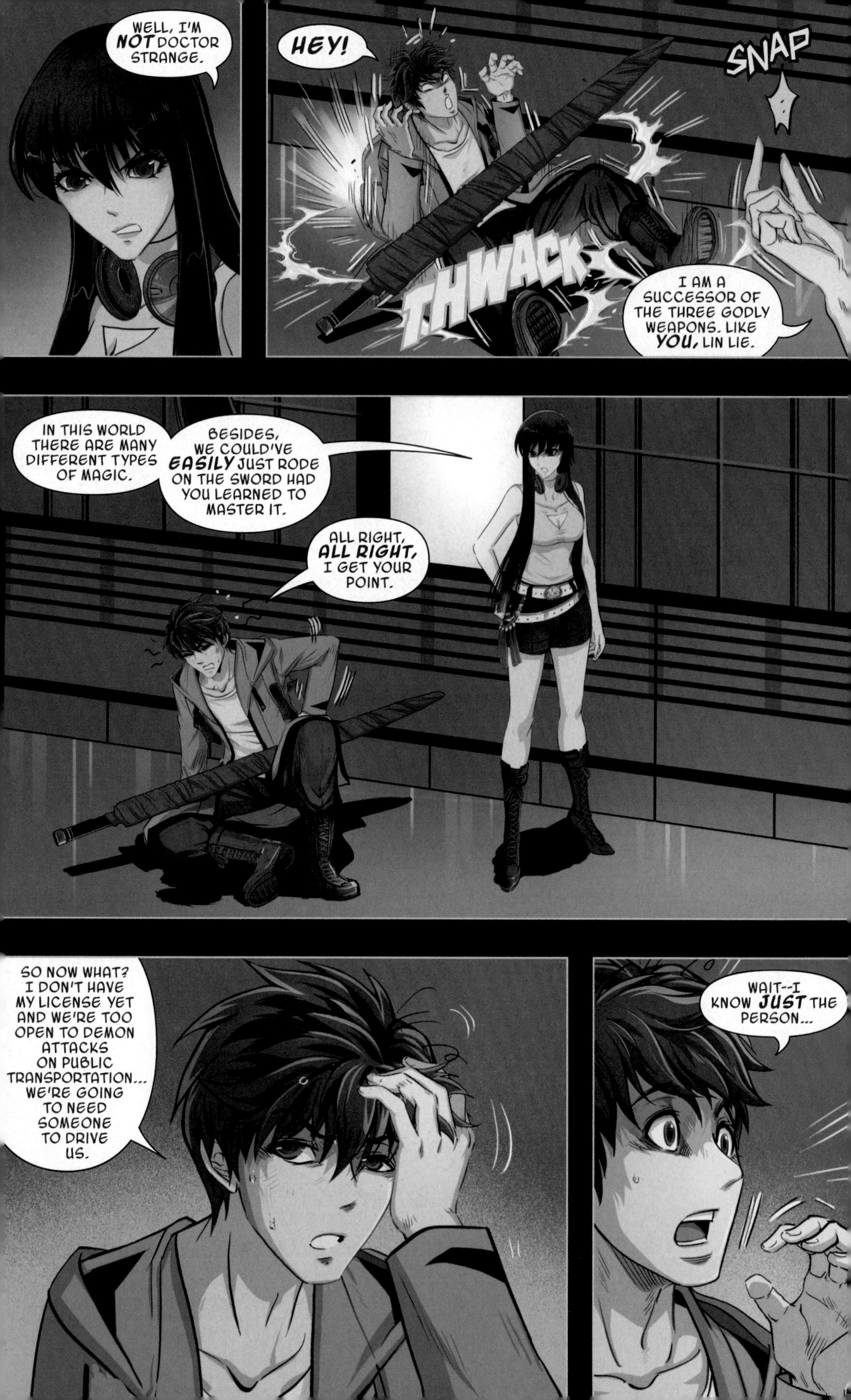
WELL, I'M NOT DOCTOR STRANGE.
HEY!
SNAP
THWACK
I AM A SUCCESSOR OF THE THREE GODLY WEAPONS. LIKE YOU, LIN LIE.
IN THIS WORLD THERE ARE MANY DIFFERENT TYPES OF MAGIC.
BESIDES, WE COULD'VE EASILY JUST RODE ON THE SWORD HAD YOU LEARNED TO MASTER IT.
ALL RIGHT, ALL RIGHT, I GET YOUR POINT.
SO NOW WHAT? I DON'T HAVE MY LICENSE YET AND WE'RE TOO OPEN TO DEMON ATTACKS ON PUBLIC TRANSPORTATION... WE'RE GOING TO NEED SOMEONE TO DRIVE US.
WAIT--I KNOW JUST THE PERSON...

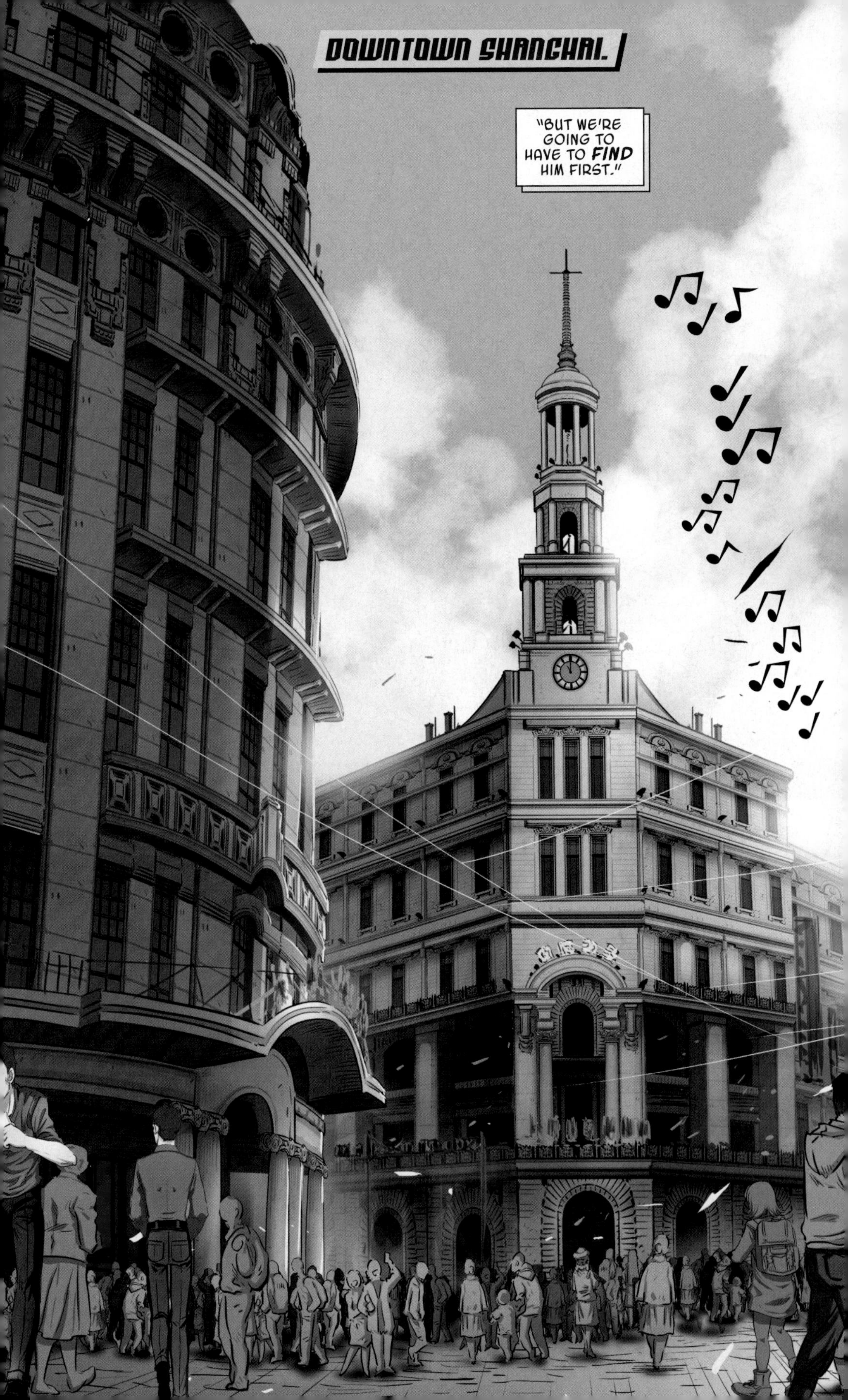
DOWNTOWN SHANGHAI.
"BUT WE'RE GOING TO HAVE TO FIND HIM FIRST."

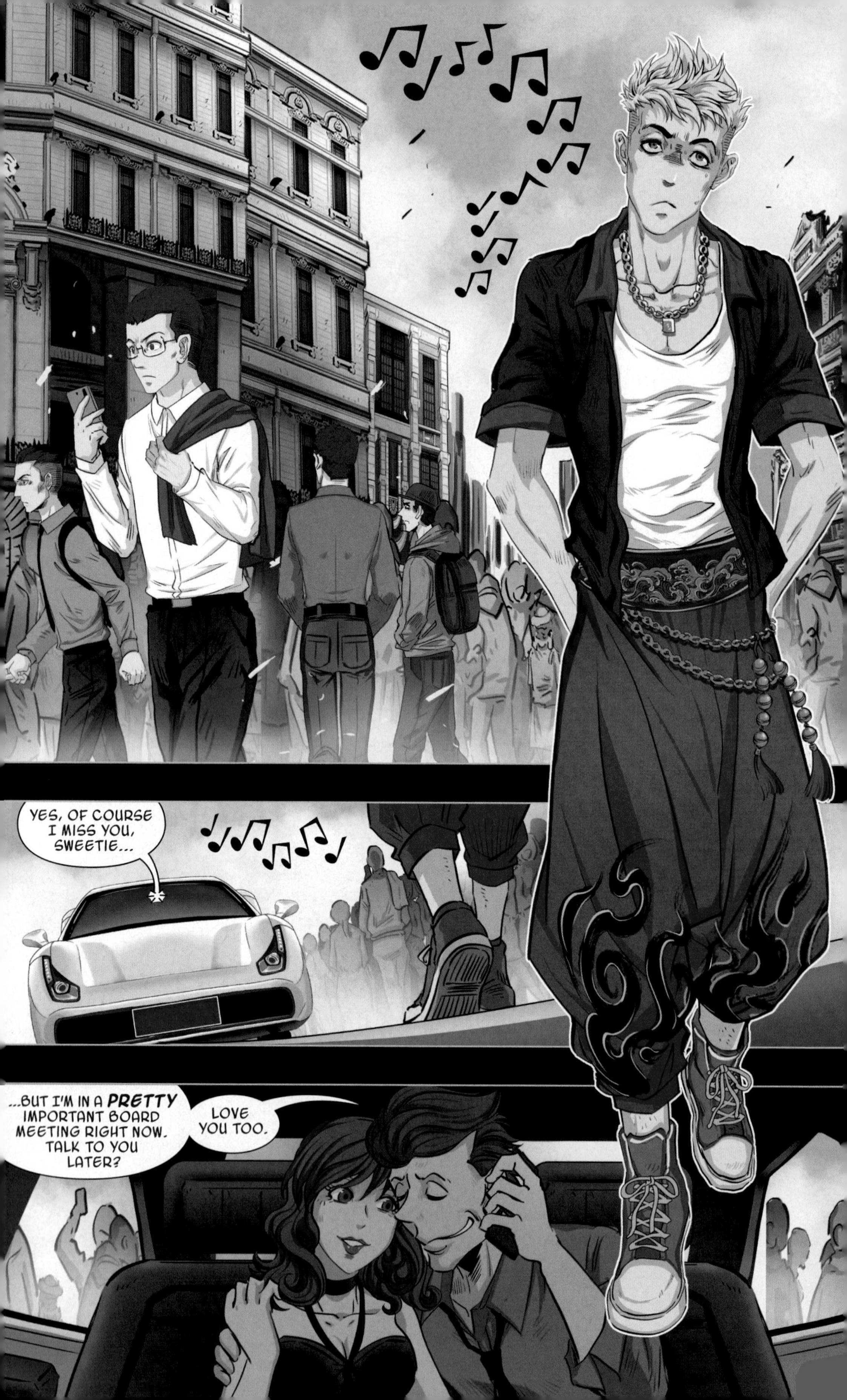
YES, OF COURSE I MISS YOU, SWEETIE...
...BUT I'M IN A PRETTY IMPORTANT BOARD MEETING RIGHT NOW. TALK TO YOU LATER?
LOVE YOU TOO.

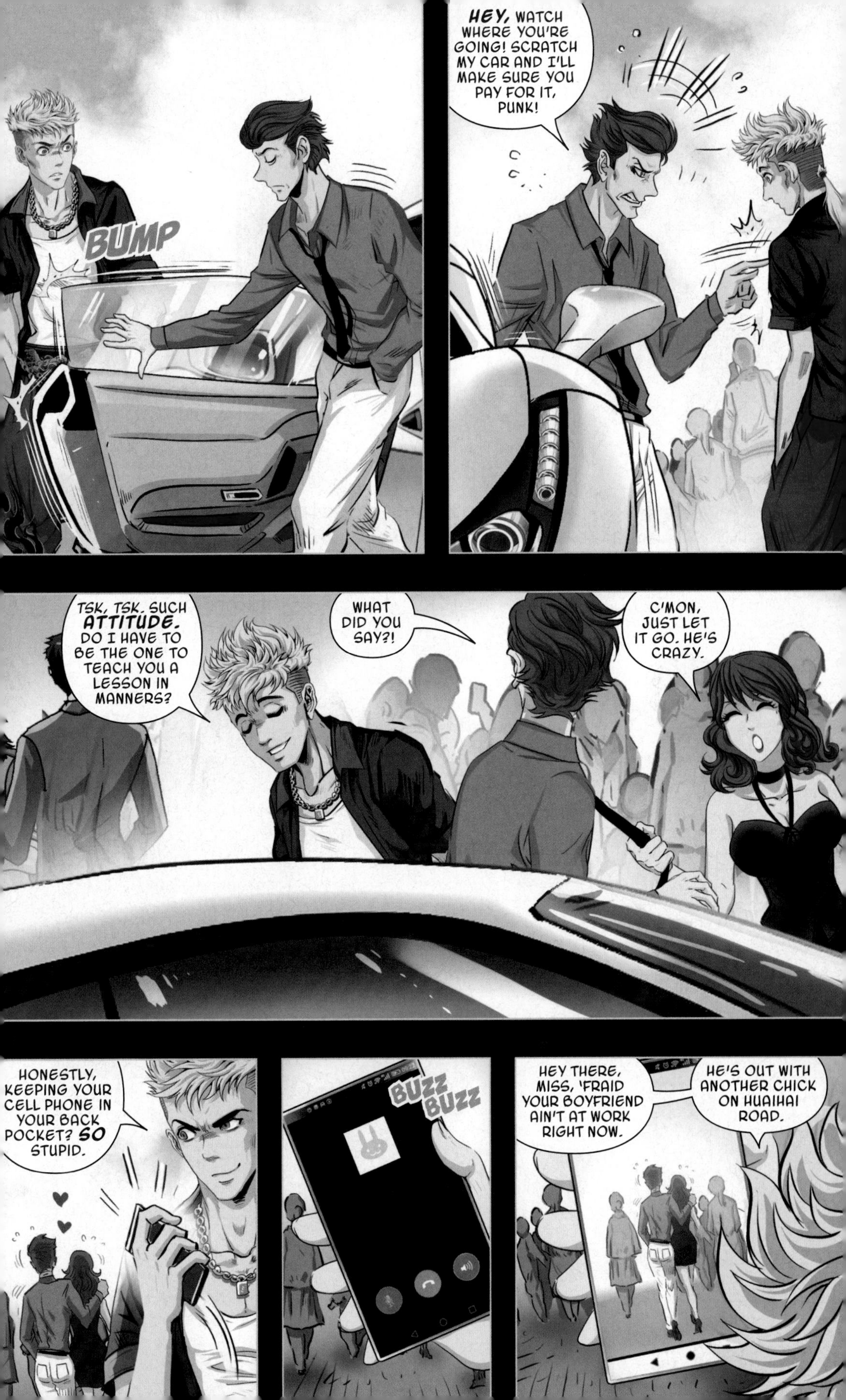
BUMP
HEY, WATCH WHERE YOU'RE GOING! SCRATCH MY CAR AND I'LL MAKE SURE YOU PAY FOR IT, PUNK!
TSK, TSK. SUCH ATTITUDE. DO I HAVE TO BE THE ONE TO TEACH YOU A LESSON IN MANNERS?
WHAT DID YOU SAY?!
C'MON, JUST LET IT GO. HE'S CRAZY.
HONESTLY, KEEPING YOUR CELL PHONE IN YOUR BACK POCKET? SO STUPID.
BUZZ BUZZ
HEY THERE, MISS, 'FRAID YOUR BOYFRIEND AIN'T AT WORK RIGHT NOW.
HE'S OUT WITH ANOTHER CHICK ON HUAIHAI ROAD.

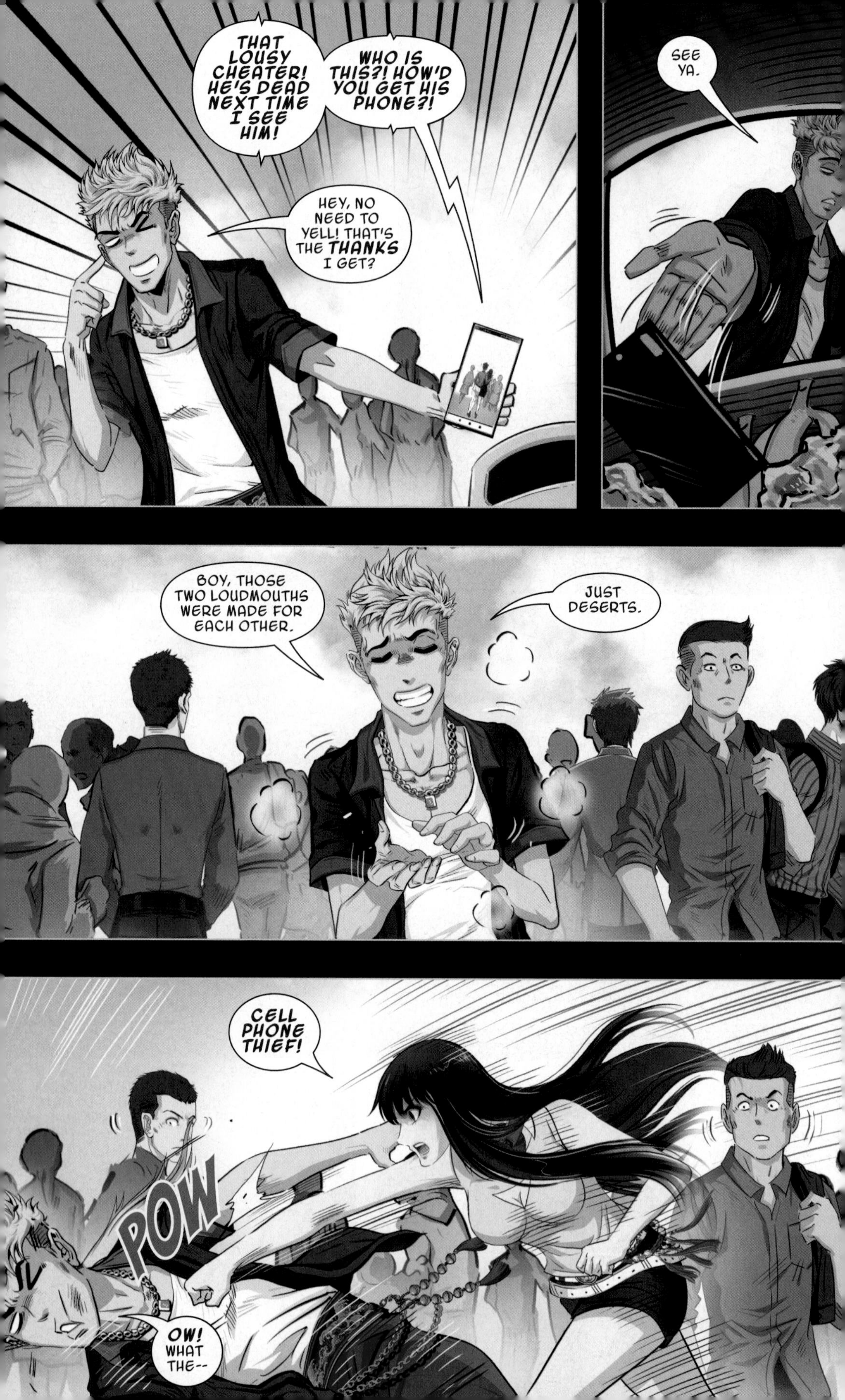
THAT LOUSY CHEATER! HE'S DEAD NEXT TIME I SEE HIM!
WHO IS THIS?! HOW'D YOU GET HIS PHONE?!
HEY, NO NEED TO YELL! THAT'S THE THANKS I GET?
SEE YA.
BOY, THOSE TWO LOUDMOUTHS WERE MADE FOR EACH OTHER.
JUST DESERTS.
CELL PHONE THIEF!
POW
OW! WHAT THE--

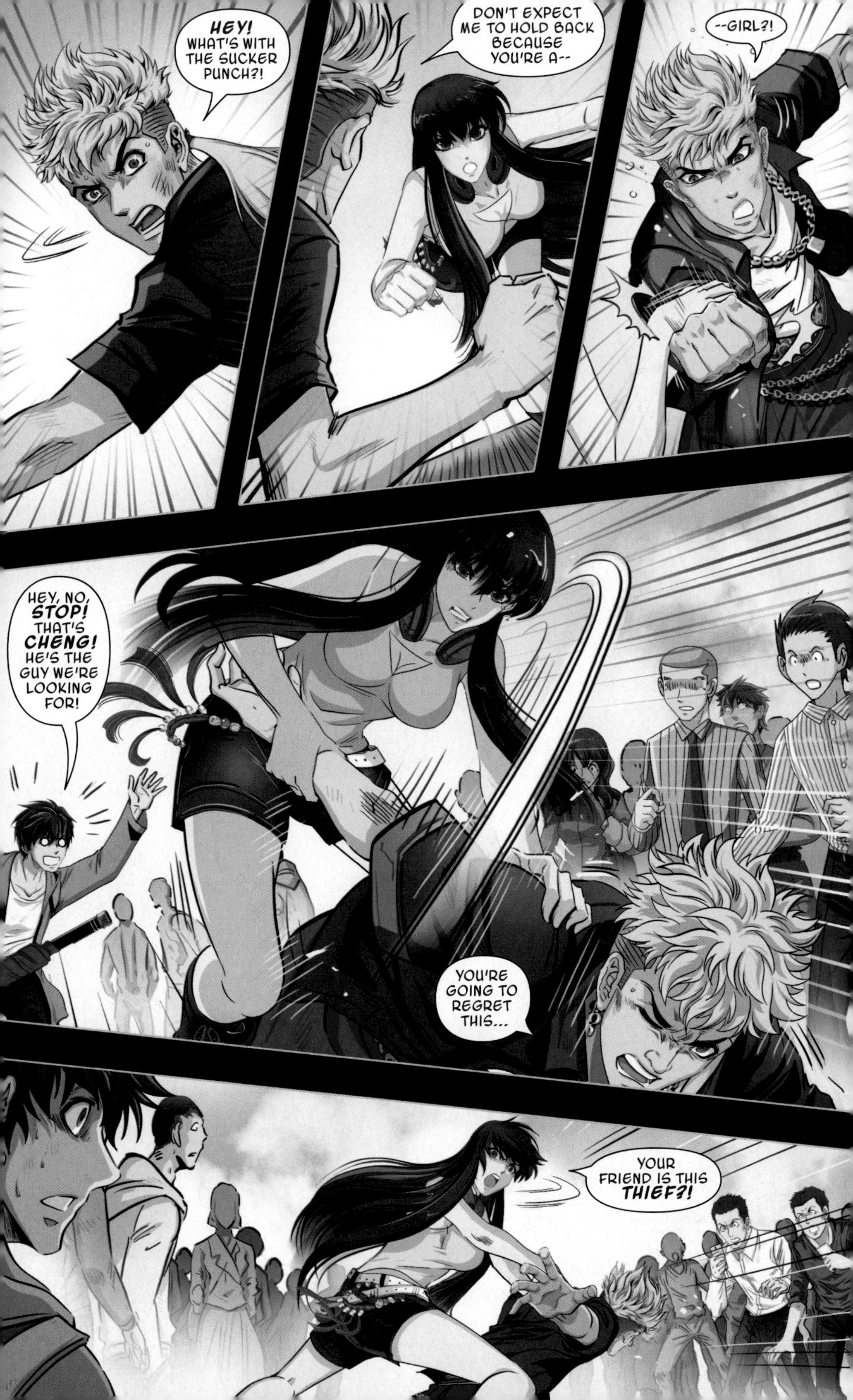

HEY! WHAT'S WITH THE SUCKER PUNCH?!
DON'T EXPECT ME TO HOLD BACK BECAUSE YOU'RE A--
--GIRL?!
HEY, NO, STOP! THAT'S CHENG! HE'S THE GUY WE'RE LOOKING FOR!
YOU'RE GOING TO REGRET THIS...
YOUR FRIEND IS THIS THIEF?!

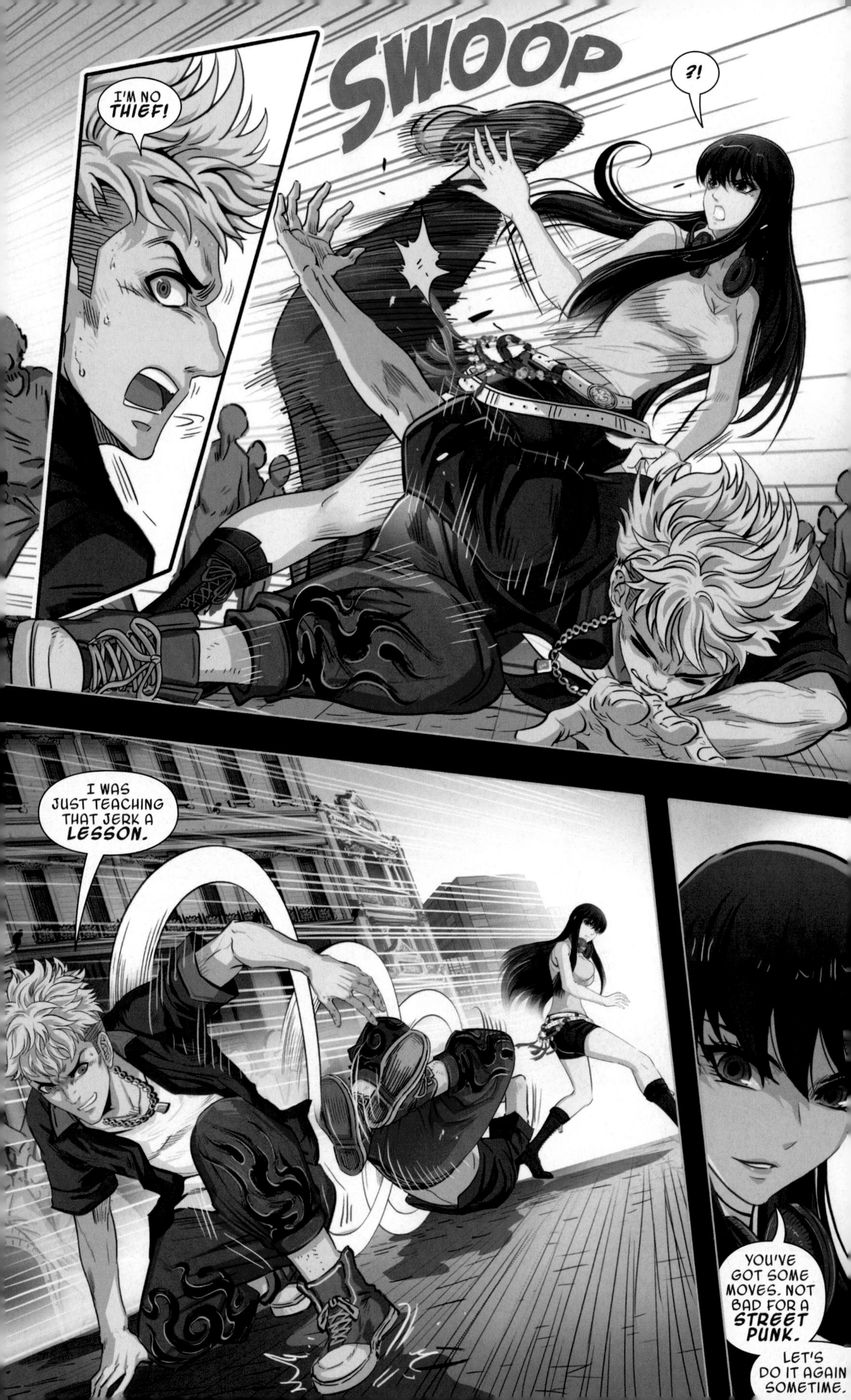
I'M NO THIEF!
SWOOP
?!
I WAS JUST TEACHING THAT JERK A LESSON.
YOU'VE GOT SOME MOVES. NOT BAD FOR A STREET PUNK.
LET'S DO IT AGAIN SOMETIME.

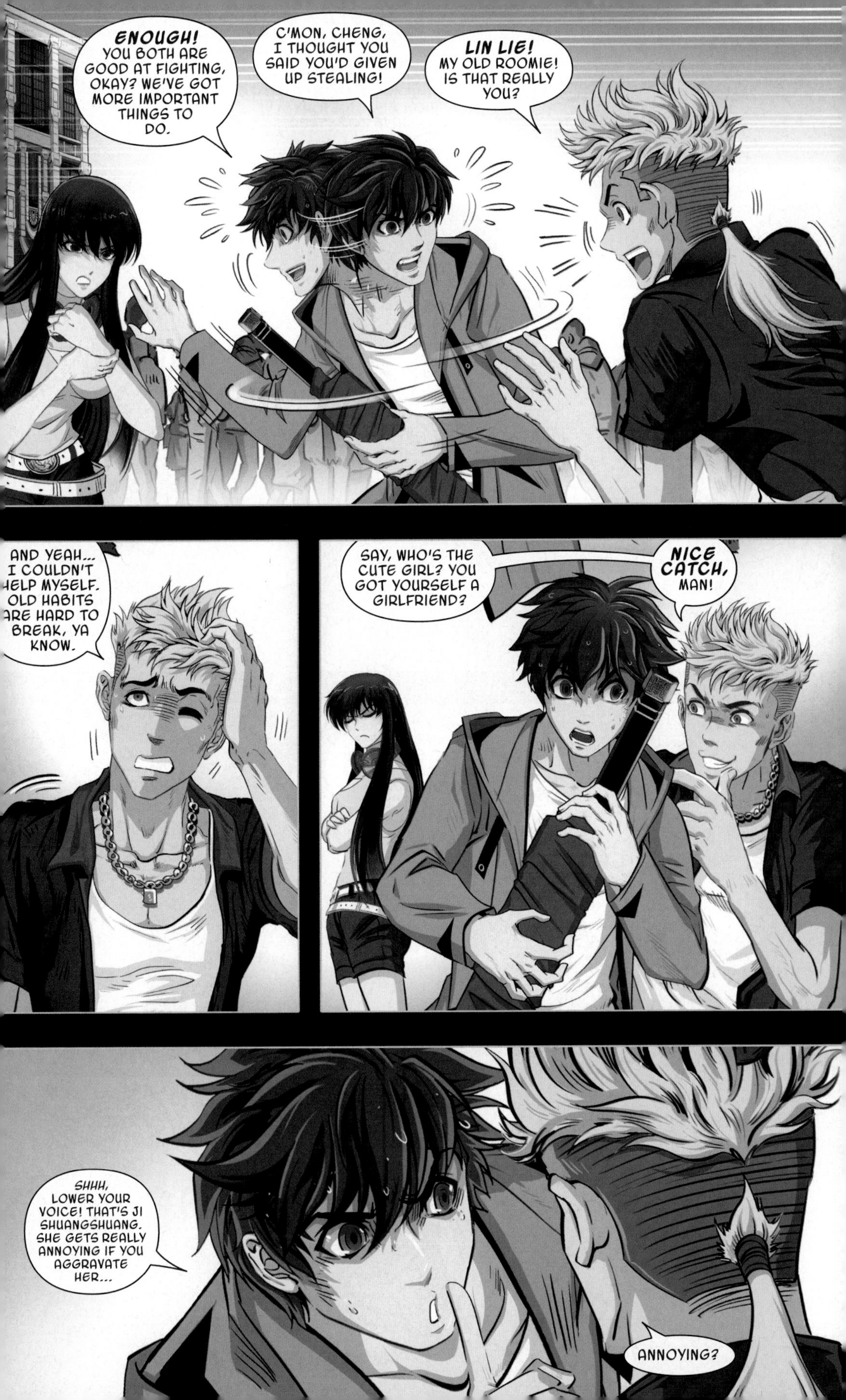
ENOUGH! YOU BOTH ARE GOOD AT FIGHTING, OKAY? WE'VE GOT MORE IMPORTANT THINGS TO DO.
C'MON, CHENG, I THOUGHT YOU SAID YOU'D GIVEN UP STEALING!
LIN LIE! MY OLD ROOMIE! IS THAT REALLY YOU?
AND YEAH... I COULDN'T HELP MYSELF. OLD HABITS ARE HARD TO BREAK, YA KNOW.
SAY, WHO'S THE CUTE GIRL? YOU GOT YOURSELF A GIRLFRIEND?
NICE CATCH, MAN!
SHHH, LOWER YOUR VOICE! THAT'S JI SHUANGSHUANG. SHE GETS REALLY ANNOYING IF YOU AGGRAVATE HER...
ANNOYING?

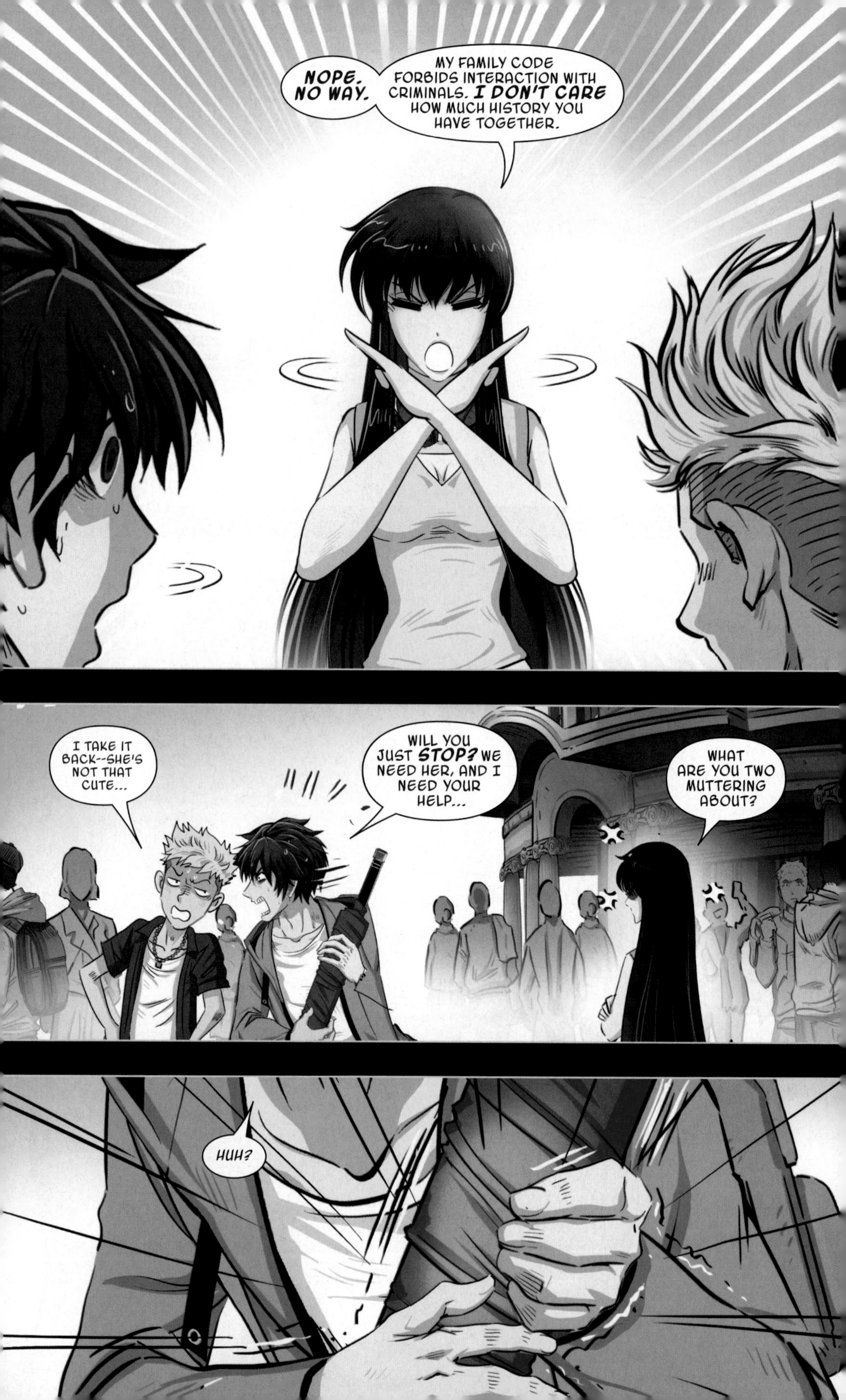
NOPE. NO WAY.
MY FAMILY CODE FORBIDS INTERACTION WITH CRIMINALS. I DON'T CARE HOW MUCH HISTORY YOU HAVE TOGETHER.
I TAKE IT BACK--SHE'S NOT THAT CUTE...
WILL YOU JUST STOP? WE NEED HER, AND I NEED YOUR HELP...
WHAT ARE YOU TWO MUTTERING ABOUT?
HUH?

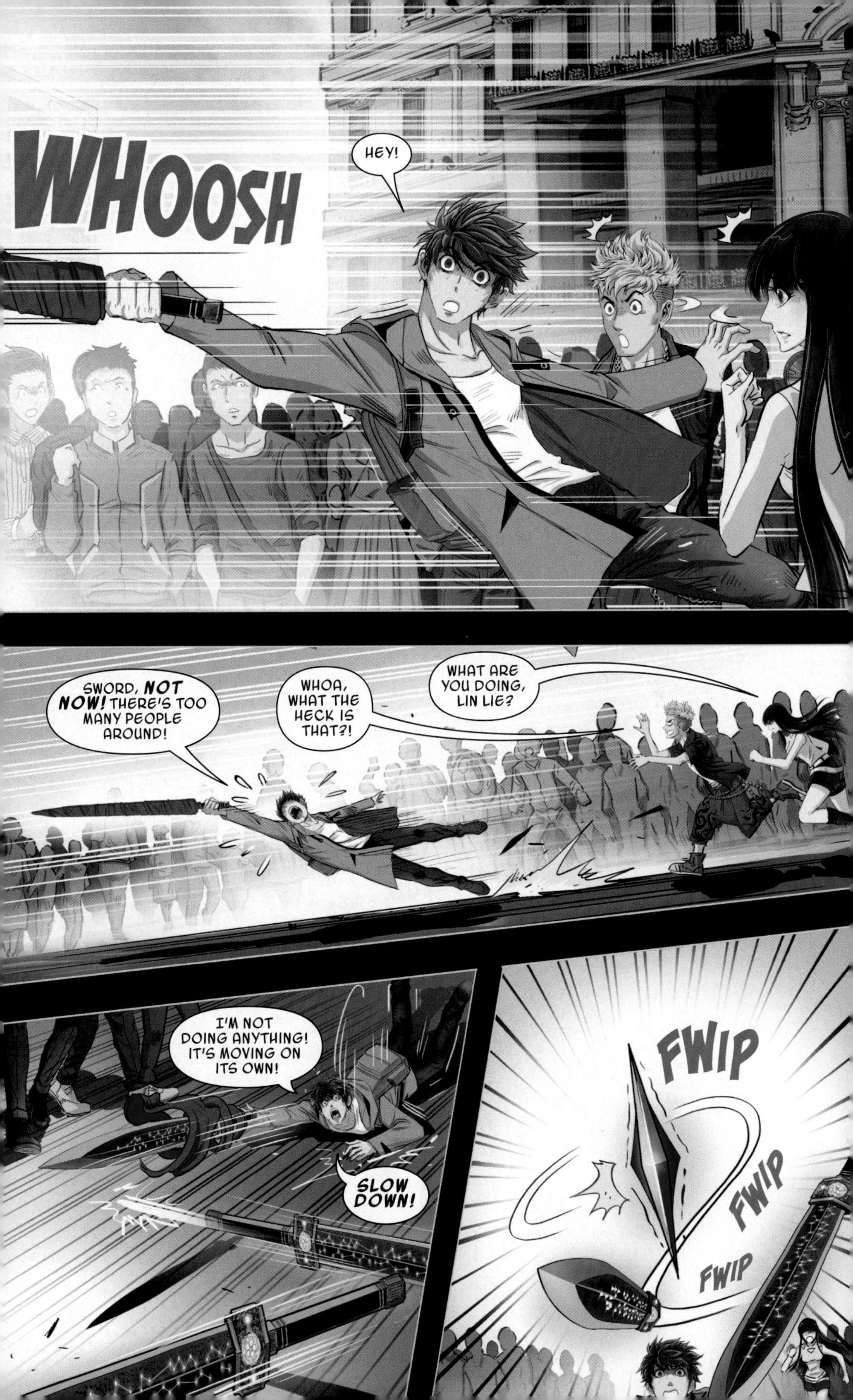

WHOOSH
HEY!
SWORD, NOT NOW! THERE'S TOO MANY PEOPLE AROUND!
WHOA, WHAT THE HECK IS THAT?!
WHAT ARE YOU DOING, LIN LIE?
I'M NOT DOING ANYTHING! IT'S MOVING ON ITS OWN!
SLOW DOWN!
FWIP
FWIP
FWIP

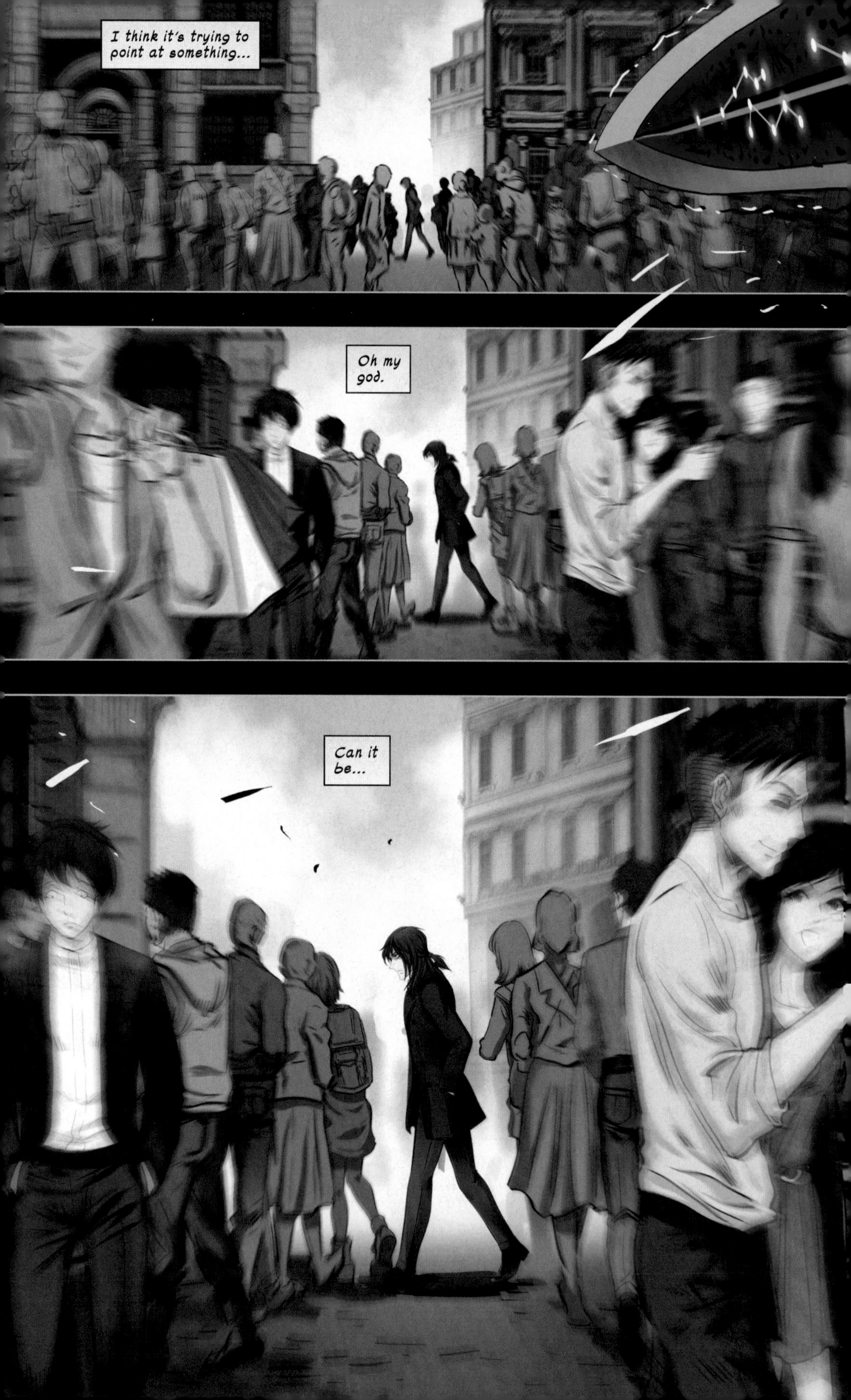
I think it's trying to point at something...
Oh my god.
Can it be...

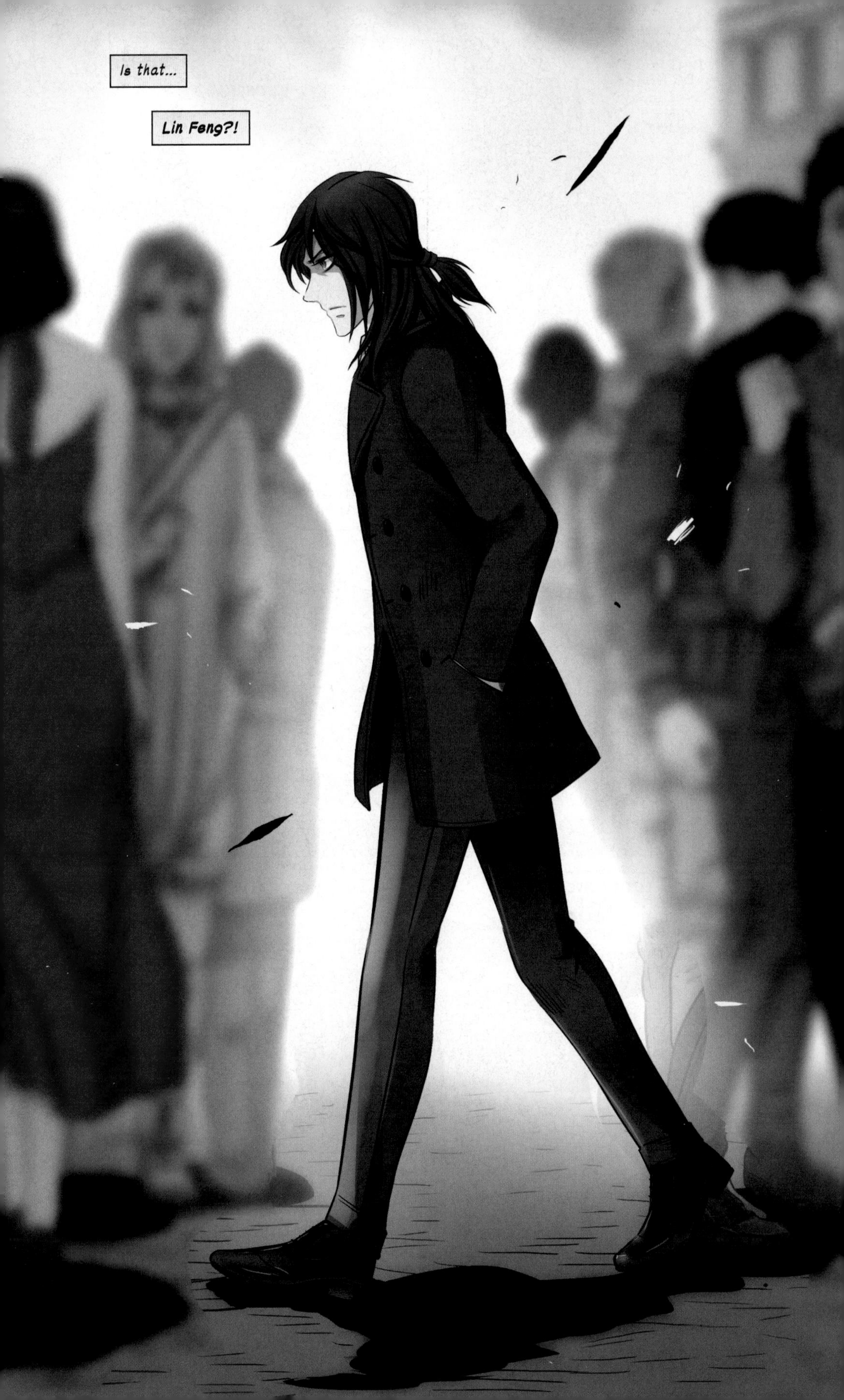
Is that...
Lin Feng?!

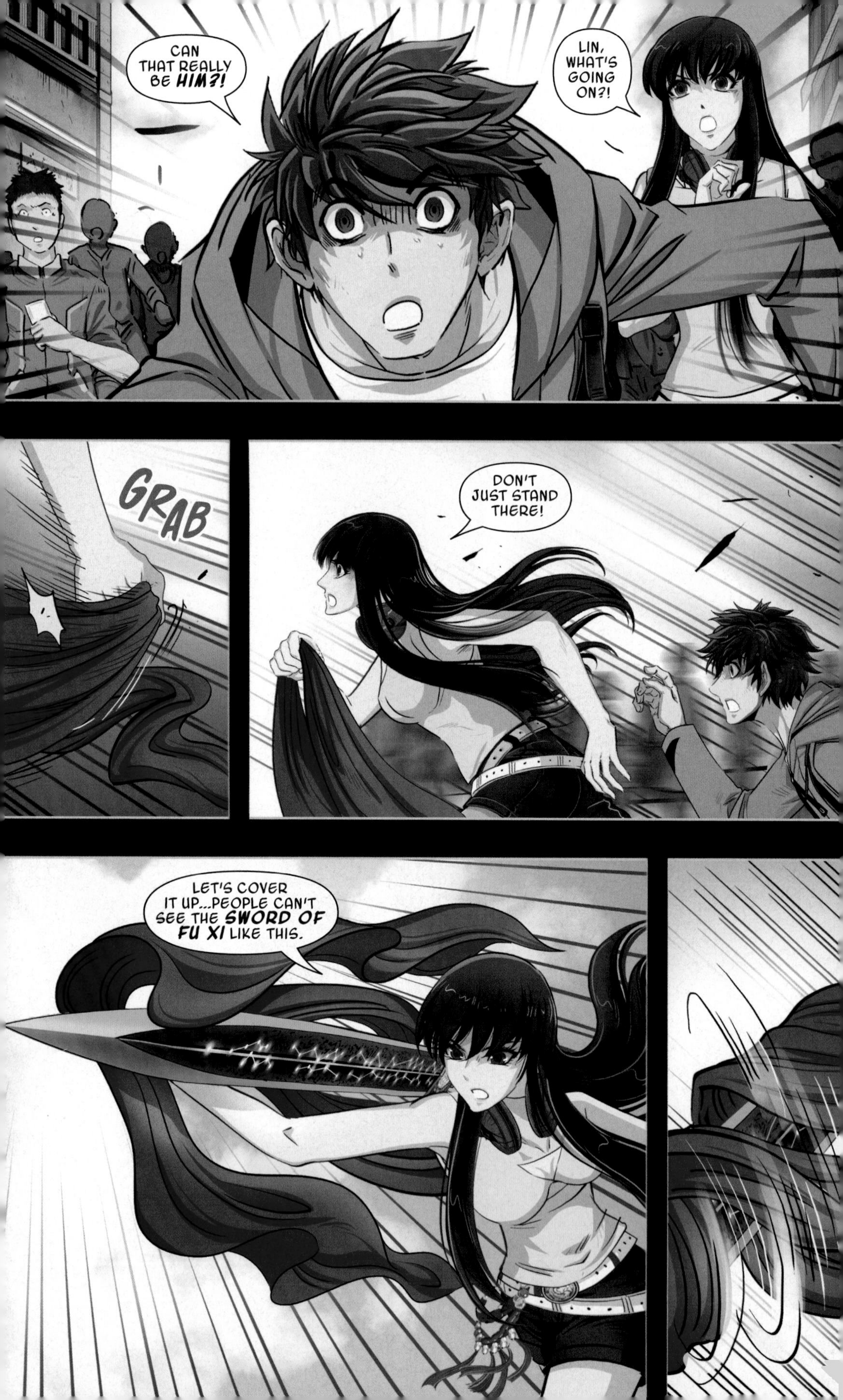
CAN THAT REALLY BE HIM?!
LIN, WHAT'S GOING ON?!
GRAB
DON'T JUST STAND THERE!
LET'S COVER IT UP...PEOPLE CAN'T SEE THE SWORD OF FU XI LIKE THIS.

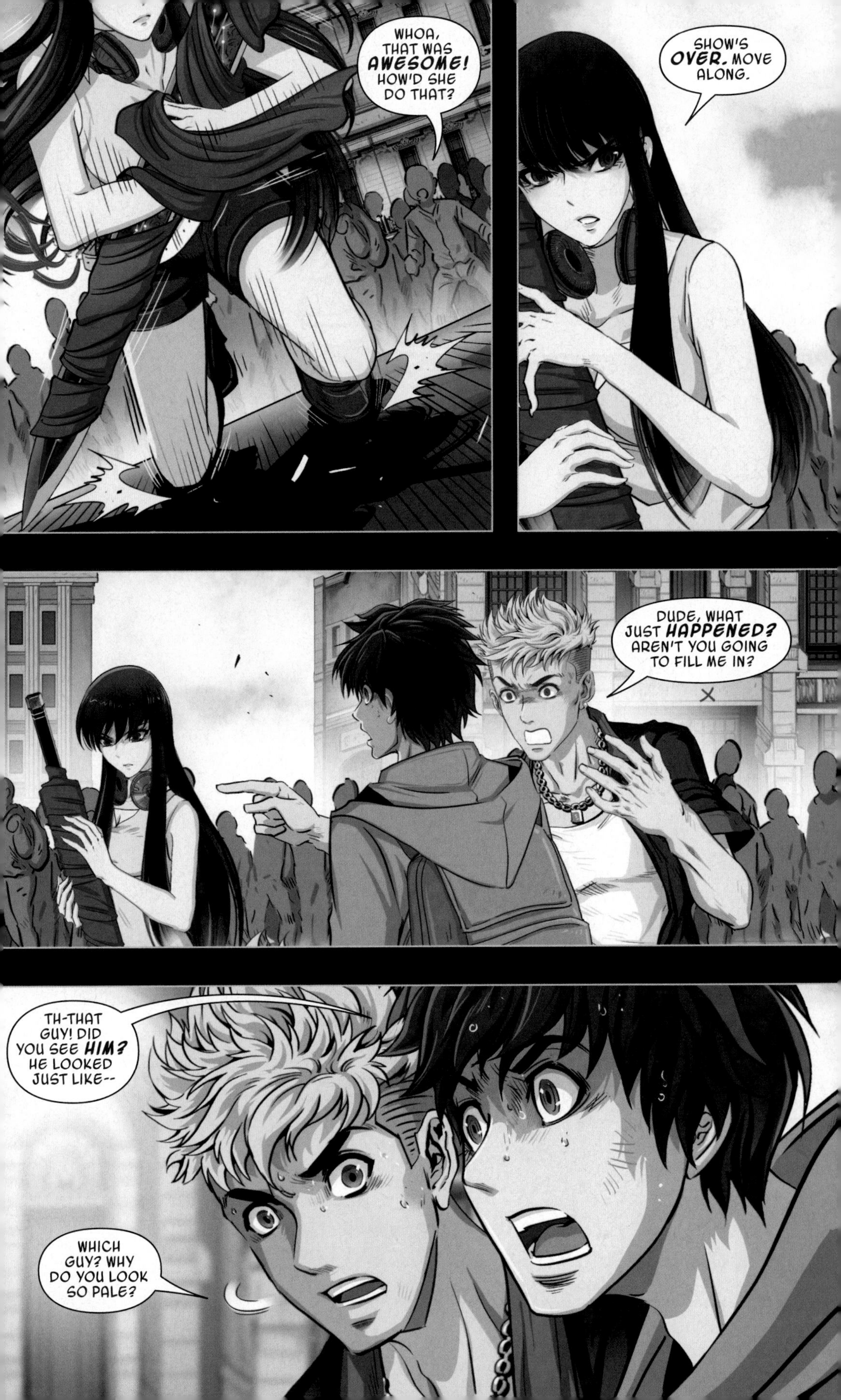
WHOA, THAT WAS AWESOME! HOW'D SHE DO THAT?
SHOW'S OVER. MOVE ALONG.
DUDE, WHAT JUST HAPPENED? AREN'T YOU GOING TO FILL ME IN?
TH-THAT GUY! DID YOU SEE HIM? HE LOOKED JUST LIKE--
WHICH GUY? WHY DO YOU LOOK SO PALE?

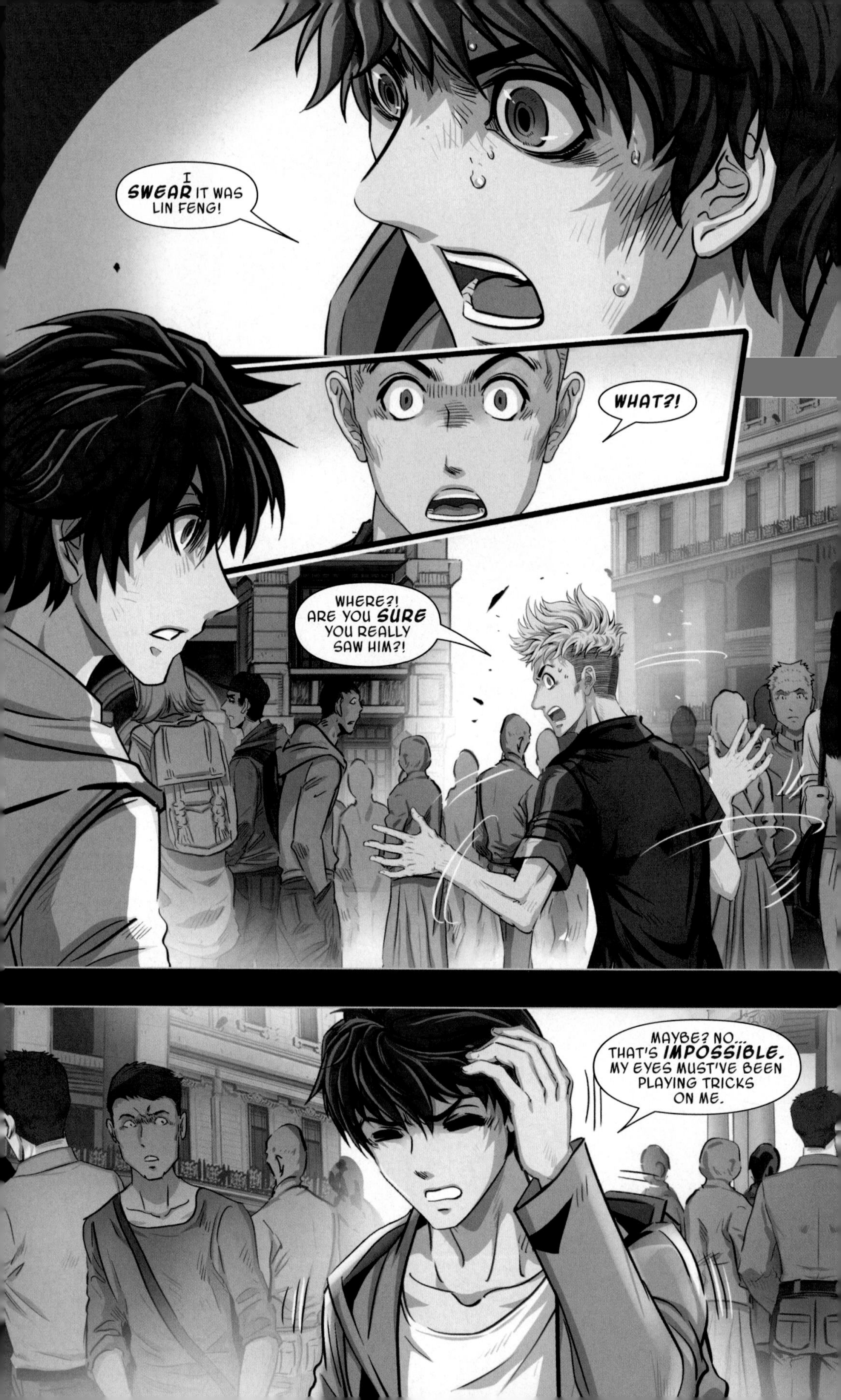

I SWEAR IT WAS LIN FENG!
WHAT?!
WHERE?! ARE YOU SURE YOU REALLY SAW HIM?!
MAYBE? NO... THAT'S IMPOSSIBLE. MY EYES MUST'VE BEEN PLAYING TRICKS ON ME.

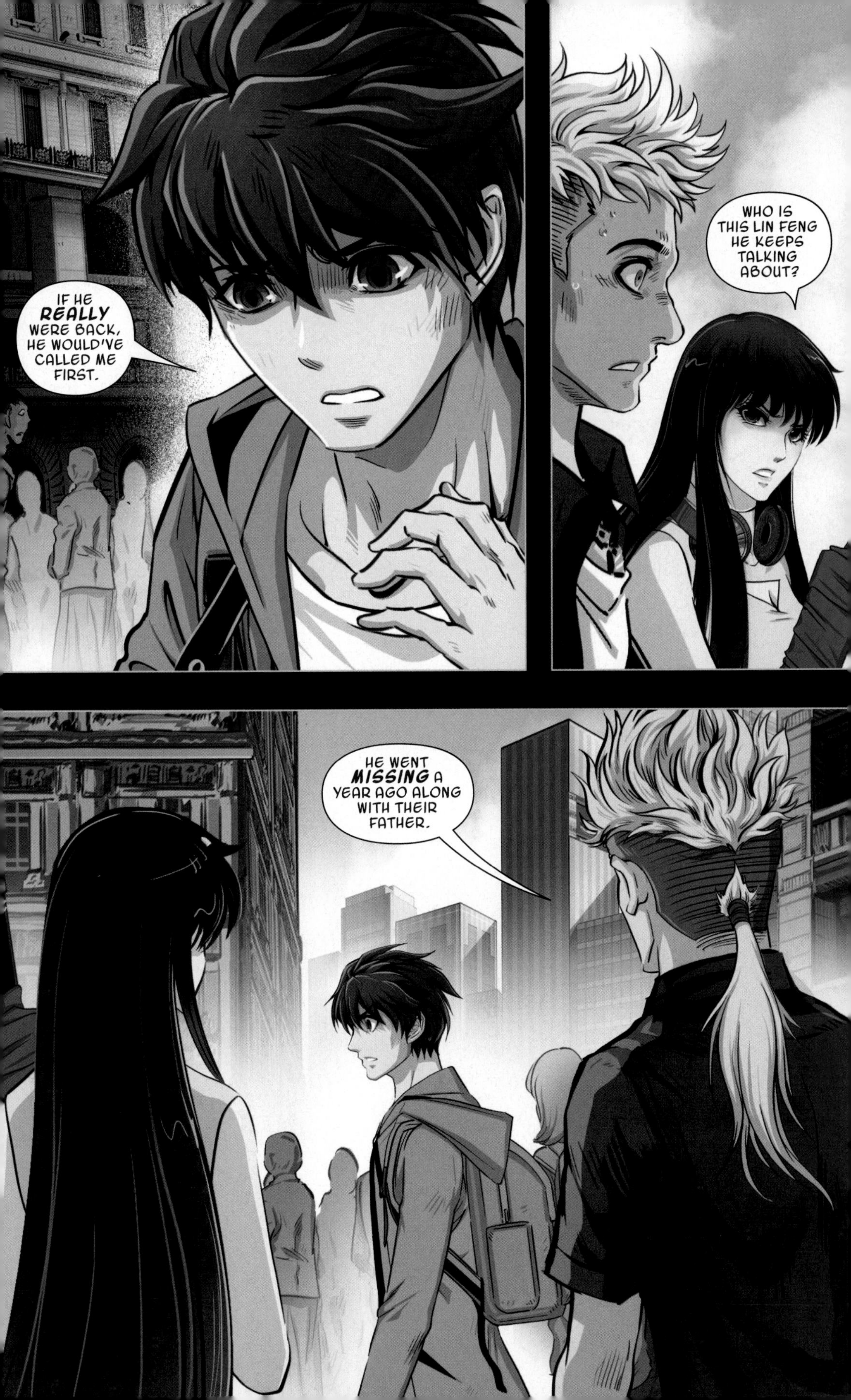
IF HE REALLY WERE BACK, HE WOULD'VE CALLED ME FIRST.
WHO IS THIS LIN FENG HE KEEPS TALKING ABOUT?
HE WENT MISSING A YEAR AGO ALONG WITH THEIR FATHER.

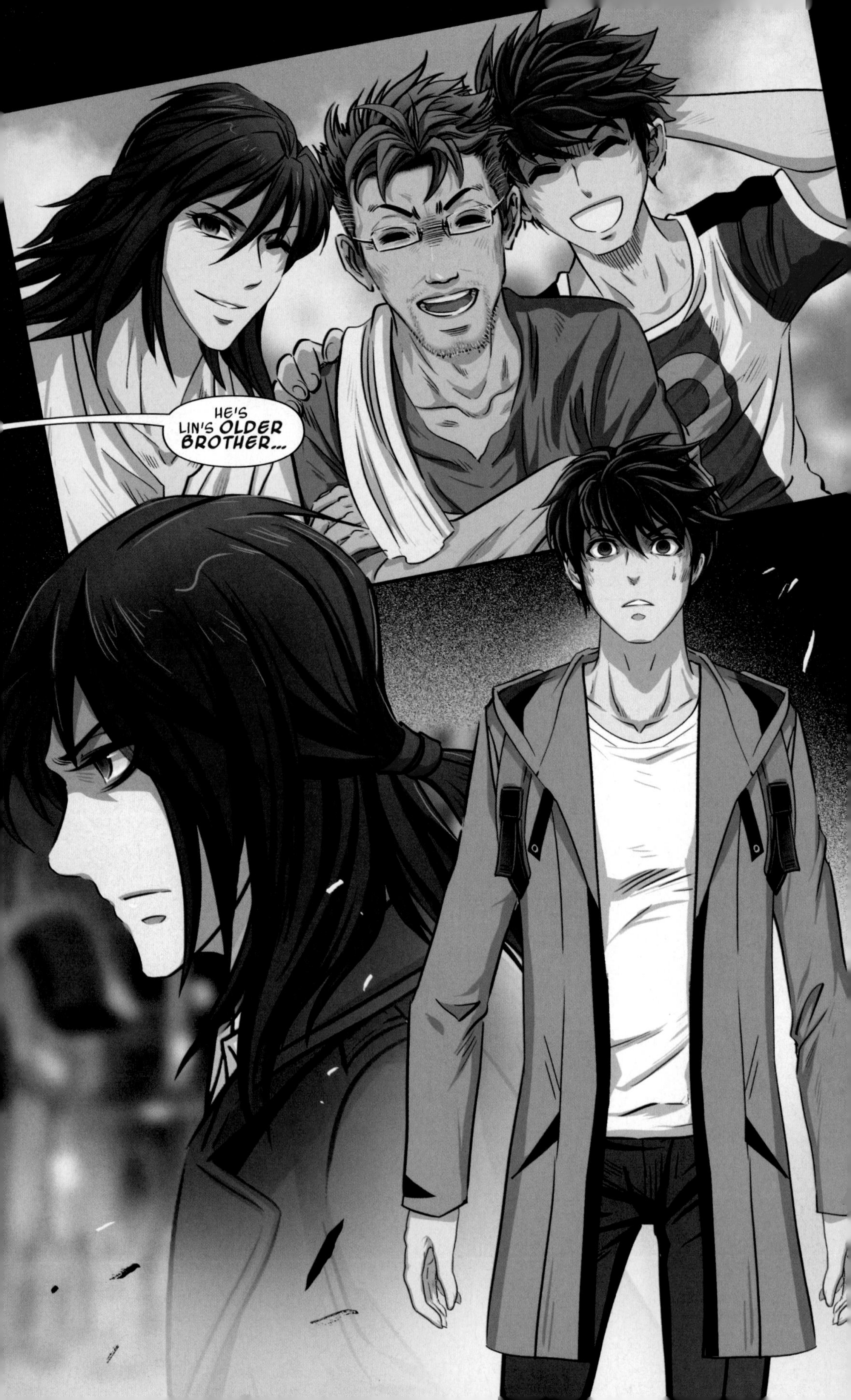
HE'S LIN'S OLDER BROTHER...

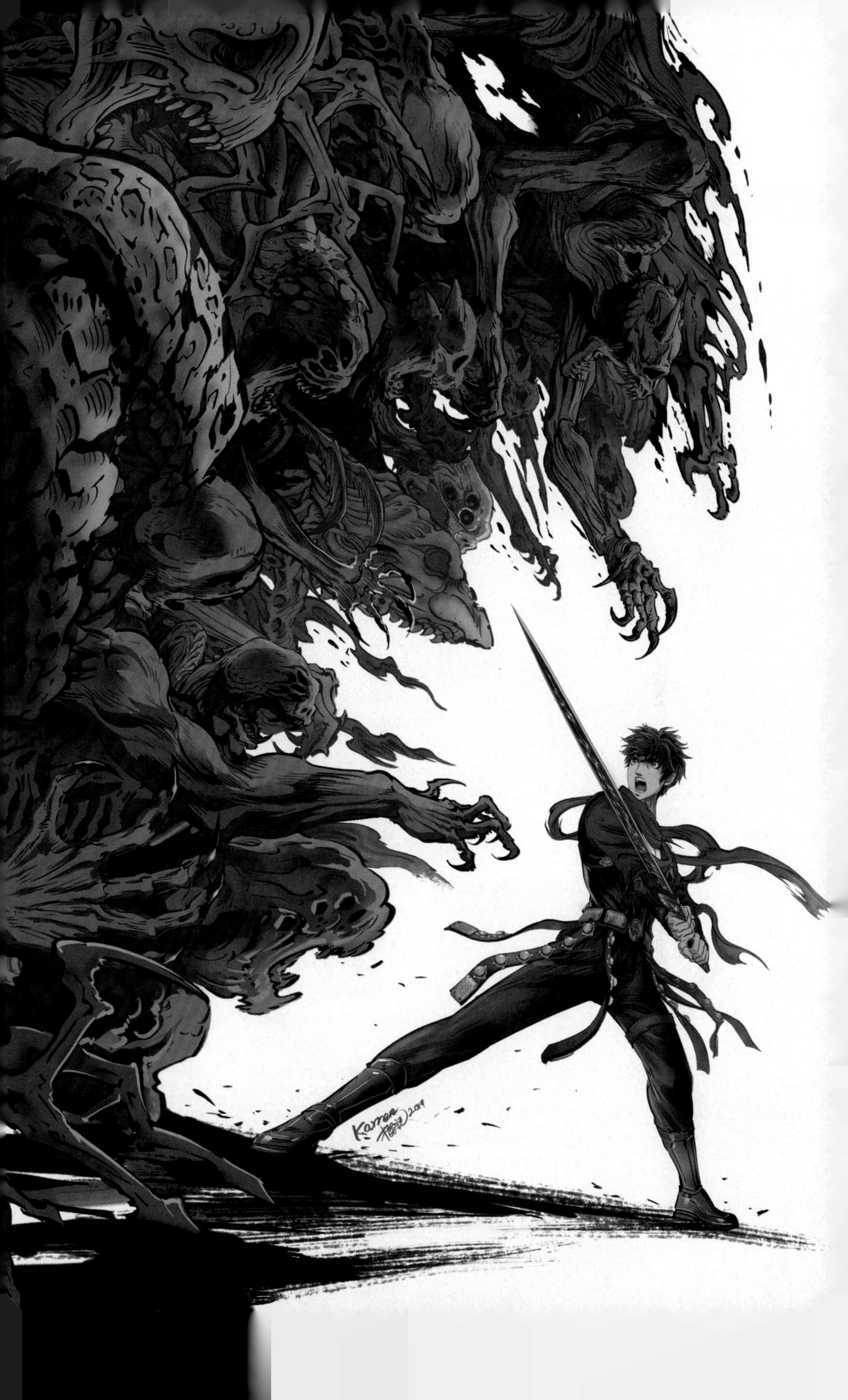
Karren 2019

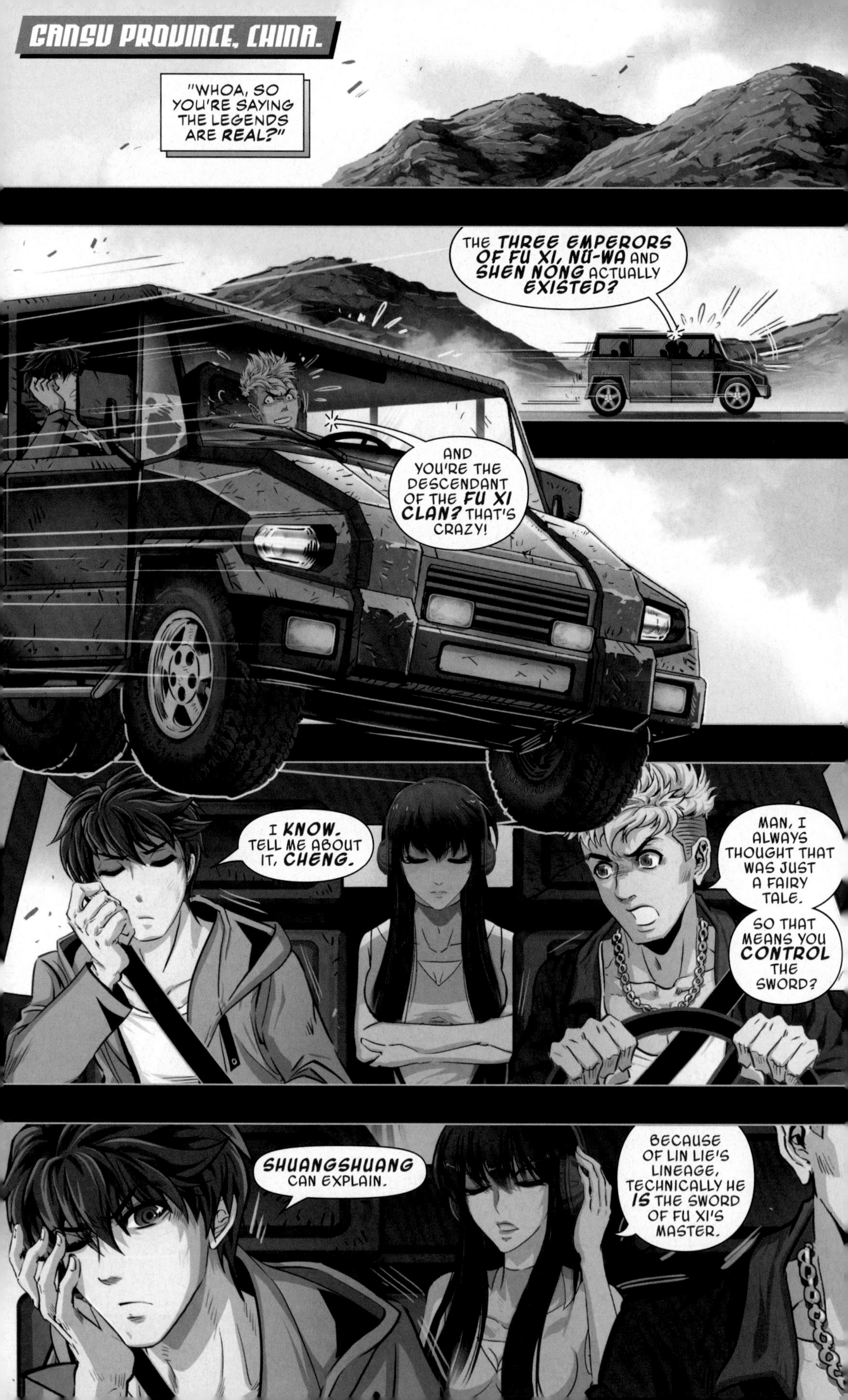
GANSU PROVINCE, CHINA.
"WHOA, SO YOU'RE SAYING THE LEGENDS ARE REAL?"
THE THREE EMPERORS OF FU XI, NÜ-WA AND SHEN NONG ACTUALLY EXISTED?
AND YOU'RE THE DESCENDANT OF THE FU XI CLAN? THAT'S CRAZY!
I KNOW. TELL ME ABOUT IT, CHENG.
MAN, I ALWAYS THOUGHT THAT WAS JUST A FAIRY TALE.
SO THAT MEANS YOU CONTROL THE SWORD?
SHUANGSHUANG CAN EXPLAIN.
BECAUSE OF LIN LIE'S LINEAGE, TECHNICALLY HE IS THE SWORD OF FU XI'S MASTER.

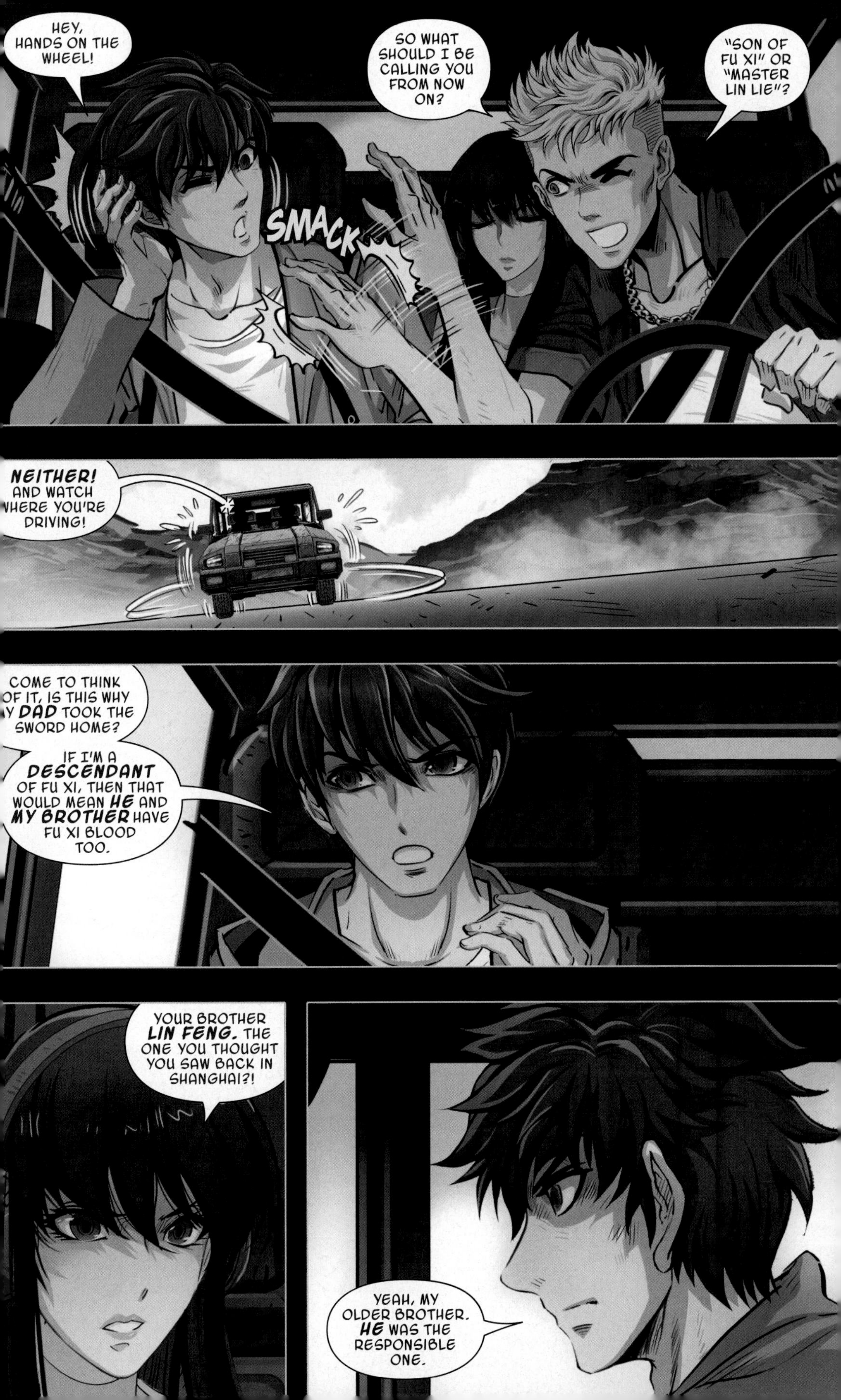
HEY, HANDS ON THE WHEEL!
SO WHAT SHOULD I BE CALLING YOU FROM NOW ON?
"SON OF FU XI" OR "MASTER LIN LIE"?
SMACK
NEITHER! AND WATCH WHERE YOU'RE DRIVING!
COME TO THINK OF IT, IS THIS WHY MY DAD TOOK THE SWORD HOME?
IF I'M A DESCENDANT OF FU XI, THEN THAT WOULD MEAN HE AND MY BROTHER HAVE FU XI BLOOD TOO.
YOUR BROTHER LIN FENG. THE ONE YOU THOUGHT YOU SAW BACK IN SHANGHAI?!
YEAH, MY OLDER BROTHER. HE WAS THE RESPONSIBLE ONE.

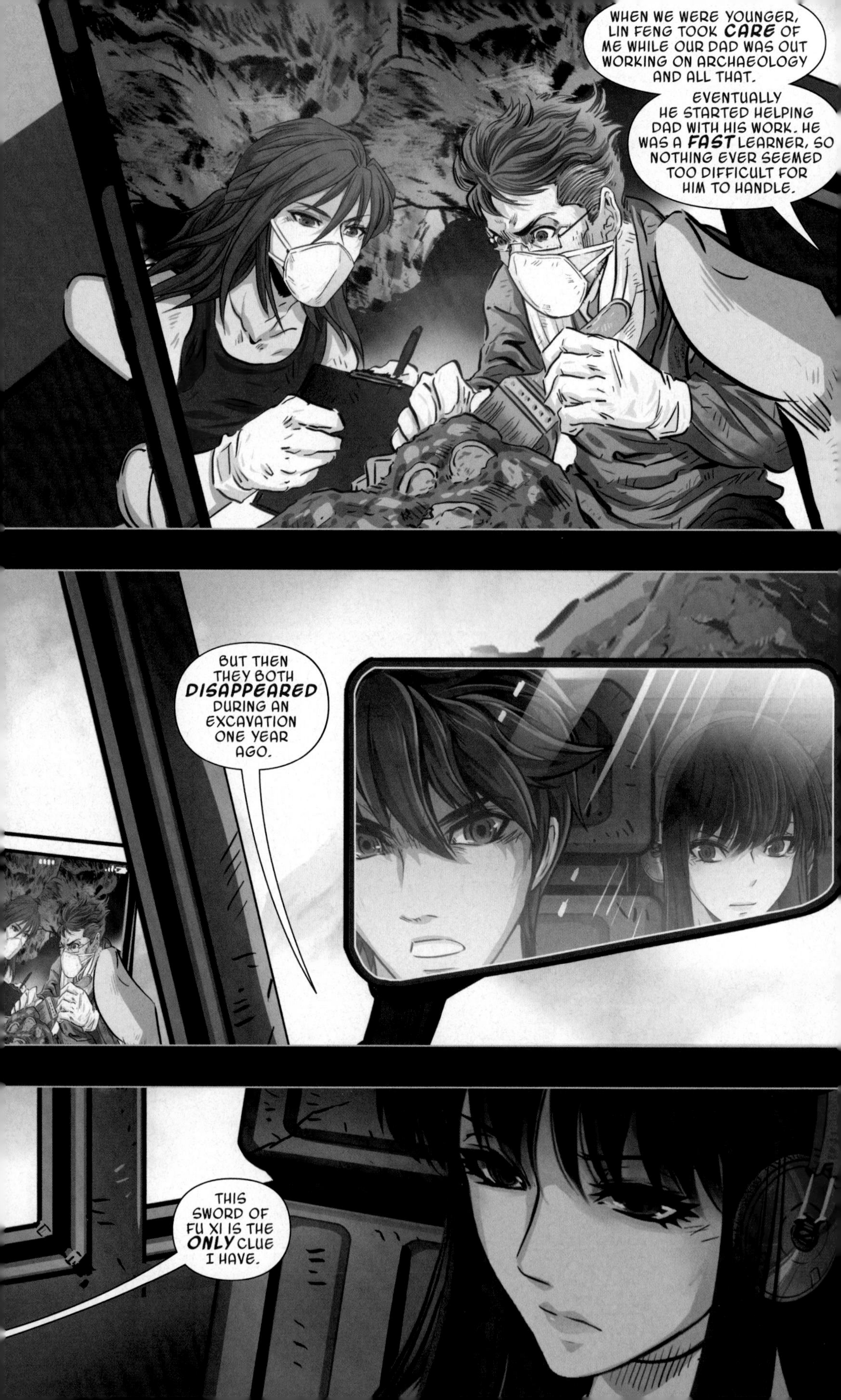

WHEN WE WERE YOUNGER, LIN FENG TOOK CARE OF ME WHILE OUR DAD WAS OUT WORKING ON ARCHAEOLOGY AND ALL THAT.
EVENTUALLY HE STARTED HELPING DAD WITH HIS WORK. HE WAS A FAST LEARNER, SO NOTHING EVER SEEMED TOO DIFFICULT FOR HIM TO HANDLE.
BUT THEN THEY BOTH DISAPPEARED DURING AN EXCAVATION ONE YEAR AGO.
THIS SWORD OF FU XI IS THE ONLY CLUE I HAVE.

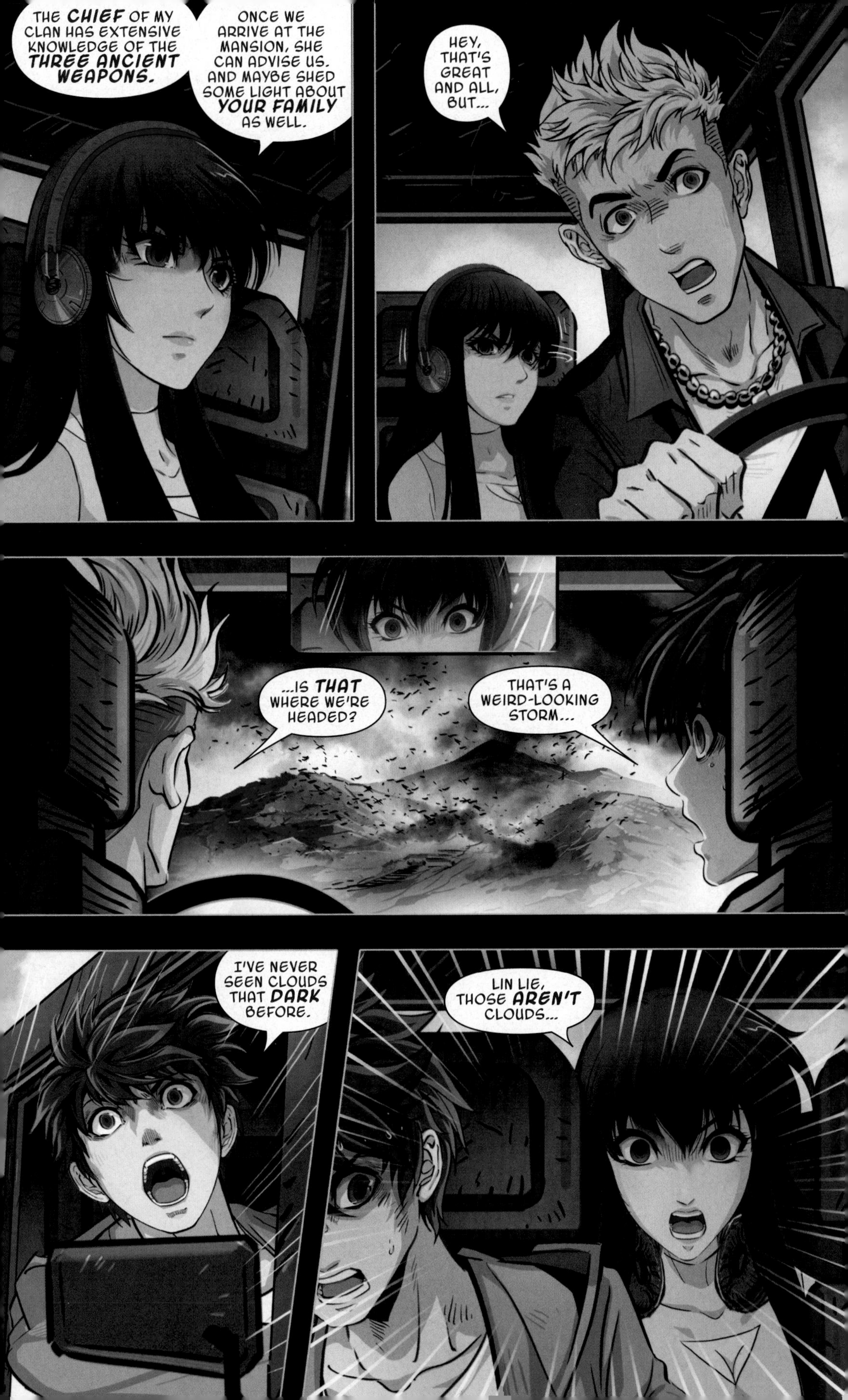
THE CHIEF OF MY CLAN HAS EXTENSIVE KNOWLEDGE OF THE THREE ANCIENT WEAPONS.
ONCE WE ARRIVE AT THE MANSION, SHE CAN ADVISE US. AND MAYBE SHED SOME LIGHT ABOUT YOUR FAMILY AS WELL.
HEY, THAT'S GREAT AND ALL, BUT...
...IS THAT WHERE WE'RE HEADED?
THAT'S A WEIRD-LOOKING STORM...
I'VE NEVER SEEN CLOUDS THAT DARK BEFORE.
LIN LIE, THOSE AREN'T CLOUDS...

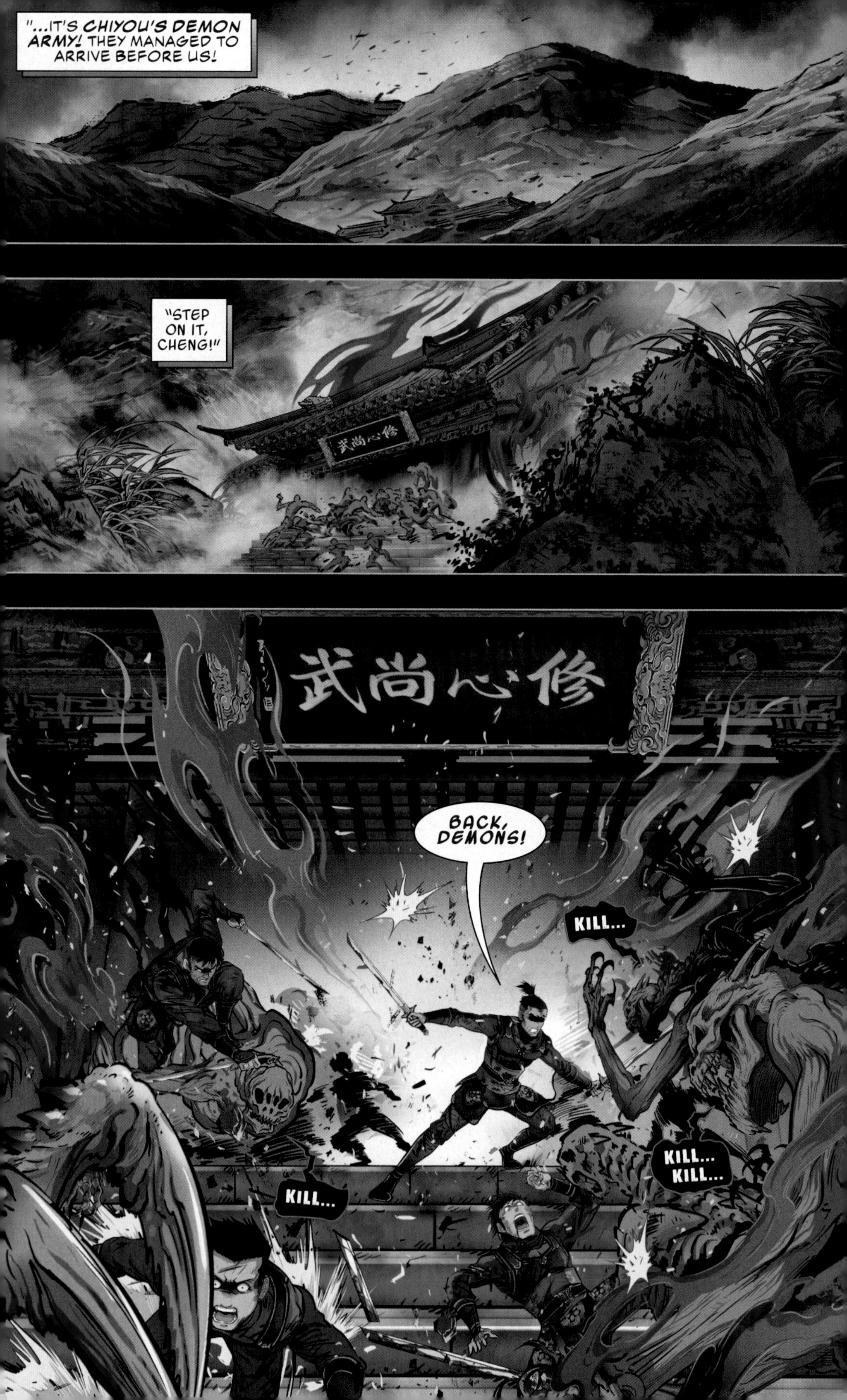
"...IT'S CHIYOU'S DEMON ARMY! THEY MANAGED TO ARRIVE BEFORE US!
"STEP ON IT, CHENG!"
武尚心修
武尚心修
BACK, DEMONS!
KILL...
KILL... KILL...
KILL...

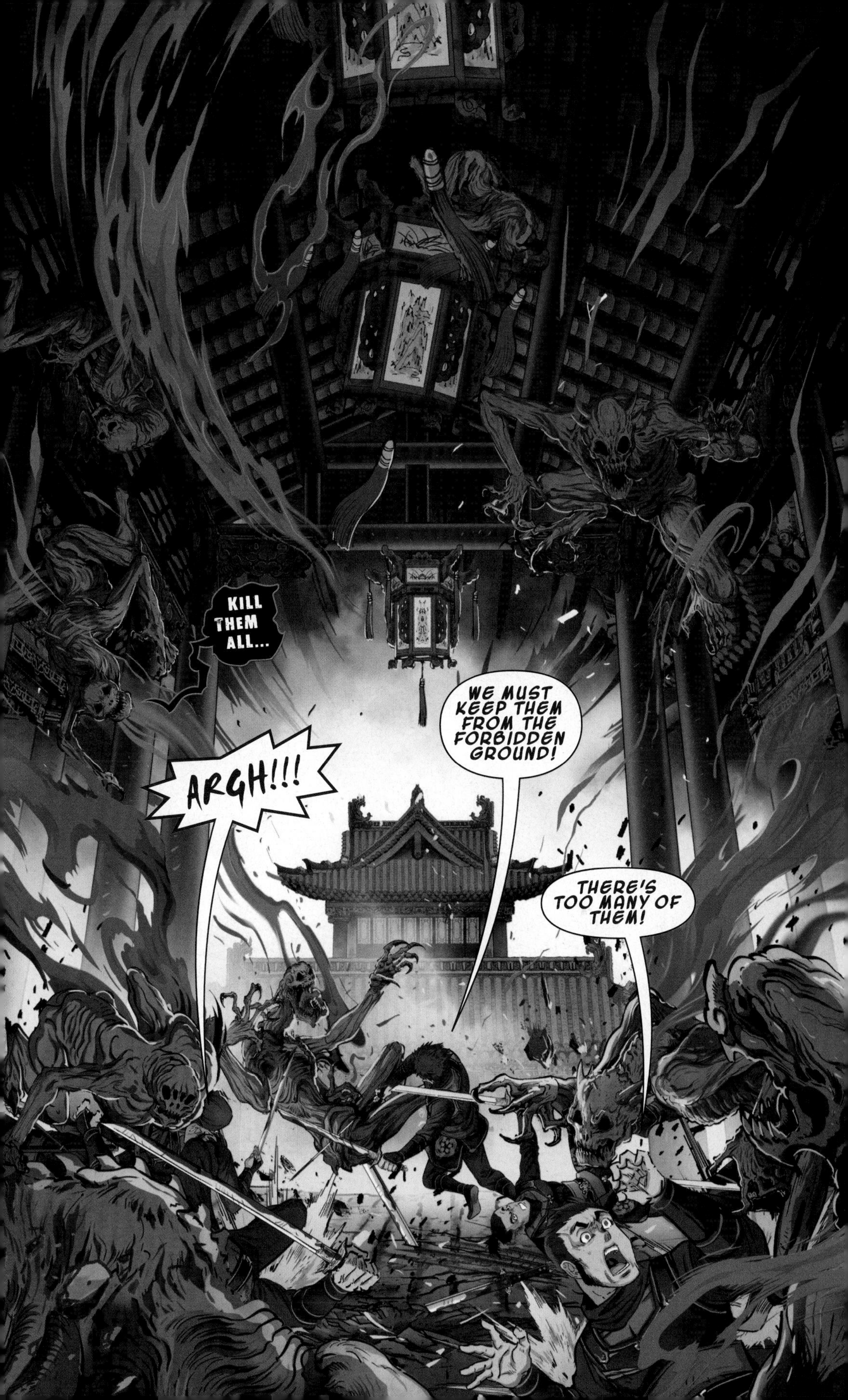

KILL THEM ALL...
ARGH!!!
WE MUST KEEP THEM FROM THE FORBIDDEN GROUND!
THERE'S TOO MANY OF THEM!

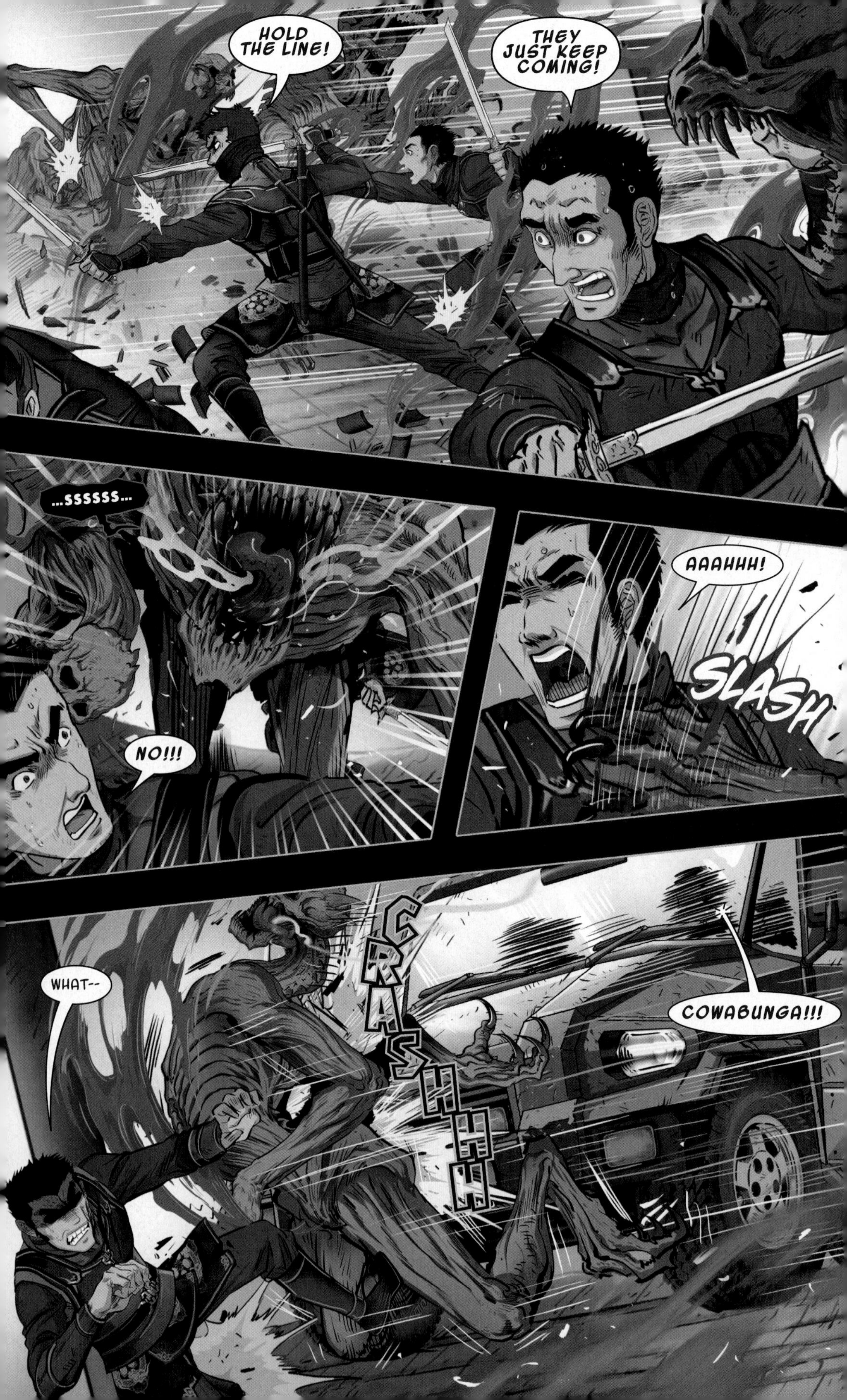
HOLD THE LINE!
THEY JUST KEEP COMING!
...SSSSSS...
NO!!!
AAAHHH!
SLASH
WHAT--
CRASHHHH
COWABUNGA!!!

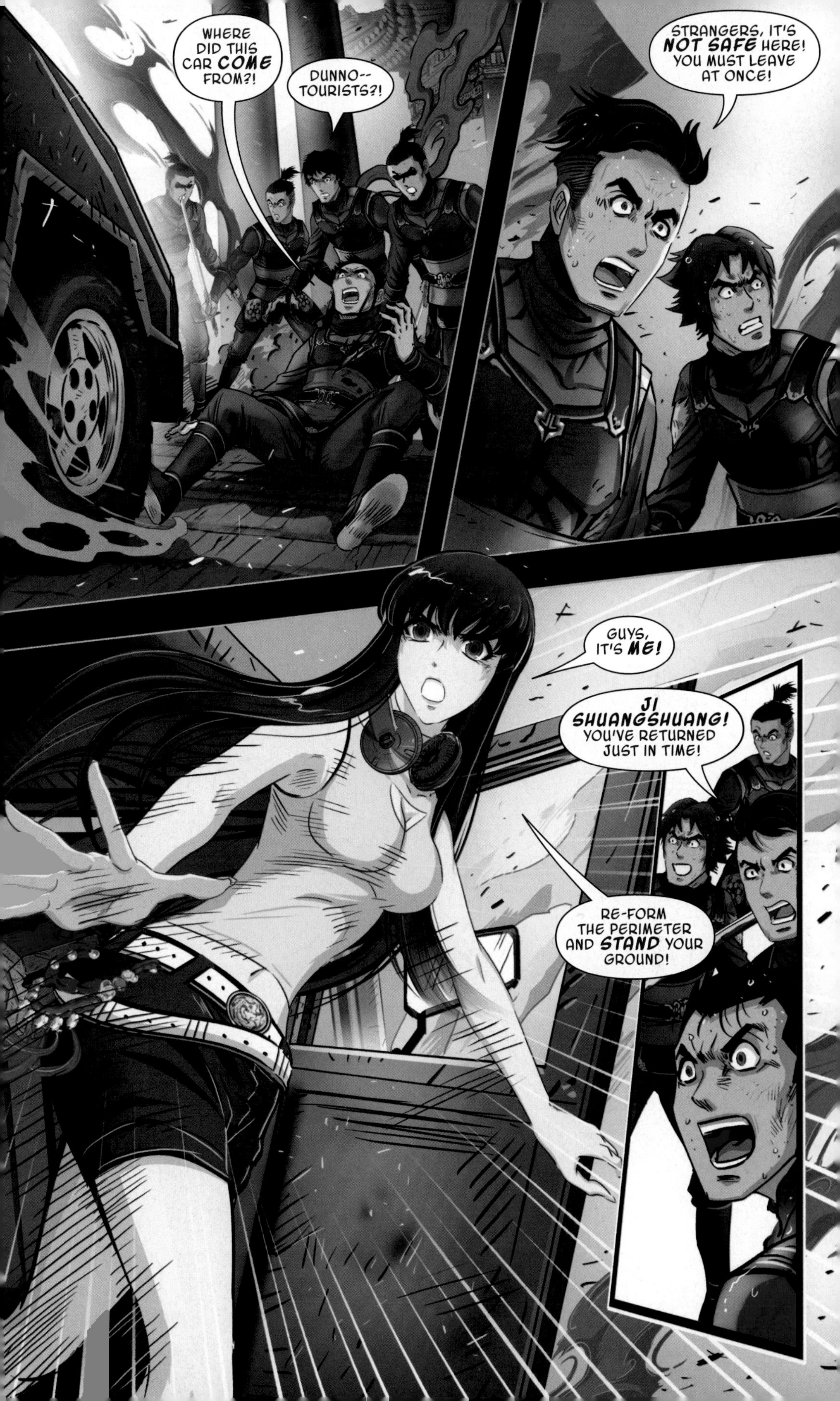
WHERE DID THIS CAR COME FROM?!
DUNNO-- TOURISTS?!
STRANGERS, IT'S NOT SAFE HERE! YOU MUST LEAVE AT ONCE!
GUYS, IT'S ME!
JI SHUANGSHUANG! YOU'VE RETURNED JUST IN TIME!
RE-FORM THE PERIMETER AND STAND YOUR GROUND!

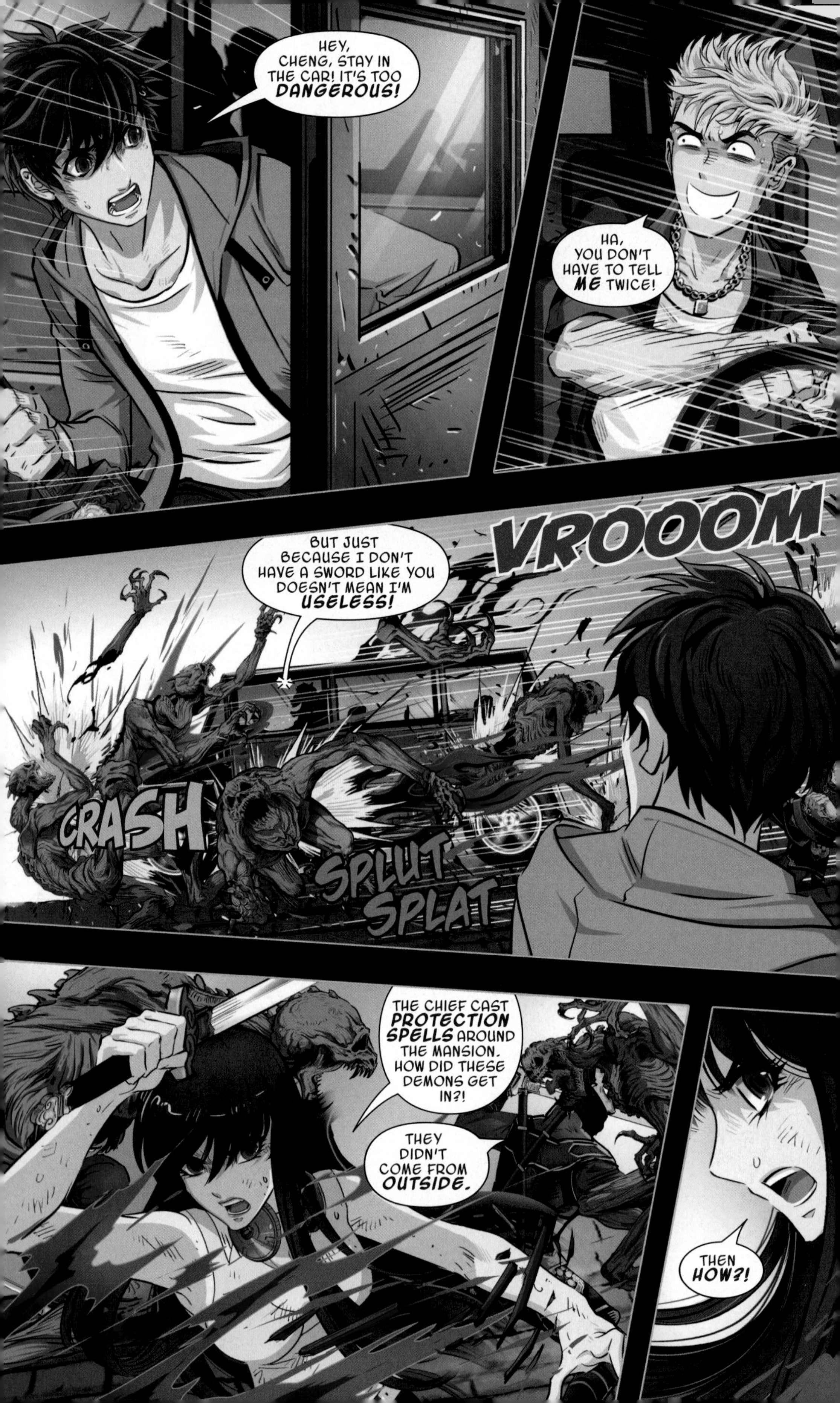
HEY, CHENG, STAY IN THE CAR! IT'S TOO DANGEROUS!
HA, YOU DON'T HAVE TO TELL ME TWICE!
VROOOM
BUT JUST BECAUSE I DON'T HAVE A SWORD LIKE YOU DOESN'T MEAN I'M USELESS!
CRASH
SPLUT
SPLAT
THE CHIEF CAST PROTECTION SPELLS AROUND THE MANSION. HOW DID THESE DEMONS GET IN?!
THEY DIDN'T COME FROM OUTSIDE.
THEN HOW?!

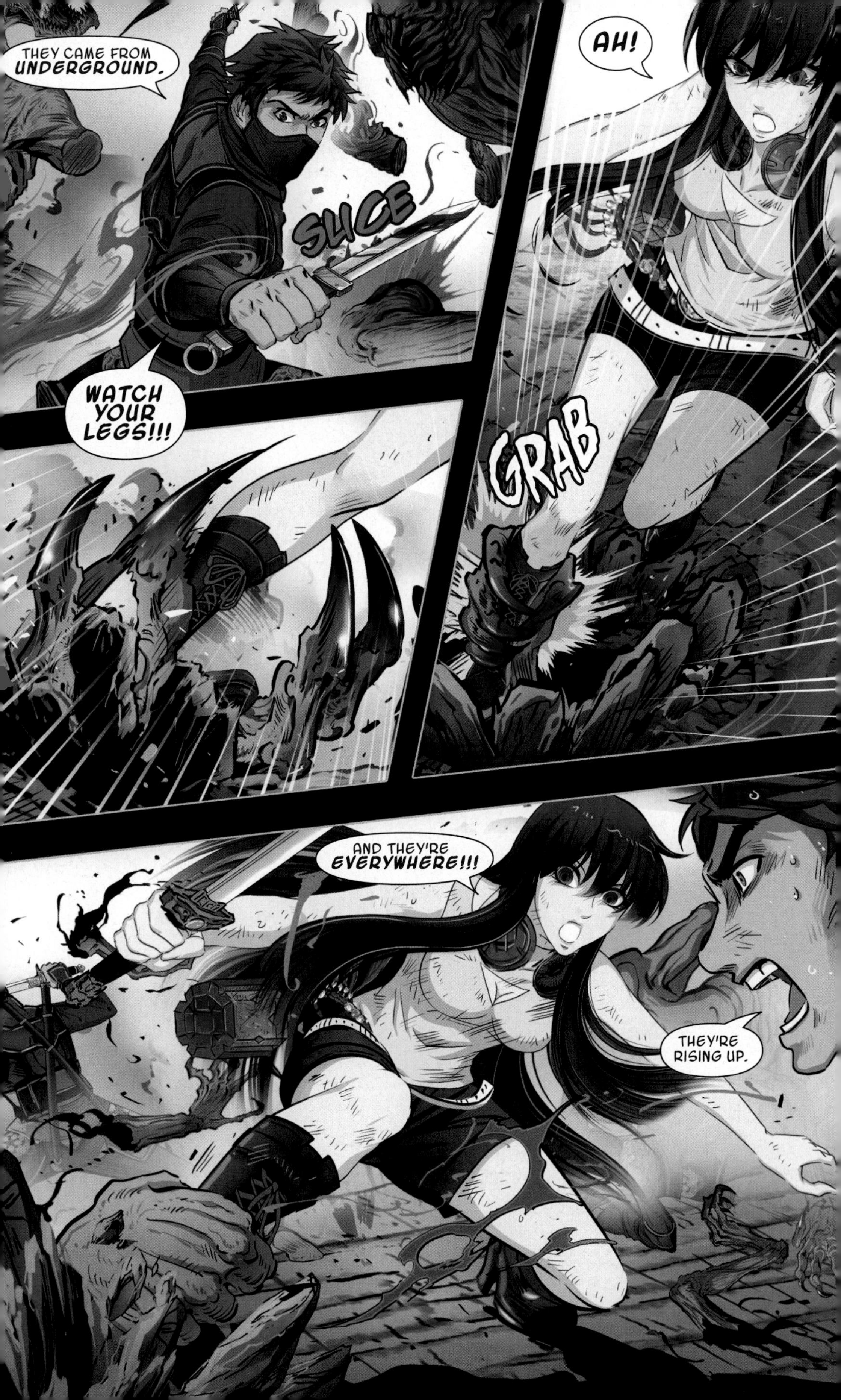
THEY CAME FROM UNDERGROUND.
SLICE
AH!
WATCH YOUR LEGS!!!
GRAB
AND THEY'RE EVERYWHERE!!!
THEY'RE RISING UP.

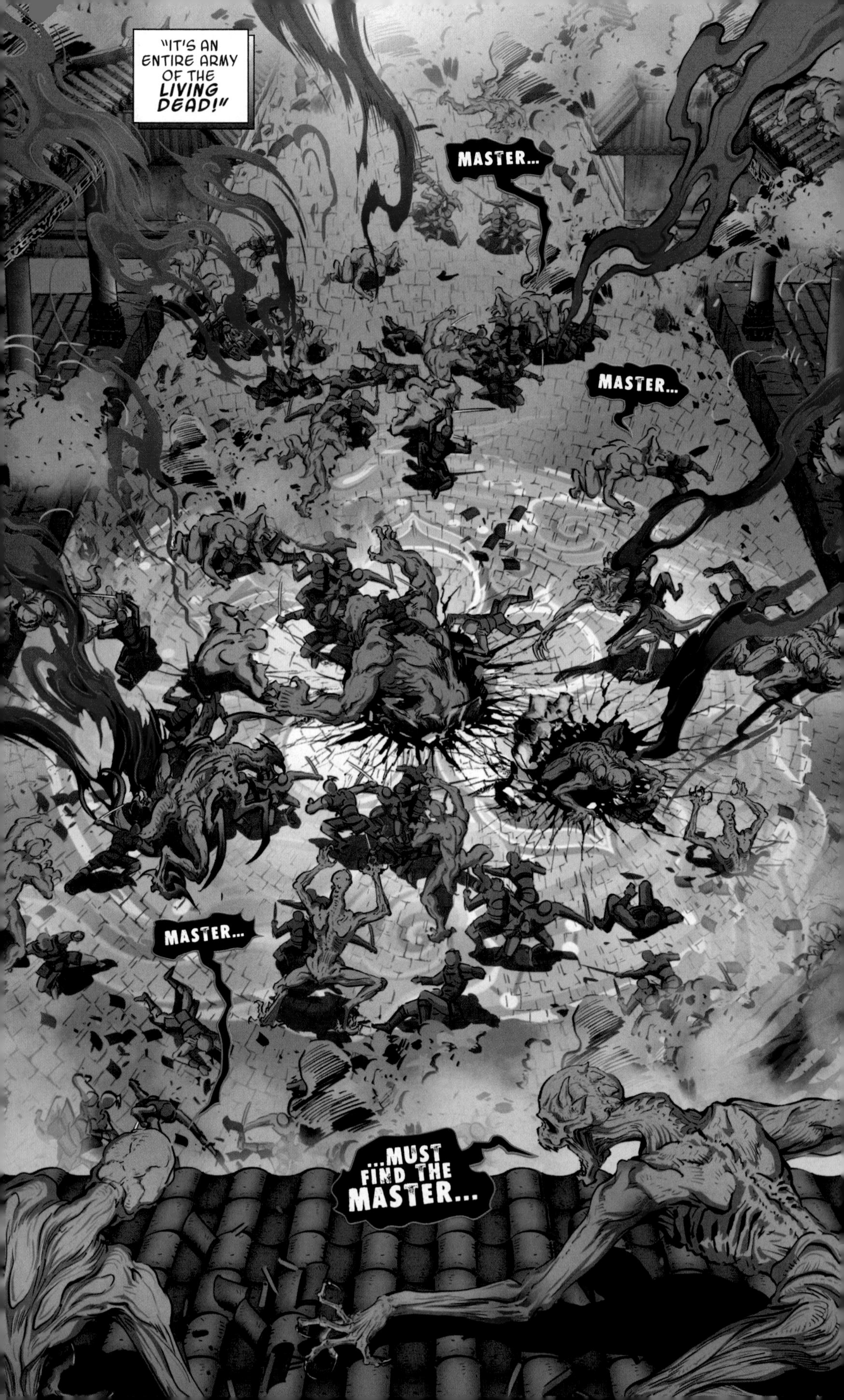
"IT'S AN ENTIRE ARMY OF THE *LIVING DEAD!*"
MASTER...
MASTER...
MASTER...
...MUST FIND THE MASTER...

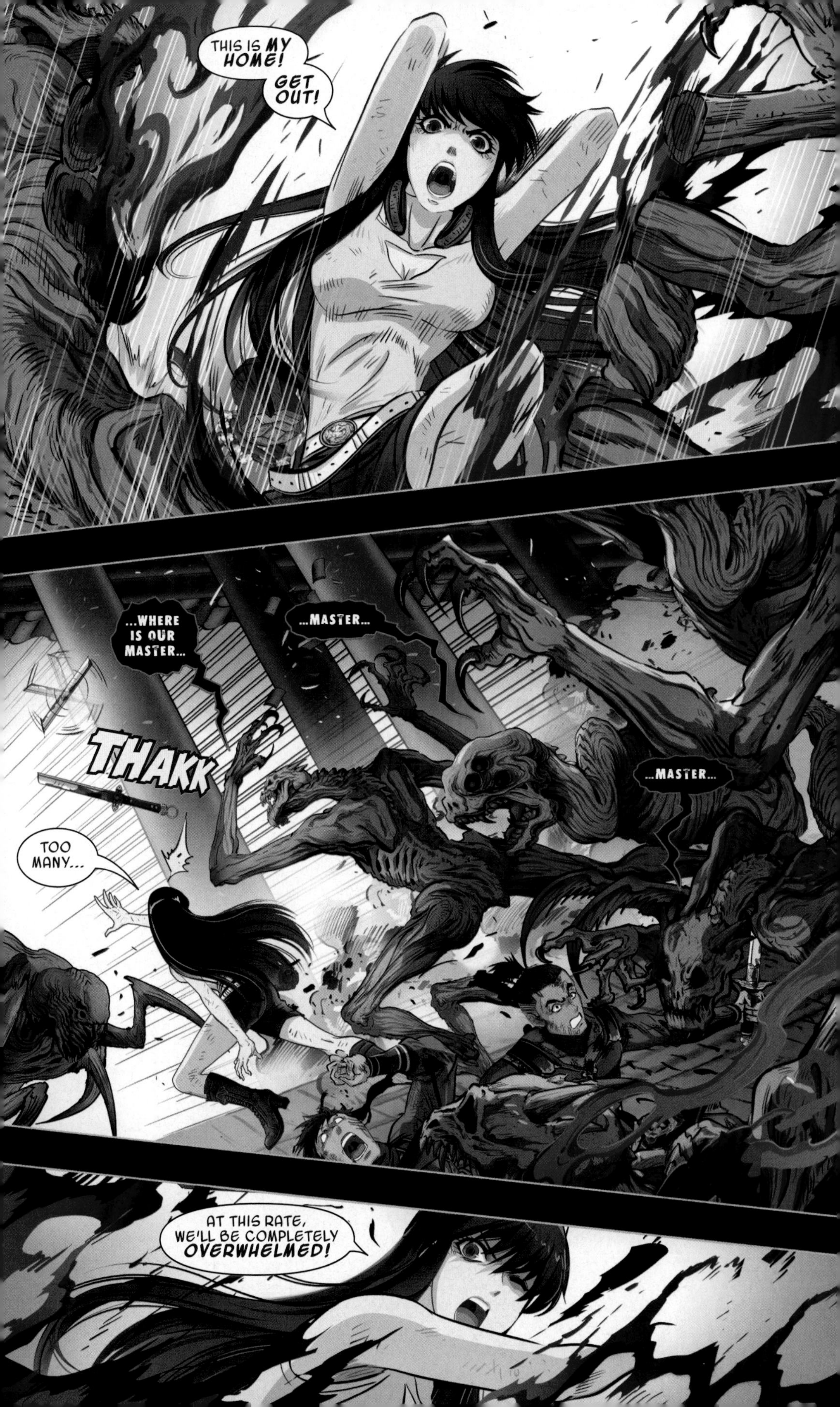
THIS IS MY HOME! GET OUT!
...WHERE IS OUR MASTER...
...MASTER...
THAKK
...MASTER...
TOO MANY...
AT THIS RATE, WE'LL BE COMPLETELY OVERWHELMED!

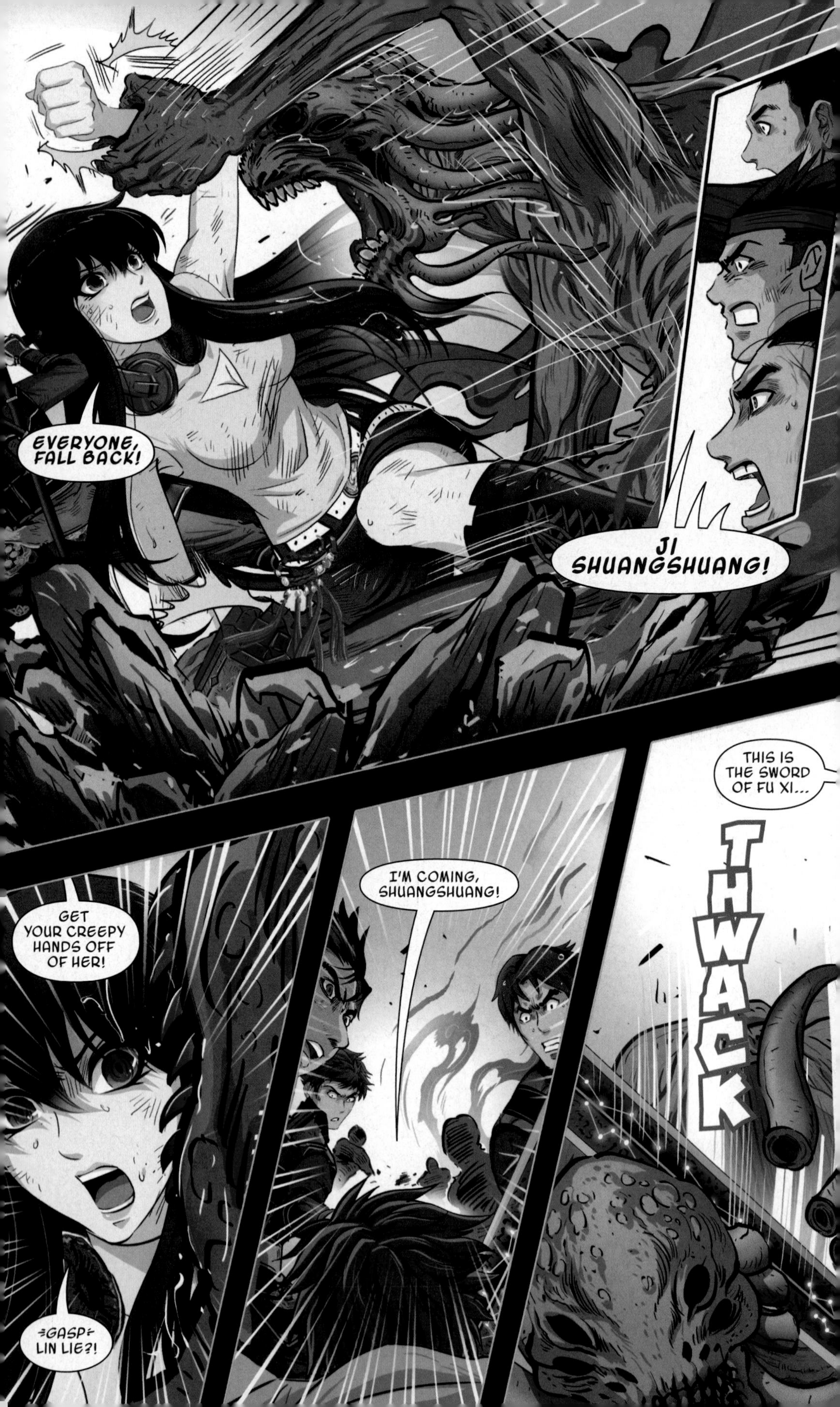
EVERYONE, FALL BACK!
JI SHUANGSHUANG!
THIS IS THE SWORD OF FU XI...
THWACK
I'M COMING, SHUANGSHUANG!
GET YOUR CREEPY HANDS OFF OF HER!
≠GASP≠ LIN LIE?!

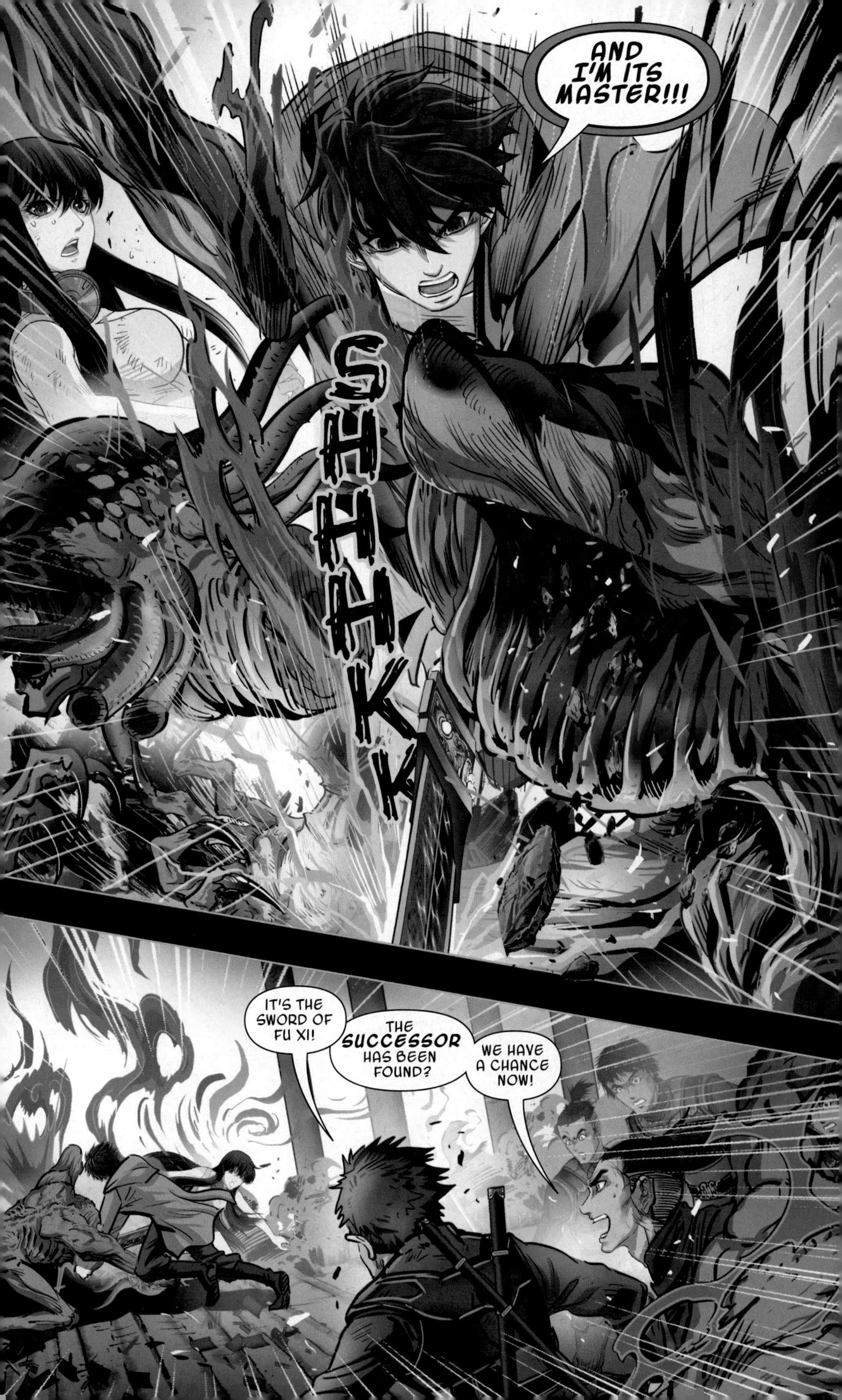
AND I'M ITS MASTER!!!
SHHHK
IT'S THE SWORD OF FU XI!
THE SUCCESSOR HAS BEEN FOUND?
WE HAVE A CHANCE NOW!

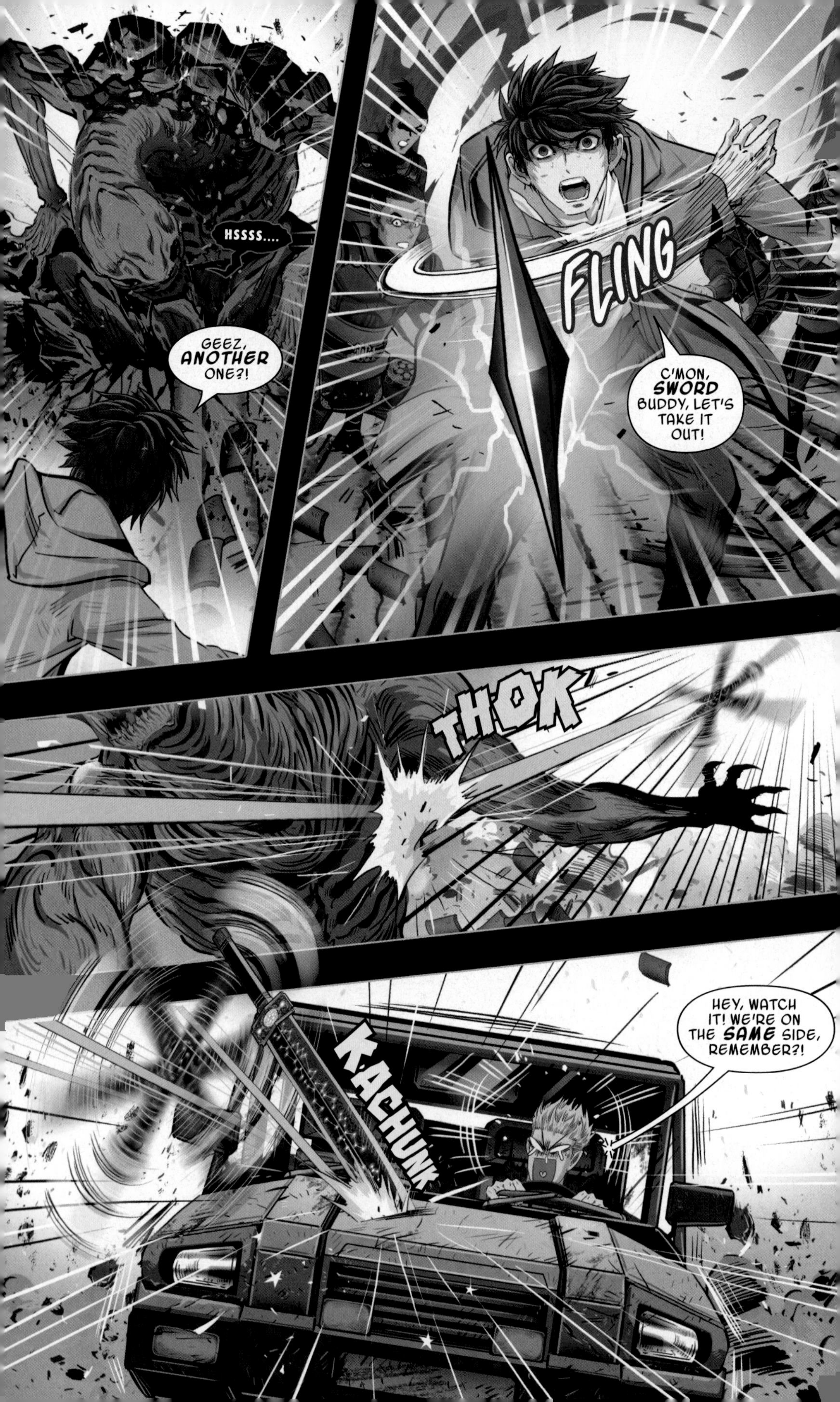
HSSSS....
GEEZ, ANOTHER ONE?!
FLING
C'MON, SWORD BUDDY, LET'S TAKE IT OUT!
THOK
KACHUNK
HEY, WATCH IT! WE'RE ON THE SAME SIDE, REMEMBER?!

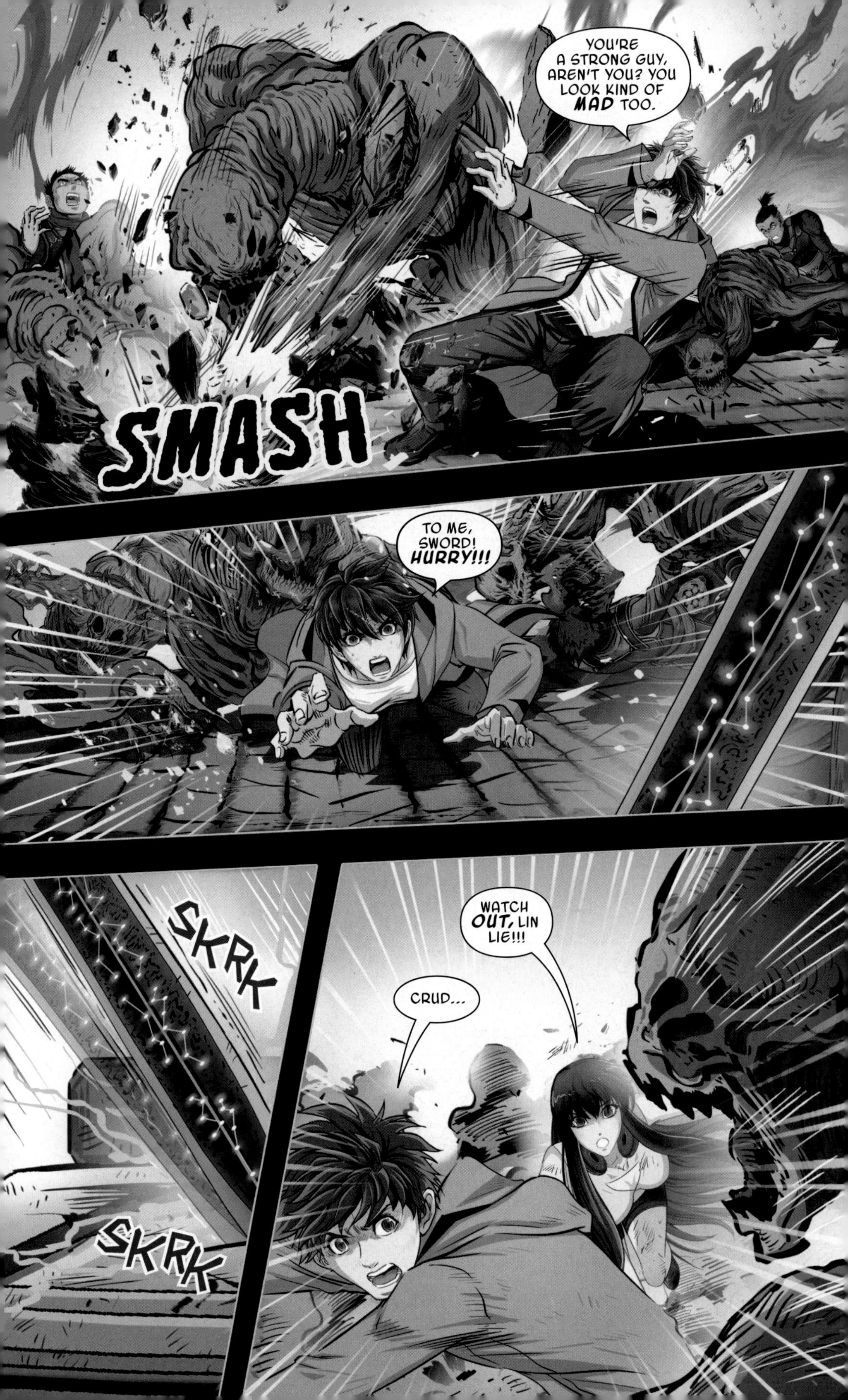
YOU'RE A STRONG GUY, AREN'T YOU? YOU LOOK KIND OF MAD TOO.
SMASH
TO ME, SWORD! HURRY!!!
SKRK
SKRK
WATCH OUT, LIN LIE!!!
CRUD...

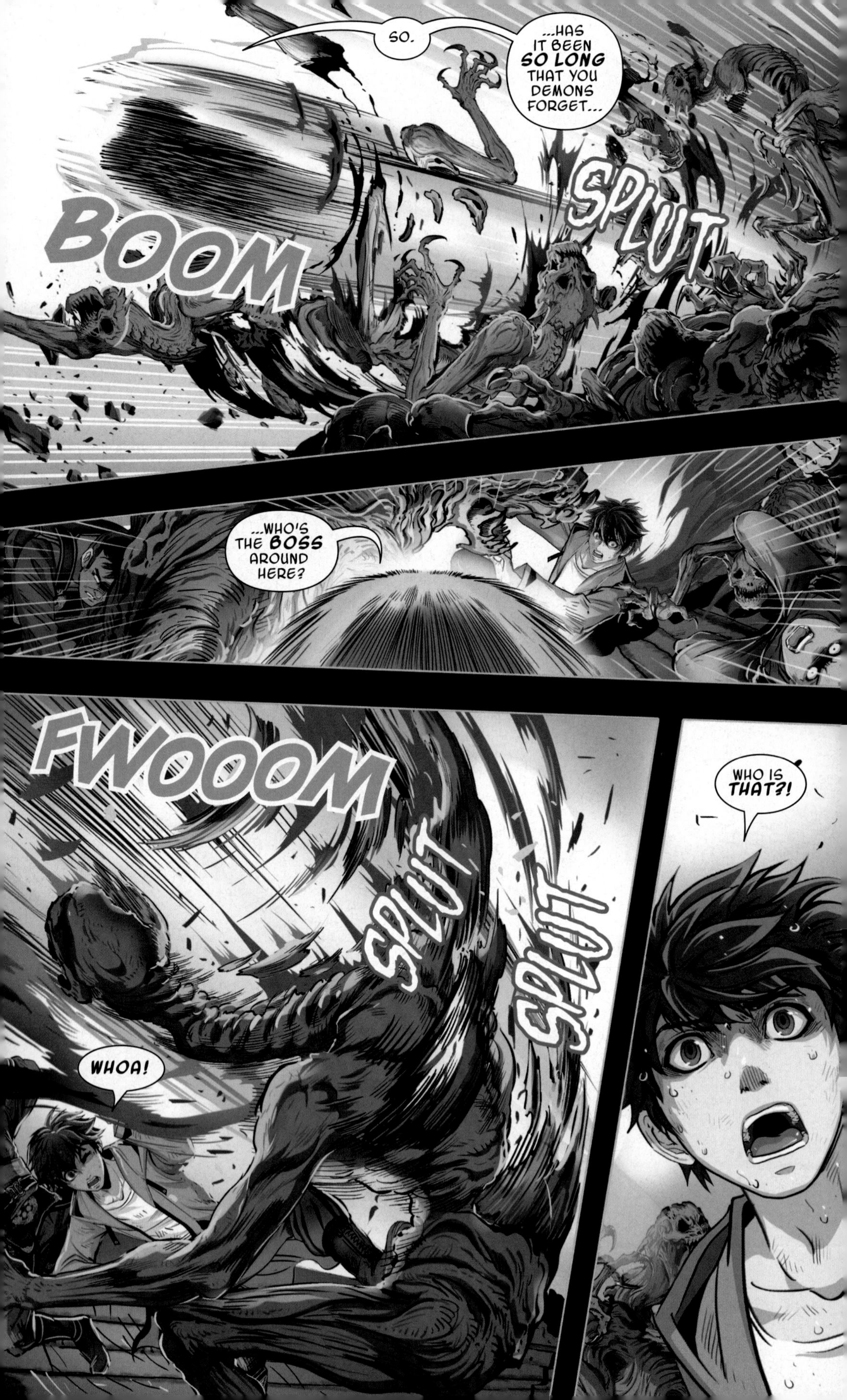
SO.
...HAS IT BEEN SO LONG THAT YOU DEMONS FORGET...
BOOM
SPLUT
...WHO'S THE BOSS AROUND HERE?
FWOOOM
SPLUT
SPLUT
WHOA!
WHO IS THAT?!

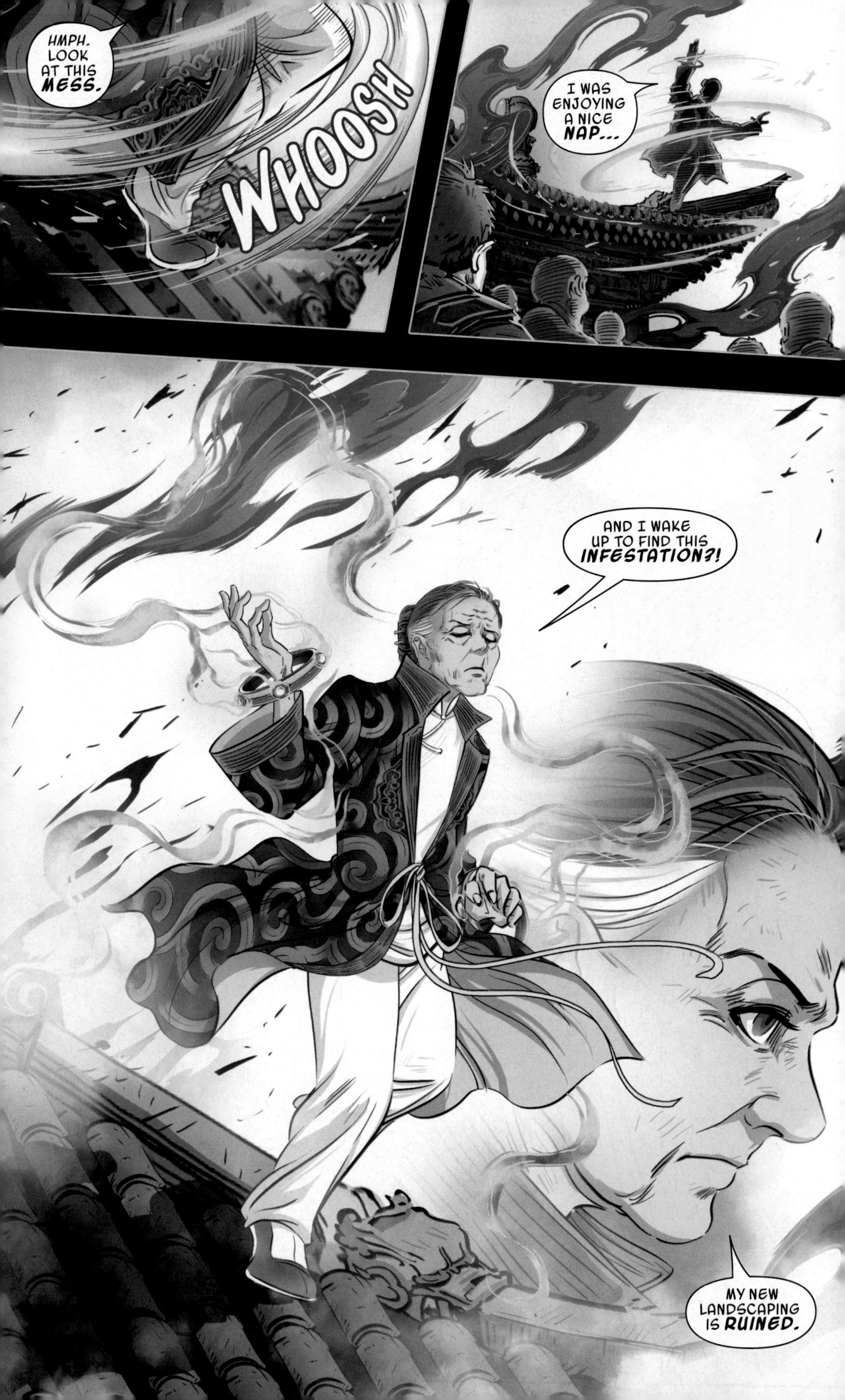
HMPH. LOOK AT THIS MESS.
WHOOSH
I WAS ENJOYING A NICE NAP...
AND I WAKE UP TO FIND THIS INFESTATION?!
MY NEW LANDSCAPING IS RUINED.

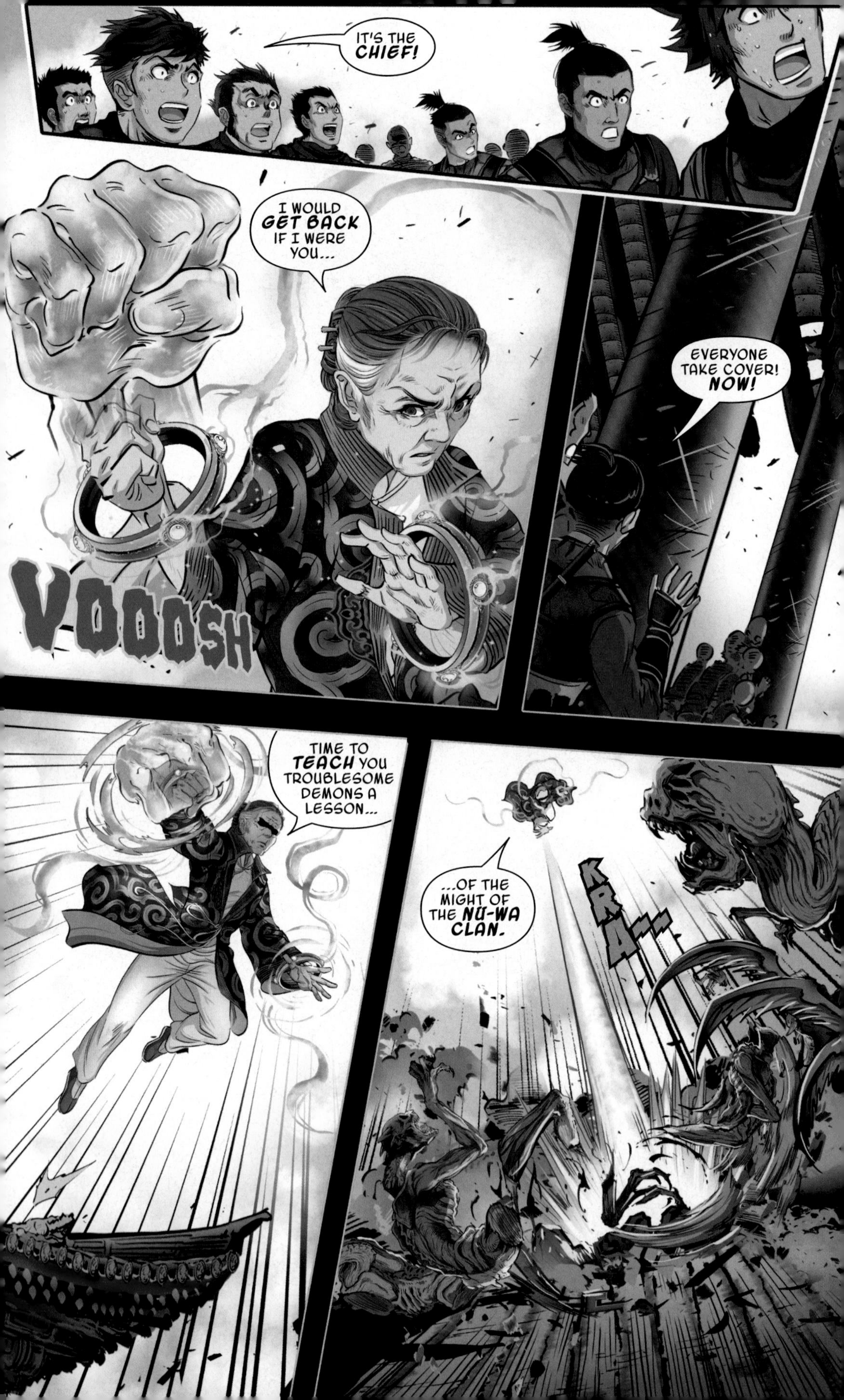
IT'S THE CHIEF!
I WOULD GET BACK IF I WERE YOU...
VOOOSH
EVERYONE TAKE COVER! NOW!
TIME TO TEACH YOU TROUBLESOME DEMONS A LESSON...
...OF THE MIGHT OF THE NÜ-WA CLAN.
KRA--

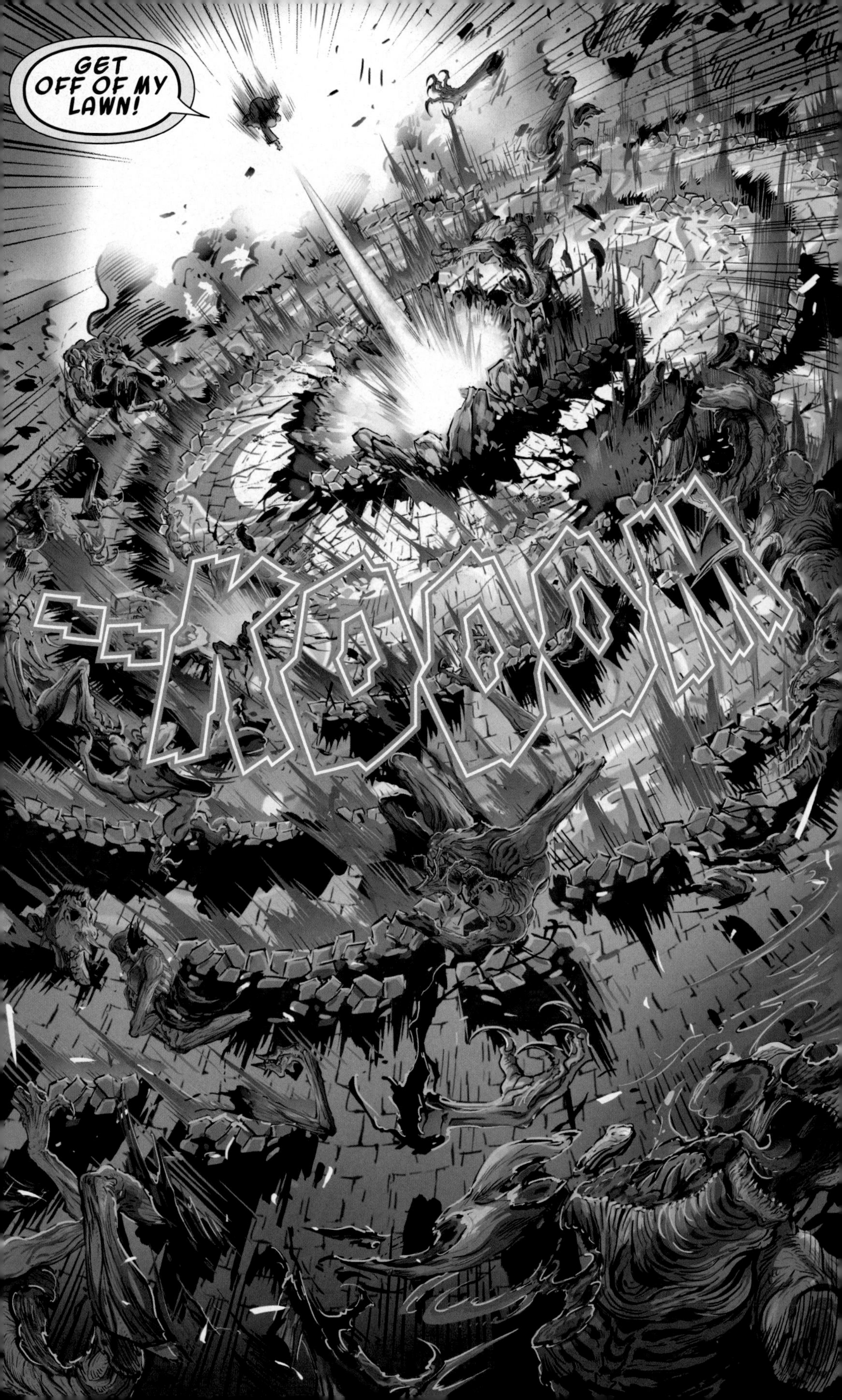
GET OFF OF MY LAWN!
KROOOM

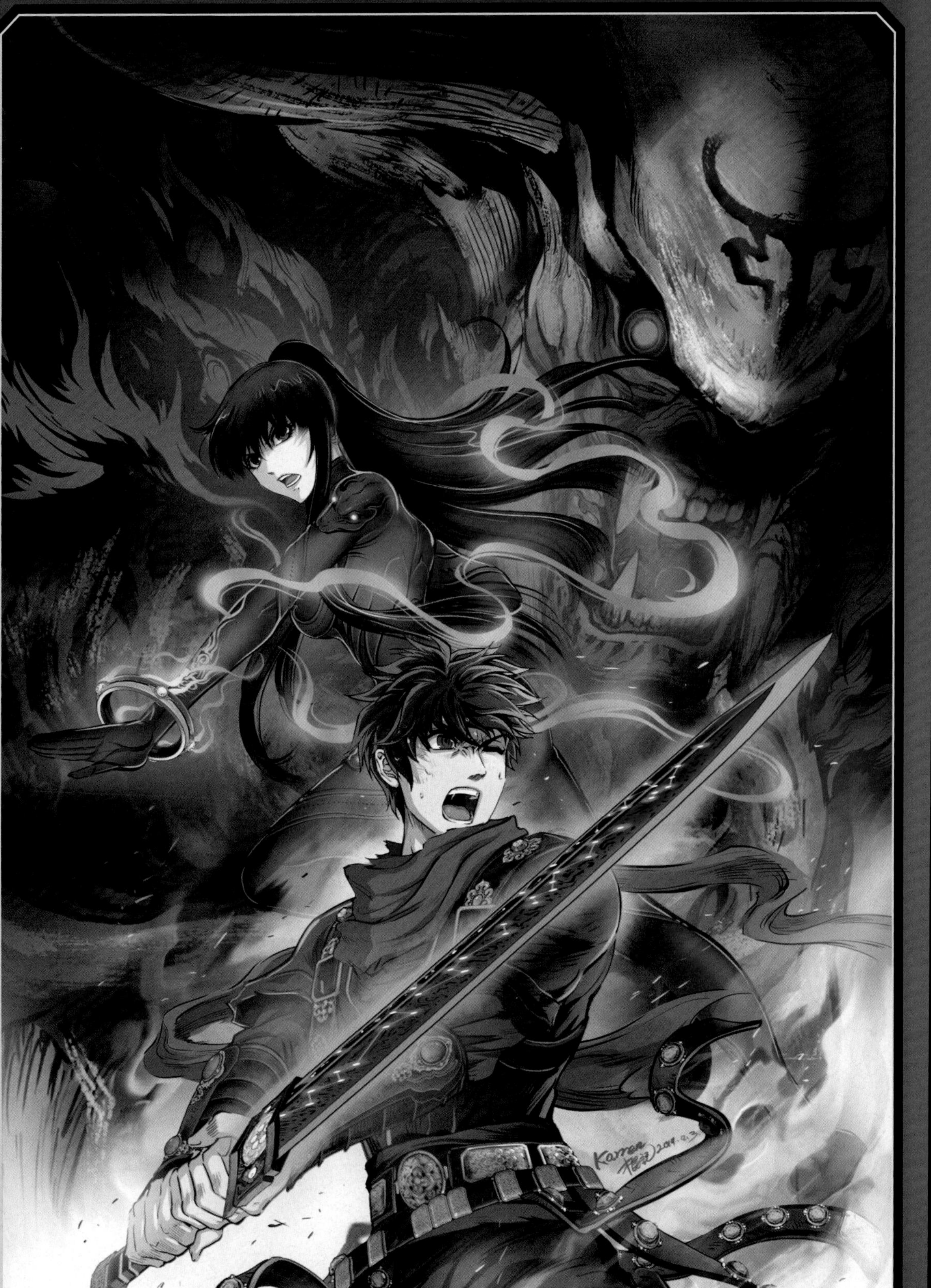

ELEVEN FRIENDS, FOES AND FAMILY

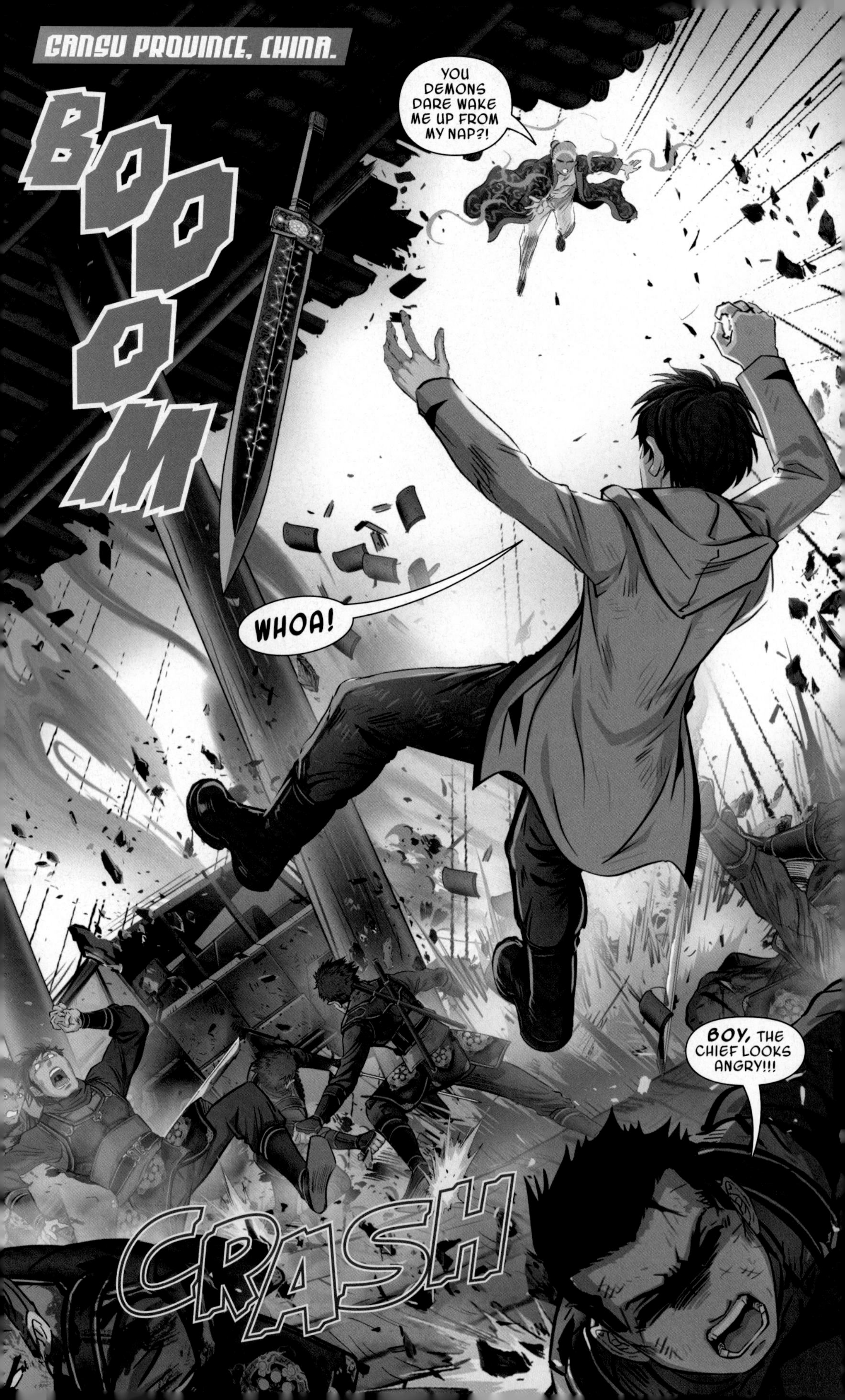
GANSU PROVINCE, CHINA.
BOOOOM
YOU DEMONS DARE WAKE ME UP FROM MY NAP?!
WHOA!
BOY, THE CHIEF LOOKS ANGRY!!!
CRASH

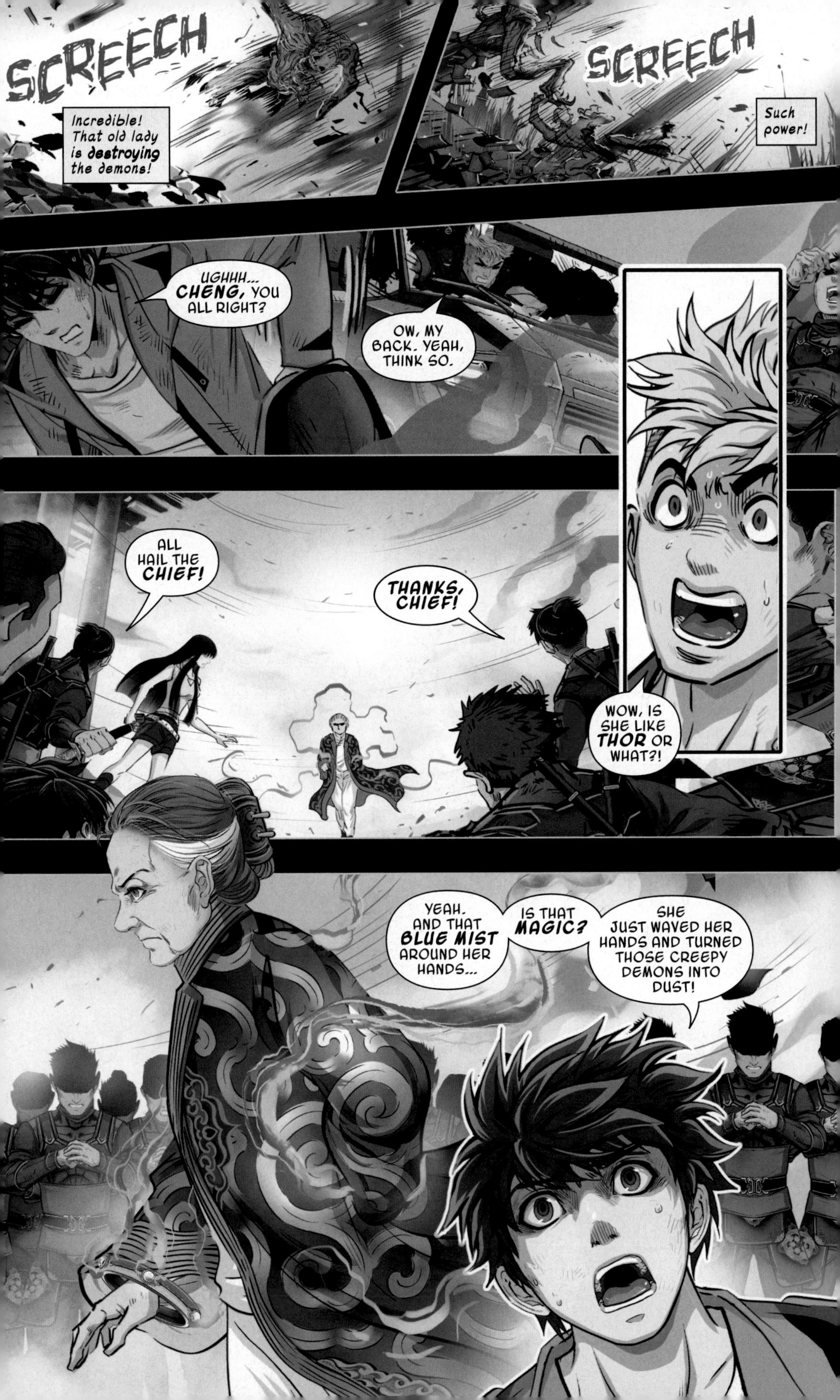
SCREECH
Incredible! That old lady is destroying the demons!
SCREECH
Such power!
UGHHH... CHENG, YOU ALL RIGHT?
OW, MY BACK. YEAH, THINK SO.
ALL HAIL THE CHIEF!
THANKS, CHIEF!
WOW, IS SHE LIKE THOR OR WHAT?!
YEAH. AND THAT BLUE MIST AROUND HER HANDS...
IS THAT MAGIC?
SHE JUST WAVED HER HANDS AND TURNED THOSE CREEPY DEMONS INTO DUST!

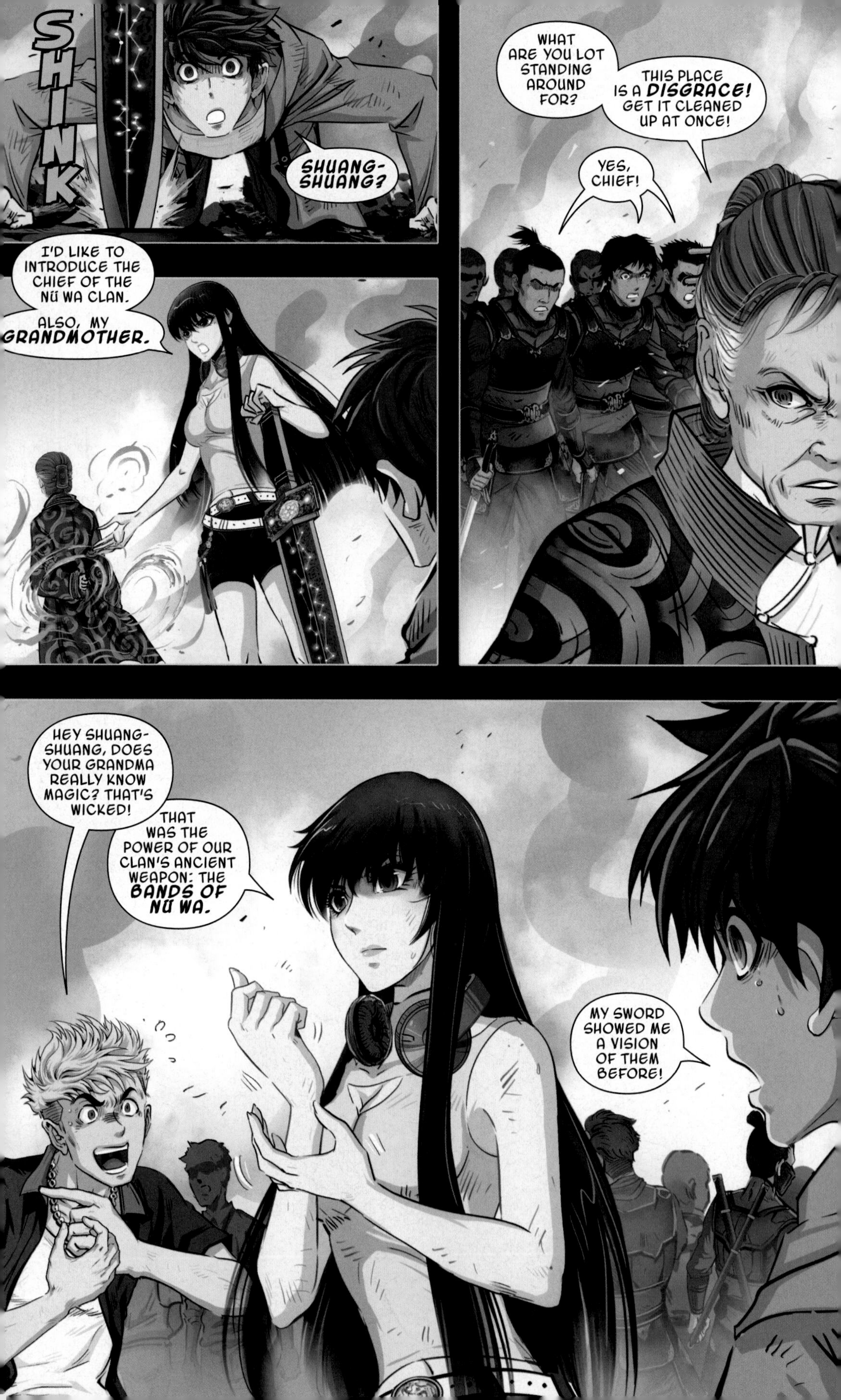
SHINK
SHUANG-SHUANG?
I'D LIKE TO INTRODUCE THE CHIEF OF THE NÜ WA CLAN.
ALSO, MY GRANDMOTHER.
WHAT ARE YOU LOT STANDING AROUND FOR?
THIS PLACE IS A DISGRACE! GET IT CLEANED UP AT ONCE!
YES, CHIEF!
HEY SHUANG-SHUANG, DOES YOUR GRANDMA REALLY KNOW MAGIC? THAT'S WICKED!
THAT WAS THE POWER OF OUR CLAN'S ANCIENT WEAPON: THE BANDS OF NÜ WA.
MY SWORD SHOWED ME A VISION OF THEM BEFORE!

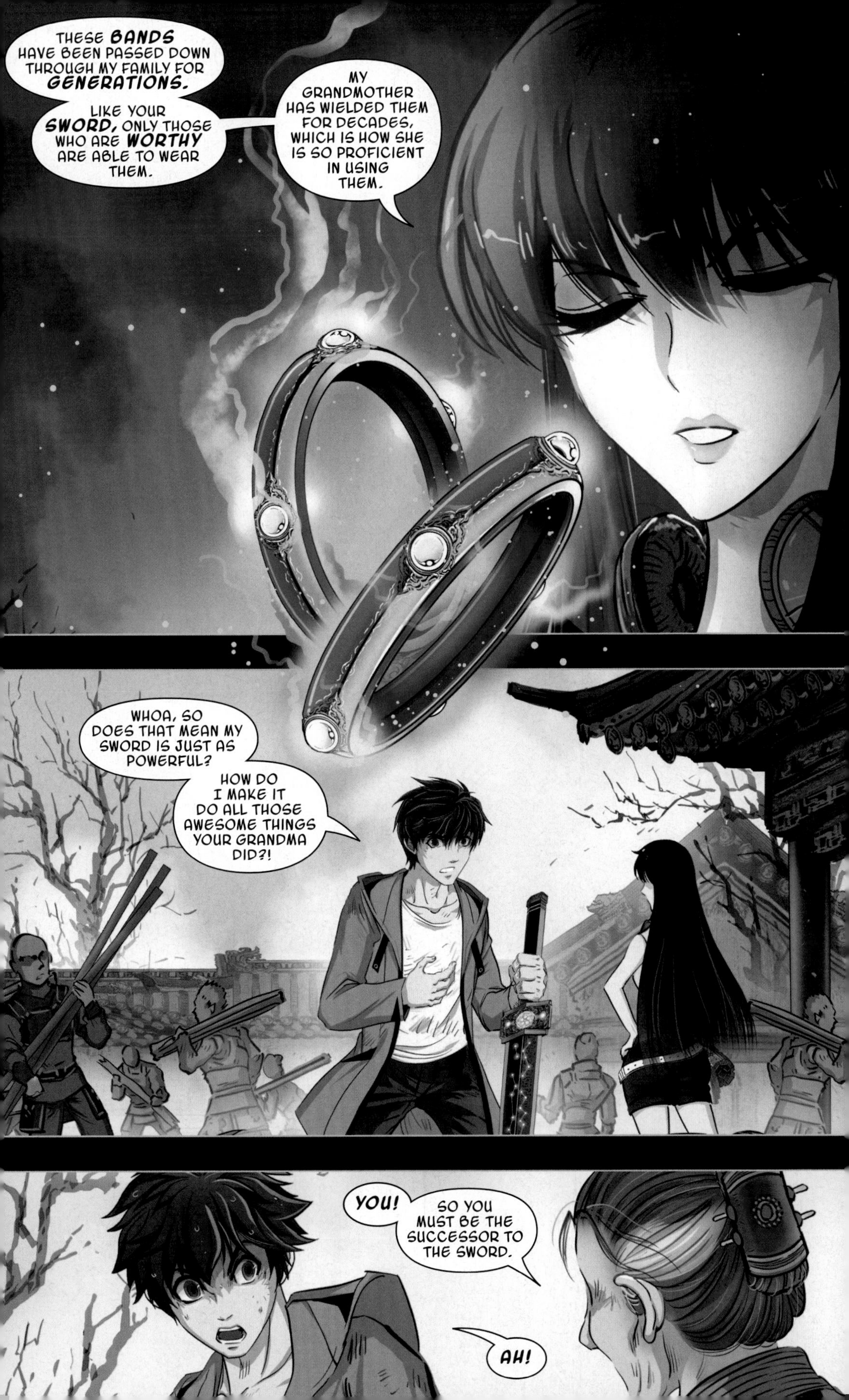
THESE BANDS HAVE BEEN PASSED DOWN THROUGH MY FAMILY FOR GENERATIONS.
LIKE YOUR SWORD, ONLY THOSE WHO ARE WORTHY ARE ABLE TO WEAR THEM.
MY GRANDMOTHER HAS WIELDED THEM FOR DECADES, WHICH IS HOW SHE IS SO PROFICIENT IN USING THEM.
WHOA, SO DOES THAT MEAN MY SWORD IS JUST AS POWERFUL?
HOW DO I MAKE IT DO ALL THOSE AWESOME THINGS YOUR GRANDMA DID?!
YOU!
SO YOU MUST BE THE SUCCESSOR TO THE SWORD.
AH!

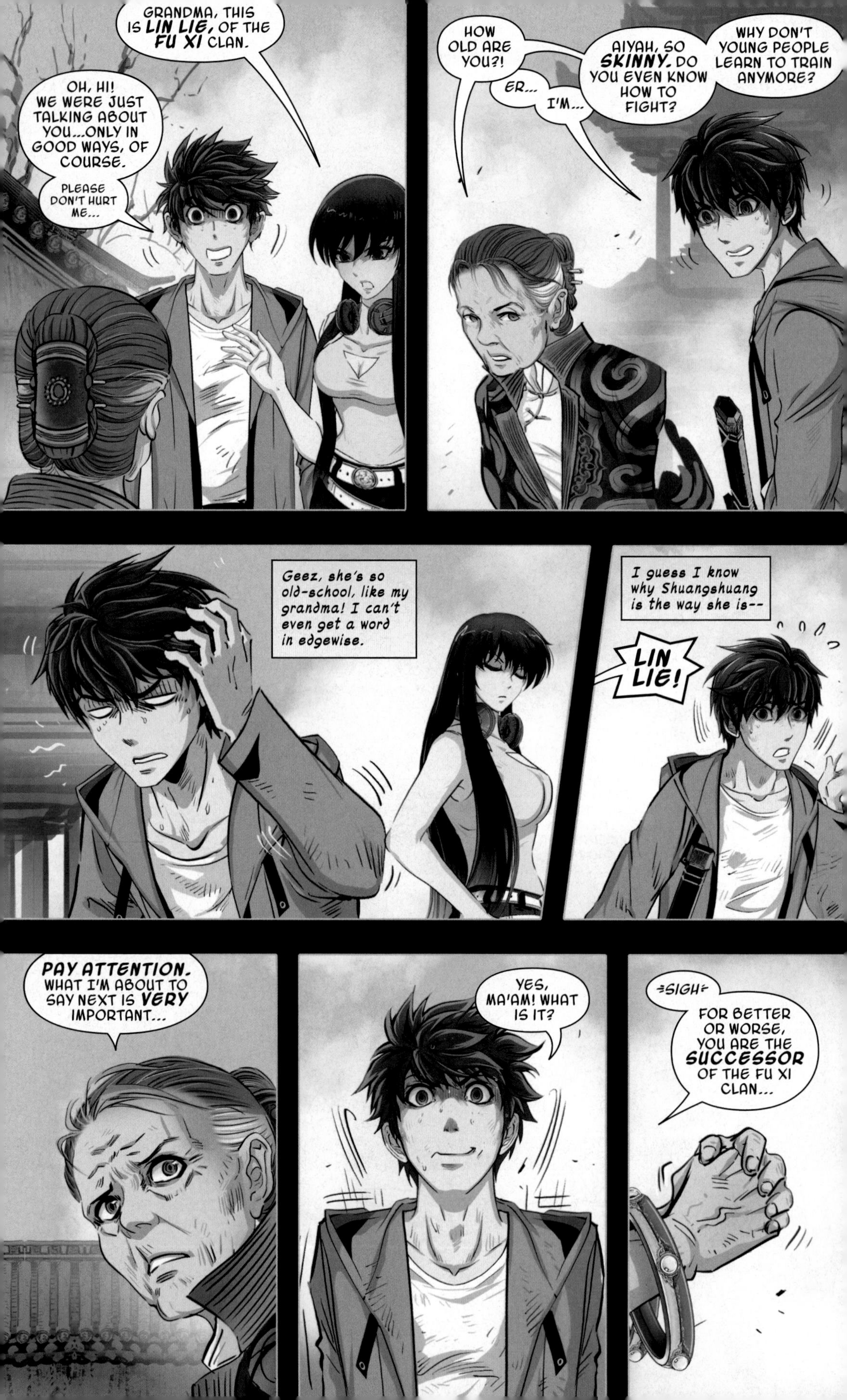
GRANDMA, THIS IS LIN LIE, OF THE FU XI CLAN.
OH, HI! WE WERE JUST TALKING ABOUT YOU...ONLY IN GOOD WAYS, OF COURSE.
PLEASE DON'T HURT ME...
HOW OLD ARE YOU?!
ER...
I'M...
AIYAH, SO SKINNY. DO YOU EVEN KNOW HOW TO FIGHT?
WHY DON'T YOUNG PEOPLE LEARN TO TRAIN ANYMORE?
Geez, she's so old-school, like my grandma! I can't even get a word in edgewise.
I guess I know why Shuangshuang is the way she is--
LIN LIE!
PAY ATTENTION. WHAT I'M ABOUT TO SAY NEXT IS VERY IMPORTANT...
YES, MA'AM! WHAT IS IT?
=SIGH=
FOR BETTER OR WORSE, YOU ARE THE SUCCESSOR OF THE FU XI CLAN...

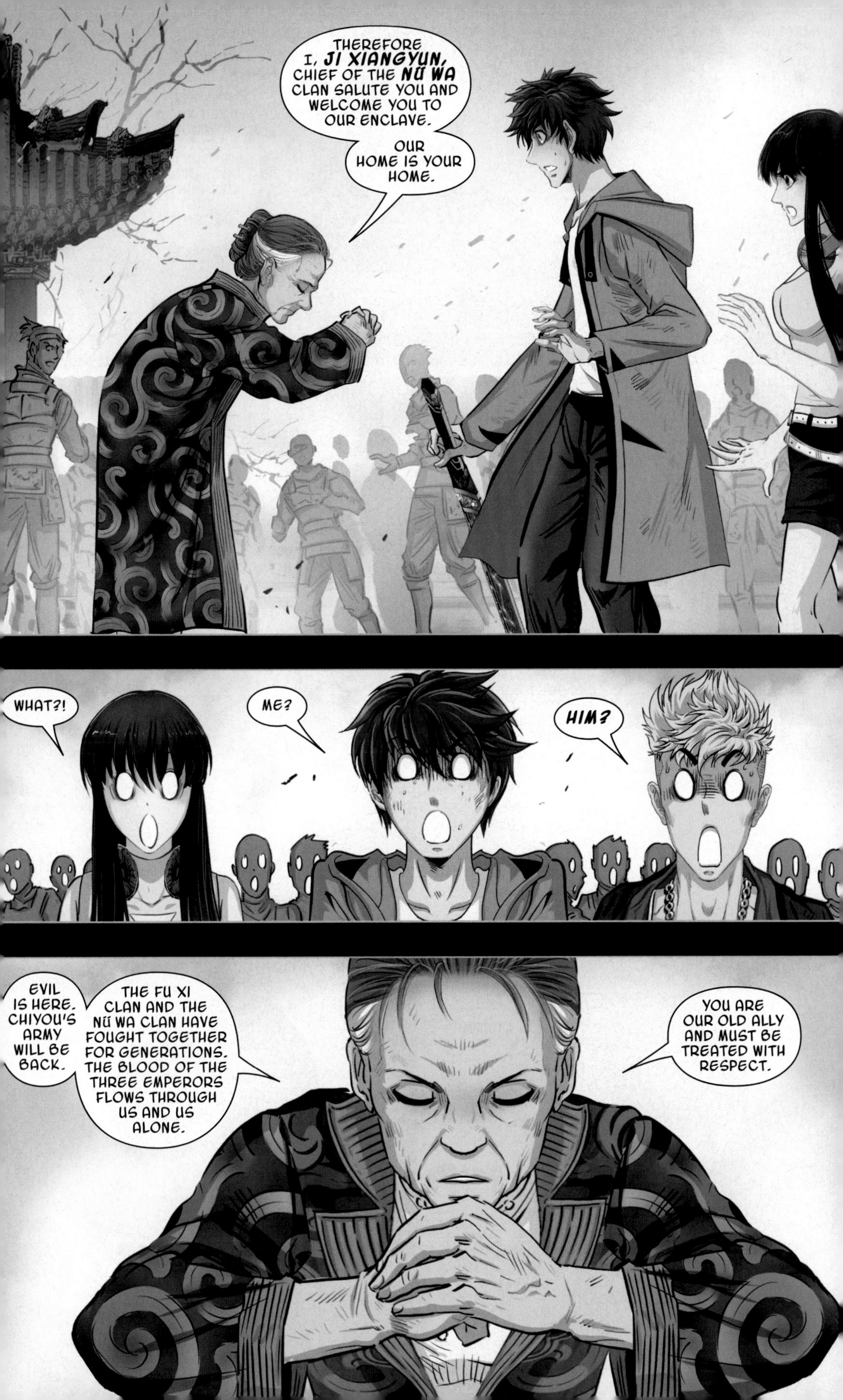
THEREFORE I, JI XIANGYUN, CHIEF OF THE NÜ WA CLAN SALUTE YOU AND WELCOME YOU TO OUR ENCLAVE.
OUR HOME IS YOUR HOME.
WHAT?!
ME?
HIM?
EVIL IS HERE. CHIYOU'S ARMY WILL BE BACK.
THE FU XI CLAN AND THE NÜ WA CLAN HAVE FOUGHT TOGETHER FOR GENERATIONS. THE BLOOD OF THE THREE EMPERORS FLOWS THROUGH US AND US ALONE.
YOU ARE OUR OLD ALLY AND MUST BE TREATED WITH RESPECT.

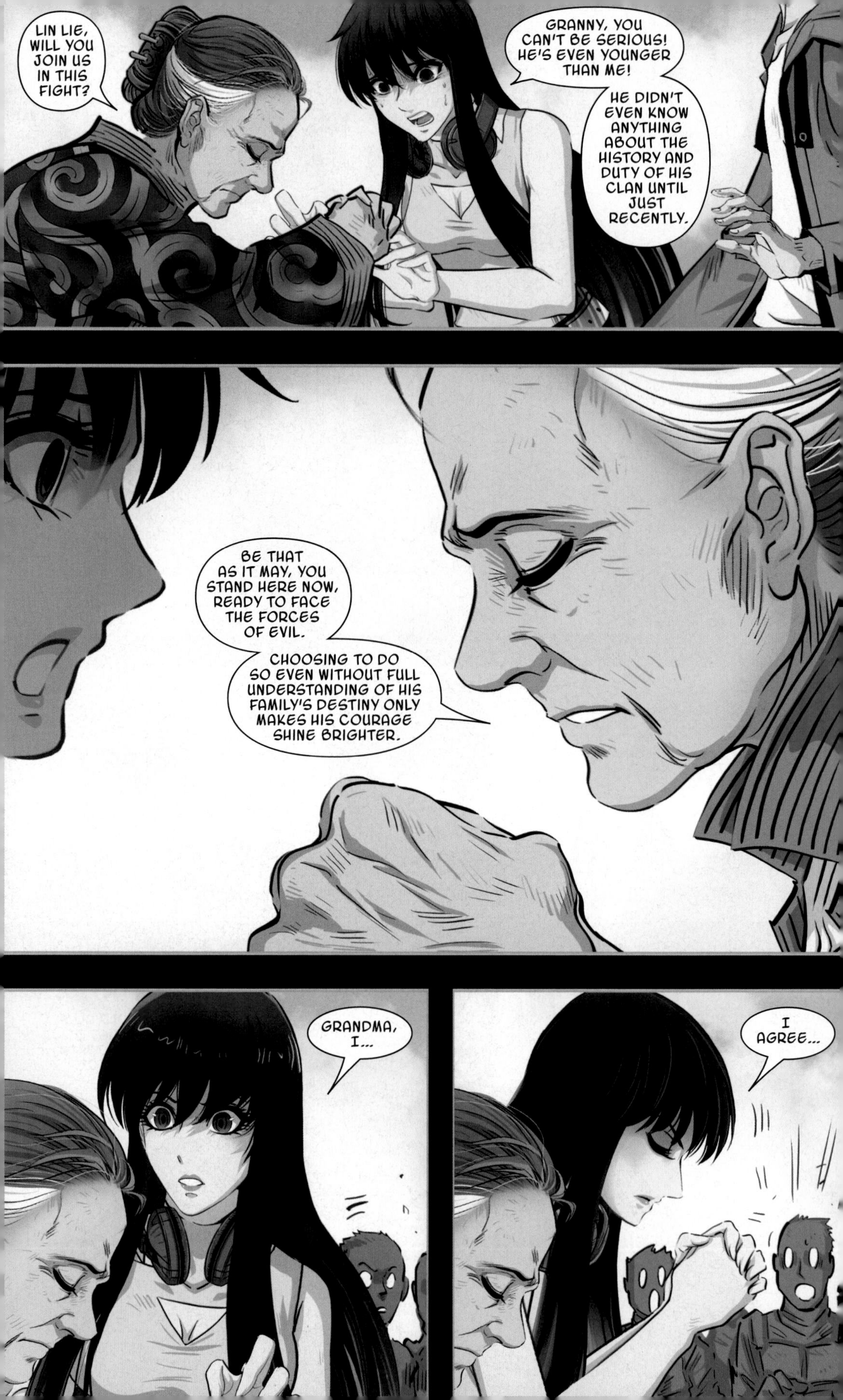
LIN LIE, WILL YOU JOIN US IN THIS FIGHT?
GRANNY, YOU CAN'T BE SERIOUS! HE'S EVEN YOUNGER THAN ME!
HE DIDN'T EVEN KNOW ANYTHING ABOUT THE HISTORY AND DUTY OF HIS CLAN UNTIL JUST RECENTLY.
BE THAT AS IT MAY, YOU STAND HERE NOW, READY TO FACE THE FORCES OF EVIL.
CHOOSING TO DO SO EVEN WITHOUT FULL UNDERSTANDING OF HIS FAMILY'S DESTINY ONLY MAKES HIS COURAGE SHINE BRIGHTER.
GRANDMA, I...
I AGREE...

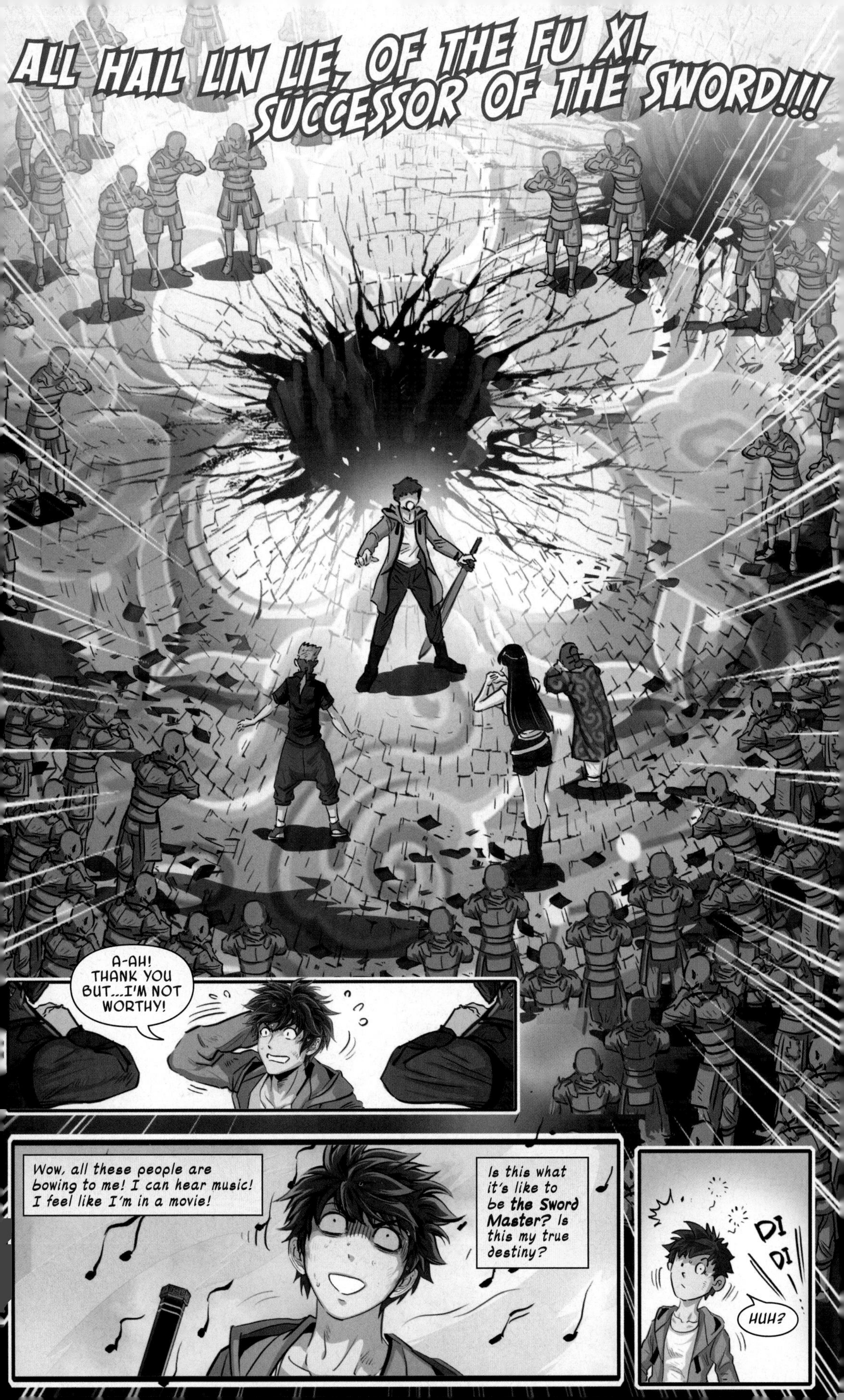
ALL HAIL LIN LIE, OF THE FU XI, SUCCESSOR OF THE SWORD!!!
A-AH! THANK YOU BUT...I'M NOT WORTHY!
Wow, all these people are bowing to me! I can hear music! I feel like I'm in a movie!
Is this what it's like to be **the Sword Master?** Is this my true destiny?
DI
DI
HUH?

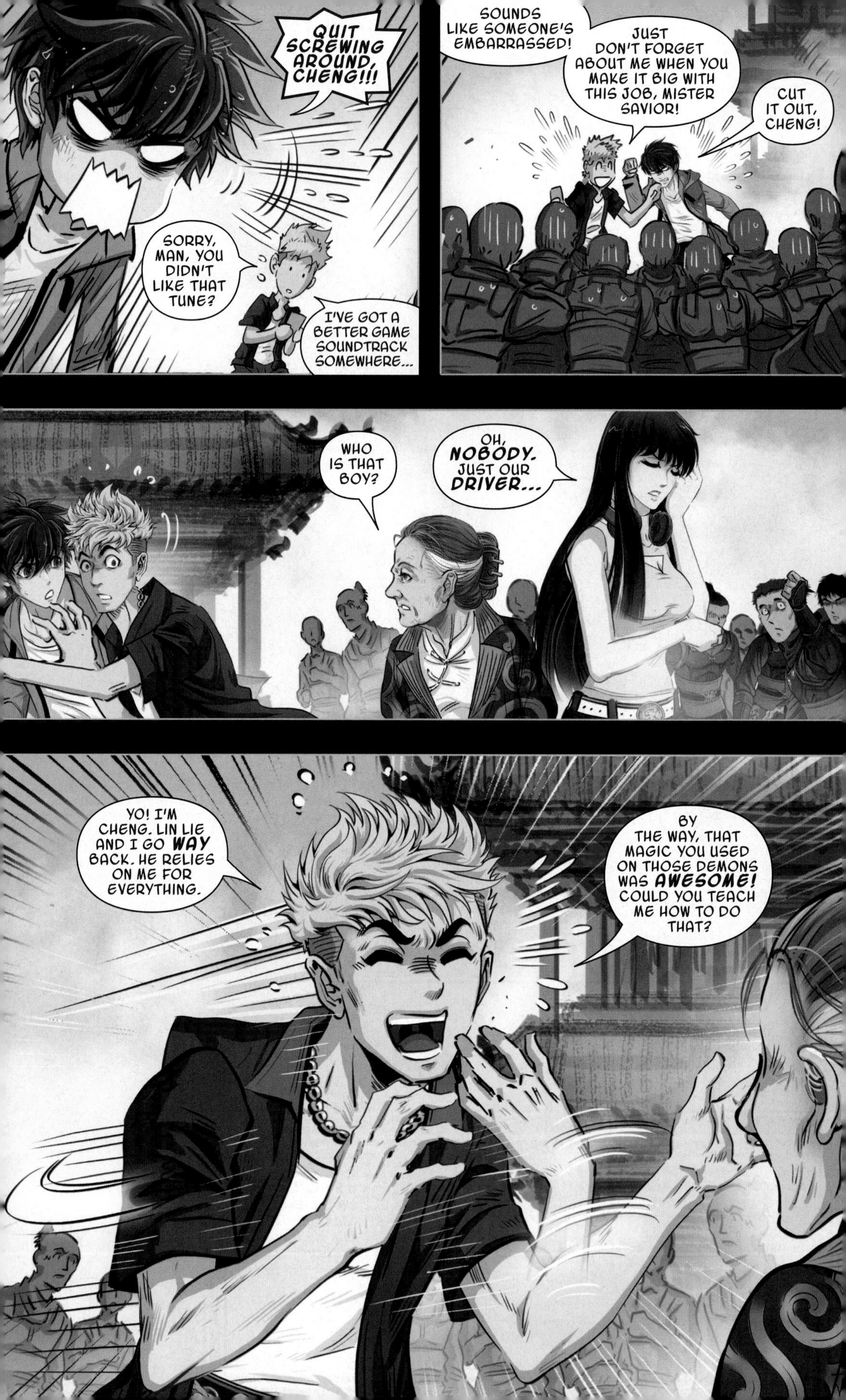
QUIT SCREWING AROUND, CHENG!!!
SORRY, MAN, YOU DIDN'T LIKE THAT TUNE?
I'VE GOT A BETTER GAME SOUNDTRACK SOMEWHERE...
SOUNDS LIKE SOMEONE'S EMBARRASSED!
JUST DON'T FORGET ABOUT ME WHEN YOU MAKE IT BIG WITH THIS JOB, MISTER SAVIOR!
CUT IT OUT, CHENG!
WHO IS THAT BOY?
OH, NOBODY. JUST OUR DRIVER...
YO! I'M CHENG. LIN LIE AND I GO WAY BACK. HE RELIES ON ME FOR EVERYTHING.
BY THE WAY, THAT MAGIC YOU USED ON THOSE DEMONS WAS AWESOME! COULD YOU TEACH ME HOW TO DO THAT?

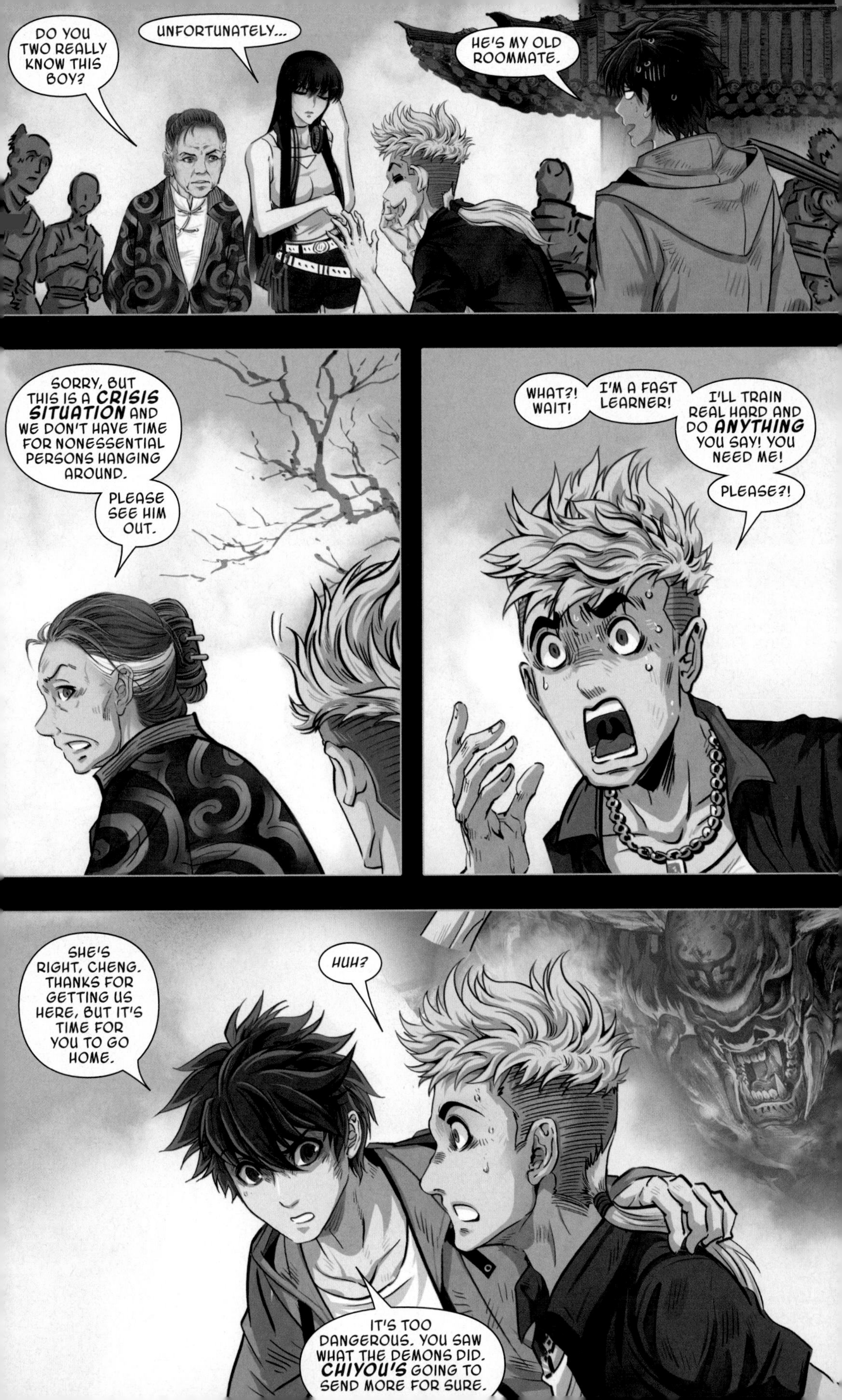
DO YOU TWO REALLY KNOW THIS BOY?
UNFORTUNATELY...
HE'S MY OLD ROOMMATE.
SORRY, BUT THIS IS A **CRISIS SITUATION** AND WE DON'T HAVE TIME FOR NONESSENTIAL PERSONS HANGING AROUND.
PLEASE SEE HIM OUT.
WHAT?! WAIT!
I'M A FAST LEARNER!
I'LL TRAIN REAL HARD AND DO **ANYTHING** YOU SAY! YOU NEED ME!
PLEASE?!
SHE'S RIGHT, CHENG. THANKS FOR GETTING US HERE, BUT IT'S TIME FOR YOU TO GO HOME.
HUH?
IT'S TOO DANGEROUS. YOU SAW WHAT THE DEMONS DID. **CHIYOU'S** GOING TO SEND MORE FOR SURE.

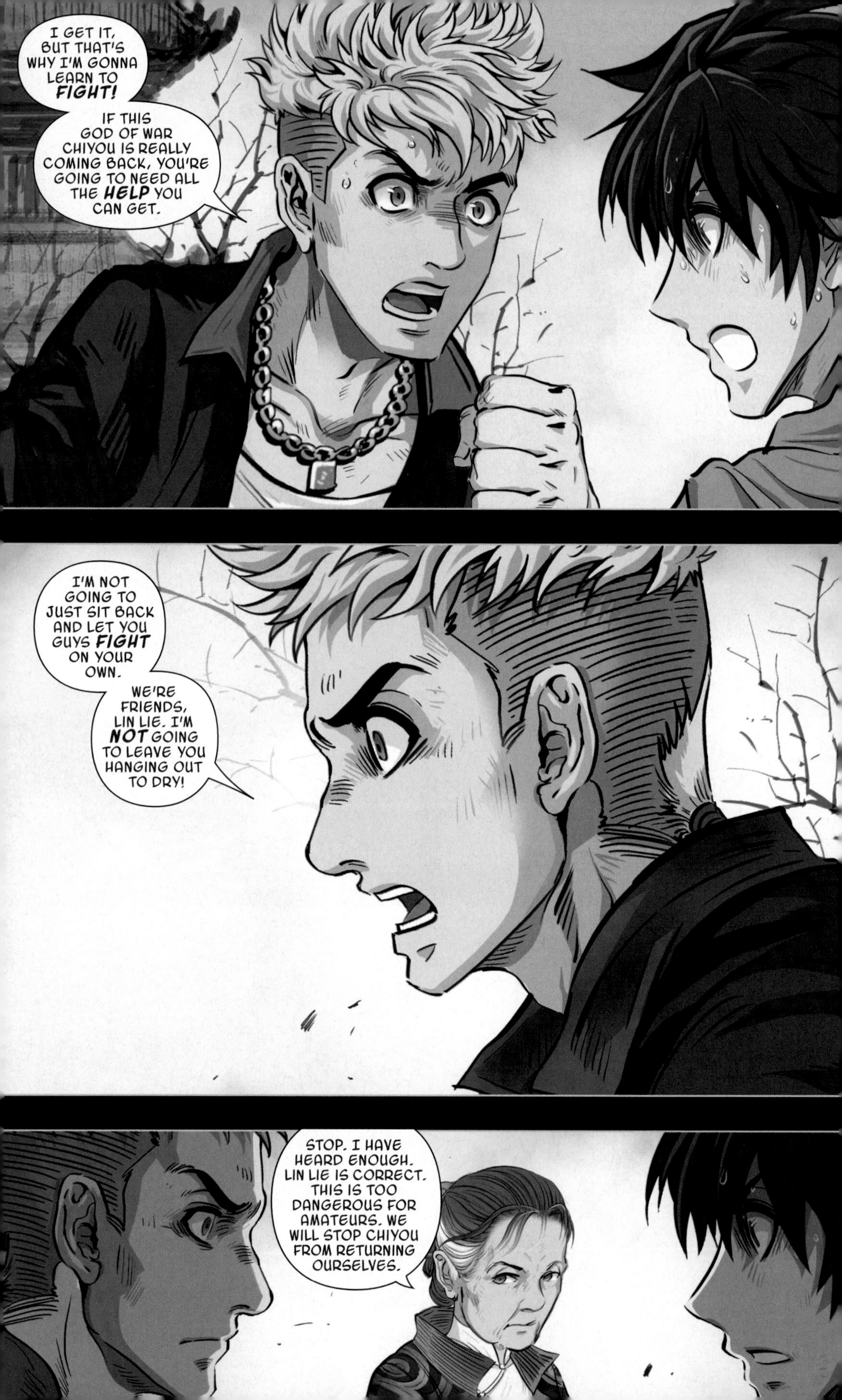
I GET IT, BUT THAT'S WHY I'M GONNA LEARN TO FIGHT!
IF THIS GOD OF WAR CHIYOU IS REALLY COMING BACK, YOU'RE GOING TO NEED ALL THE HELP YOU CAN GET.
I'M NOT GOING TO JUST SIT BACK AND LET YOU GUYS FIGHT ON YOUR OWN.
WE'RE FRIENDS, LIN LIE. I'M NOT GOING TO LEAVE YOU HANGING OUT TO DRY!
STOP. I HAVE HEARD ENOUGH. LIN LIE IS CORRECT. THIS IS TOO DANGEROUS FOR AMATEURS. WE WILL STOP CHIYOU FROM RETURNING OURSELVES.

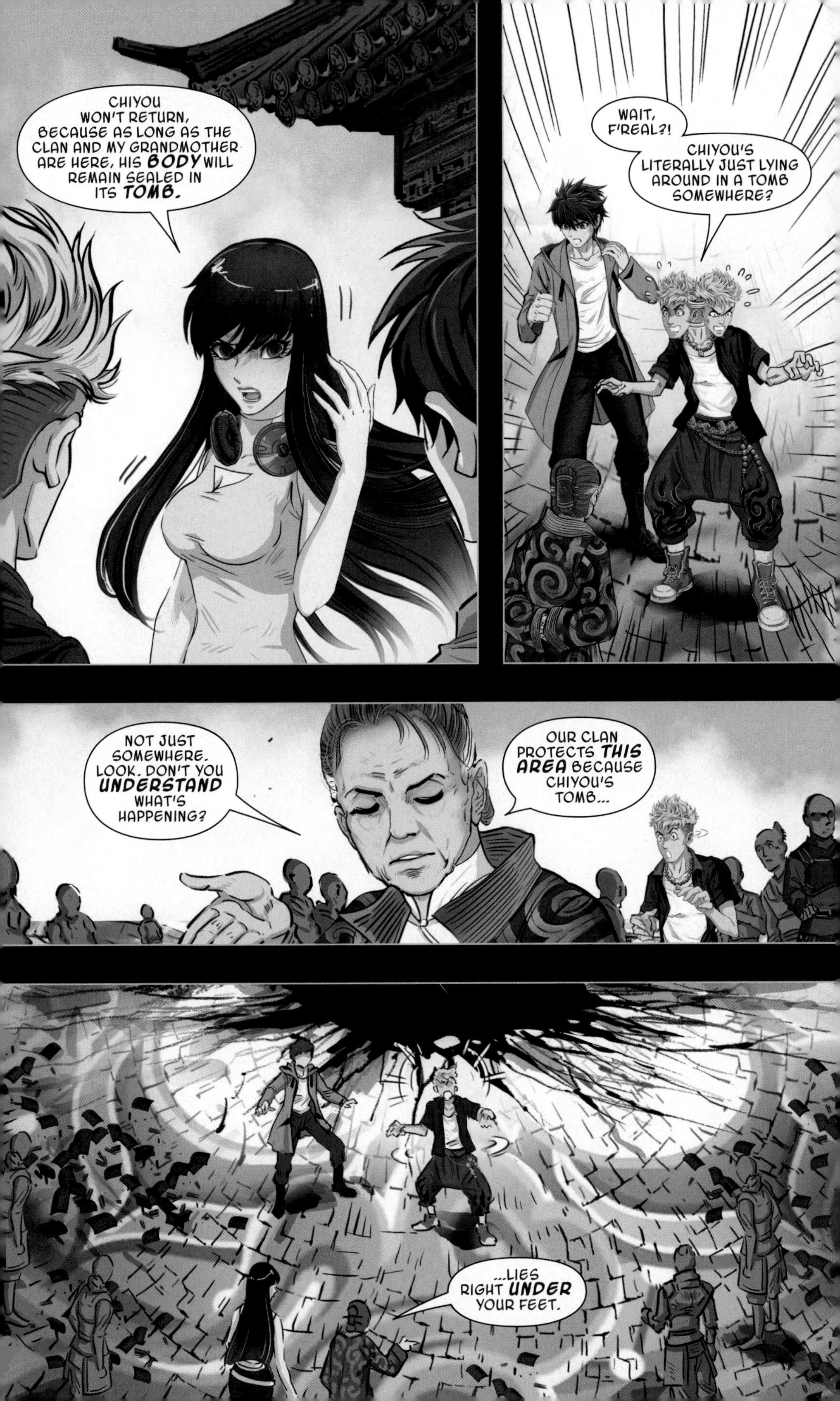
CHIYOU WON'T RETURN, BECAUSE AS LONG AS THE CLAN AND MY GRANDMOTHER ARE HERE, HIS BODY WILL REMAIN SEALED IN ITS TOMB.
WAIT, F'REAL?!
CHIYOU'S LITERALLY JUST LYING AROUND IN A TOMB SOMEWHERE?
NOT JUST SOMEWHERE. LOOK. DON'T YOU UNDERSTAND WHAT'S HAPPENING?
OUR CLAN PROTECTS THIS AREA BECAUSE CHIYOU'S TOMB...
...LIES RIGHT UNDER YOUR FEET.

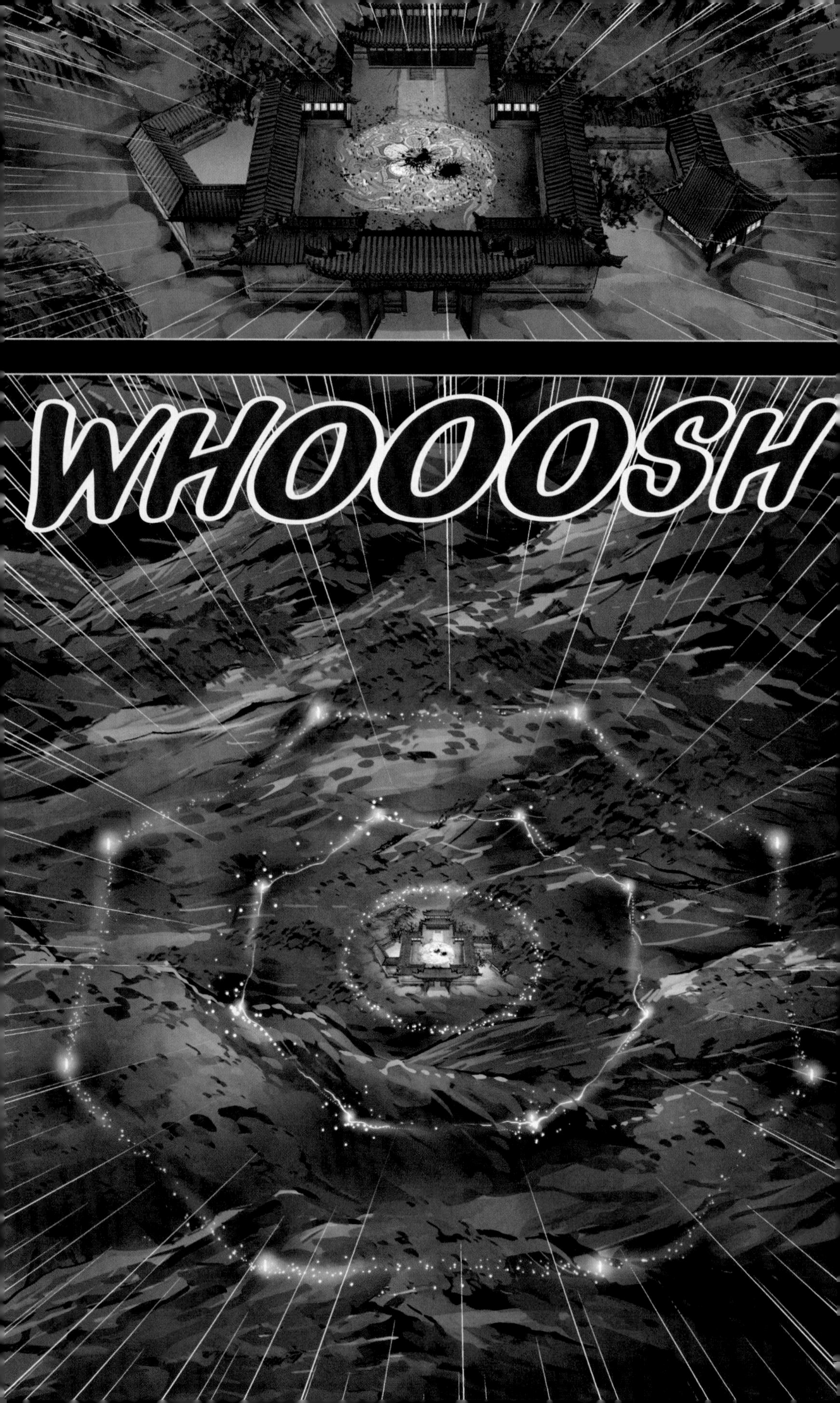
WHOOOSH

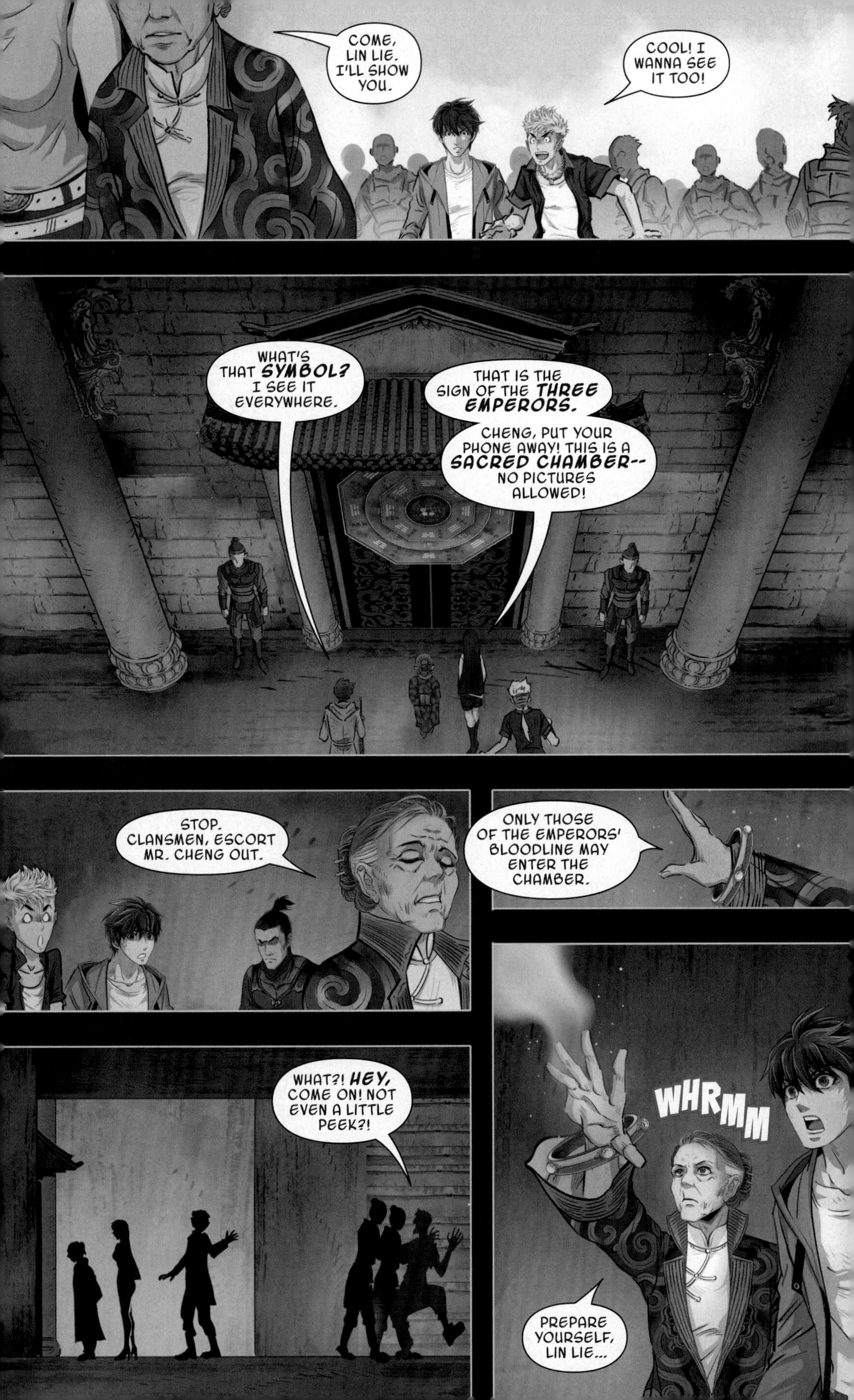
COME, LIN LIE. I'LL SHOW YOU.
COOL! I WANNA SEE IT TOO!
WHAT'S THAT SYMBOL? I SEE IT EVERYWHERE.
THAT IS THE SIGN OF THE THREE EMPERORS.
CHENG, PUT YOUR PHONE AWAY! THIS IS A SACRED CHAMBER-- NO PICTURES ALLOWED!
STOP. CLANSMEN, ESCORT MR. CHENG OUT.
ONLY THOSE OF THE EMPERORS' BLOODLINE MAY ENTER THE CHAMBER.
WHAT?! HEY, COME ON! NOT EVEN A LITTLE PEEK?!
WHRMM
PREPARE YOURSELF, LIN LIE...

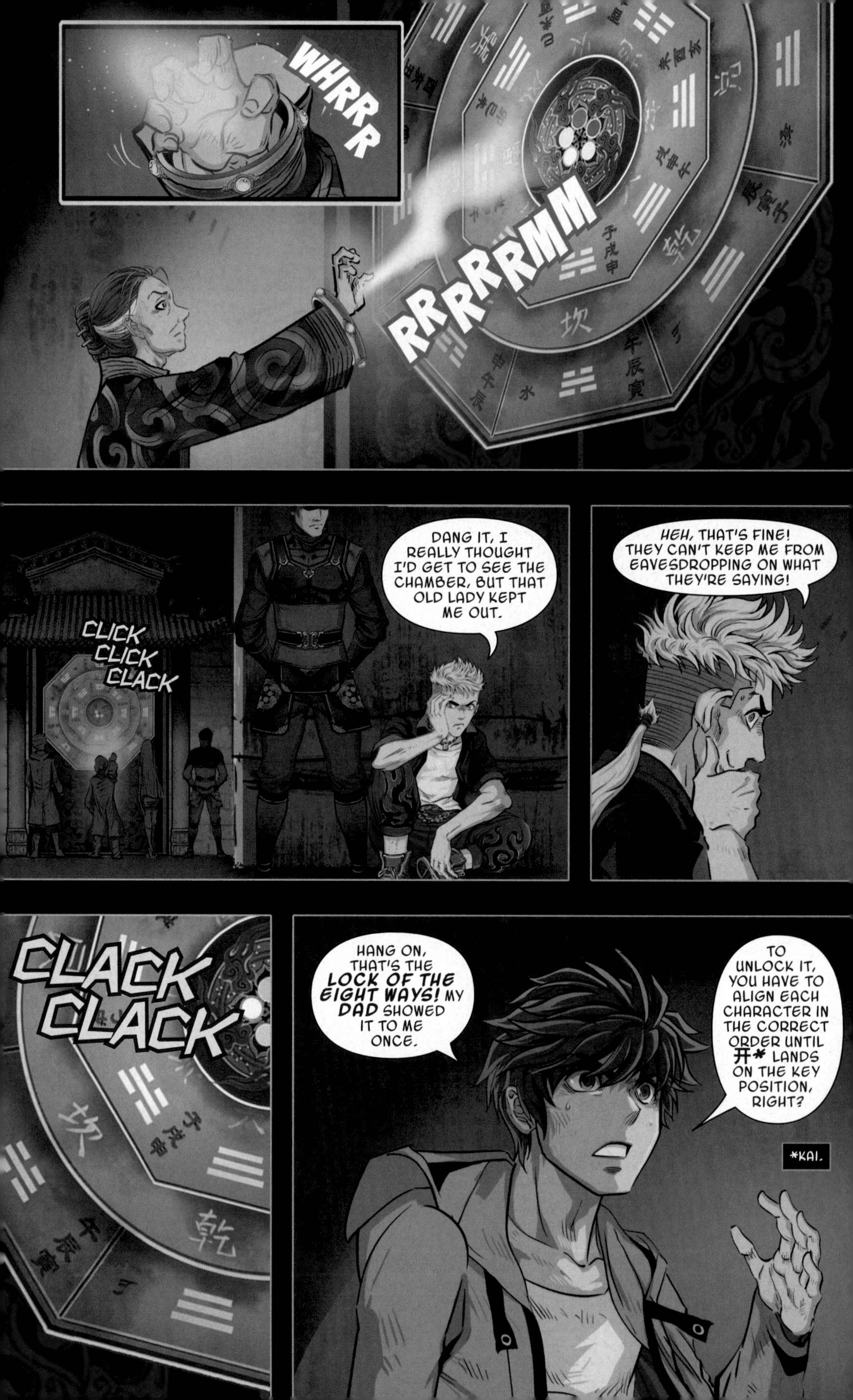
WHRRR
RRRRRMM
CLICK
CLICK
CLACK
DANG IT, I REALLY THOUGHT I'D GET TO SEE THE CHAMBER, BUT THAT OLD LADY KEPT ME OUT.
HEH, THAT'S FINE! THEY CAN'T KEEP ME FROM EAVESDROPPING ON WHAT THEY'RE SAYING!
CLACK
CLACK
HANG ON, THAT'S THE **LOCK OF THE EIGHT WAYS!** MY **DAD** SHOWED IT TO ME ONCE.
TO UNLOCK IT, YOU HAVE TO ALIGN EACH CHARACTER IN THE CORRECT ORDER UNTIL **开*** LANDS ON THE KEY POSITION, RIGHT?
*KAI.

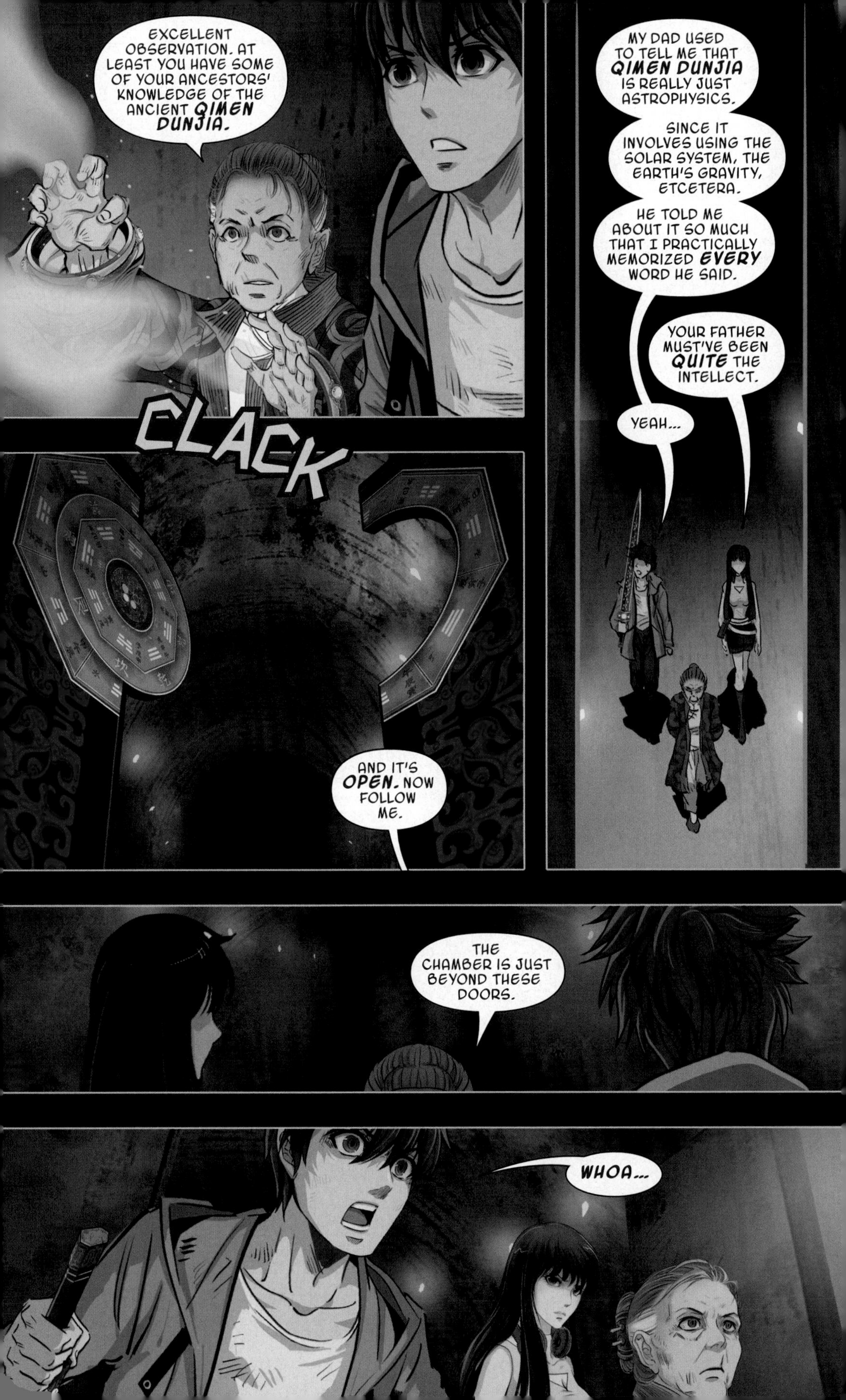
EXCELLENT OBSERVATION. AT LEAST YOU HAVE SOME OF YOUR ANCESTORS' KNOWLEDGE OF THE ANCIENT QIMEN DUNJIA.
CLACK
AND IT'S OPEN. NOW FOLLOW ME.
MY DAD USED TO TELL ME THAT QIMEN DUNJIA IS REALLY JUST ASTROPHYSICS.
SINCE IT INVOLVES USING THE SOLAR SYSTEM, THE EARTH'S GRAVITY, ETCETERA.
HE TOLD ME ABOUT IT SO MUCH THAT I PRACTICALLY MEMORIZED EVERY WORD HE SAID.
YOUR FATHER MUST'VE BEEN QUITE THE INTELLECT.
YEAH...
THE CHAMBER IS JUST BEYOND THESE DOORS.
WHOA...

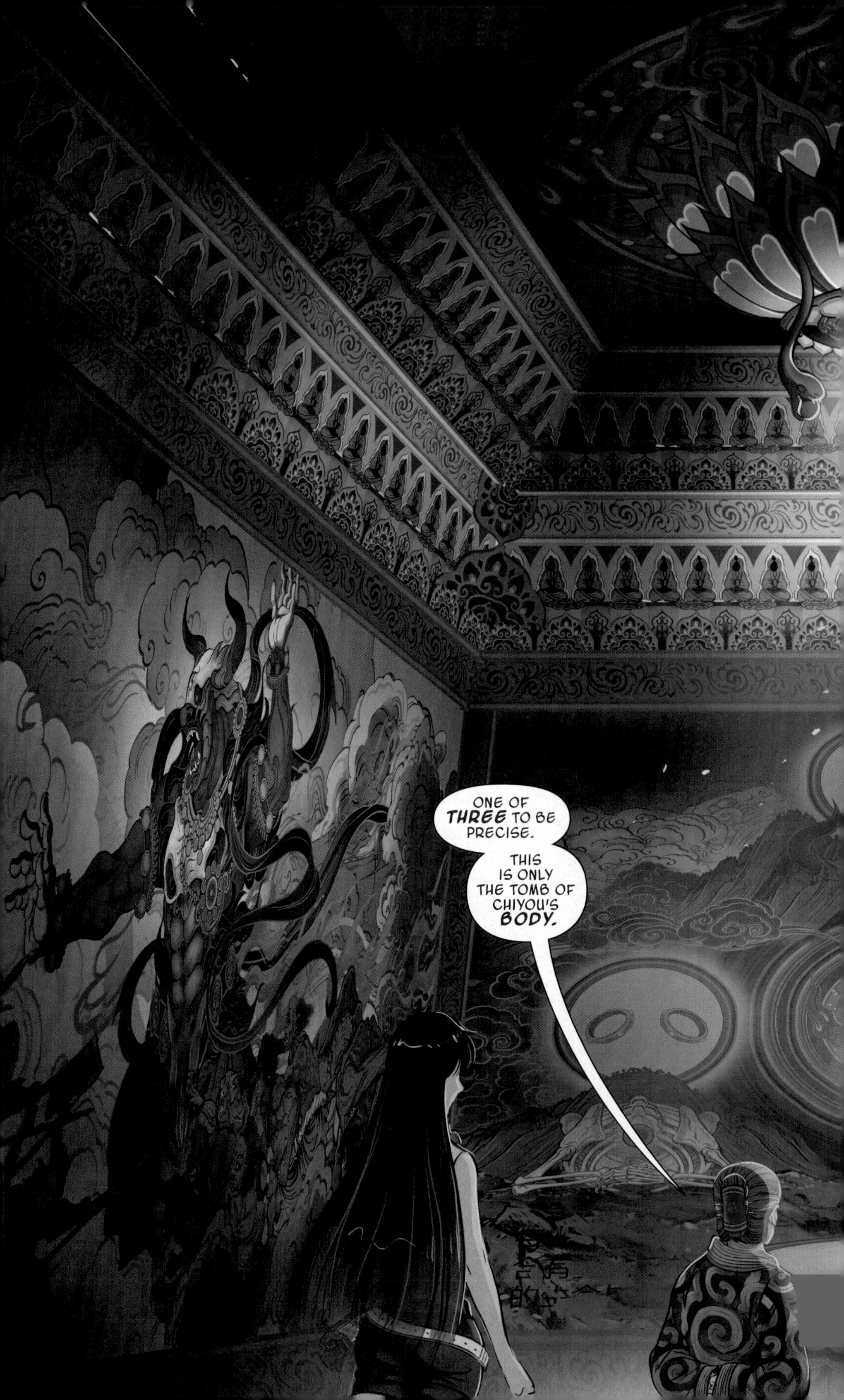
ONE OF THREE TO BE PRECISE.
THIS IS ONLY THE TOMB OF CHIYOU'S BODY.

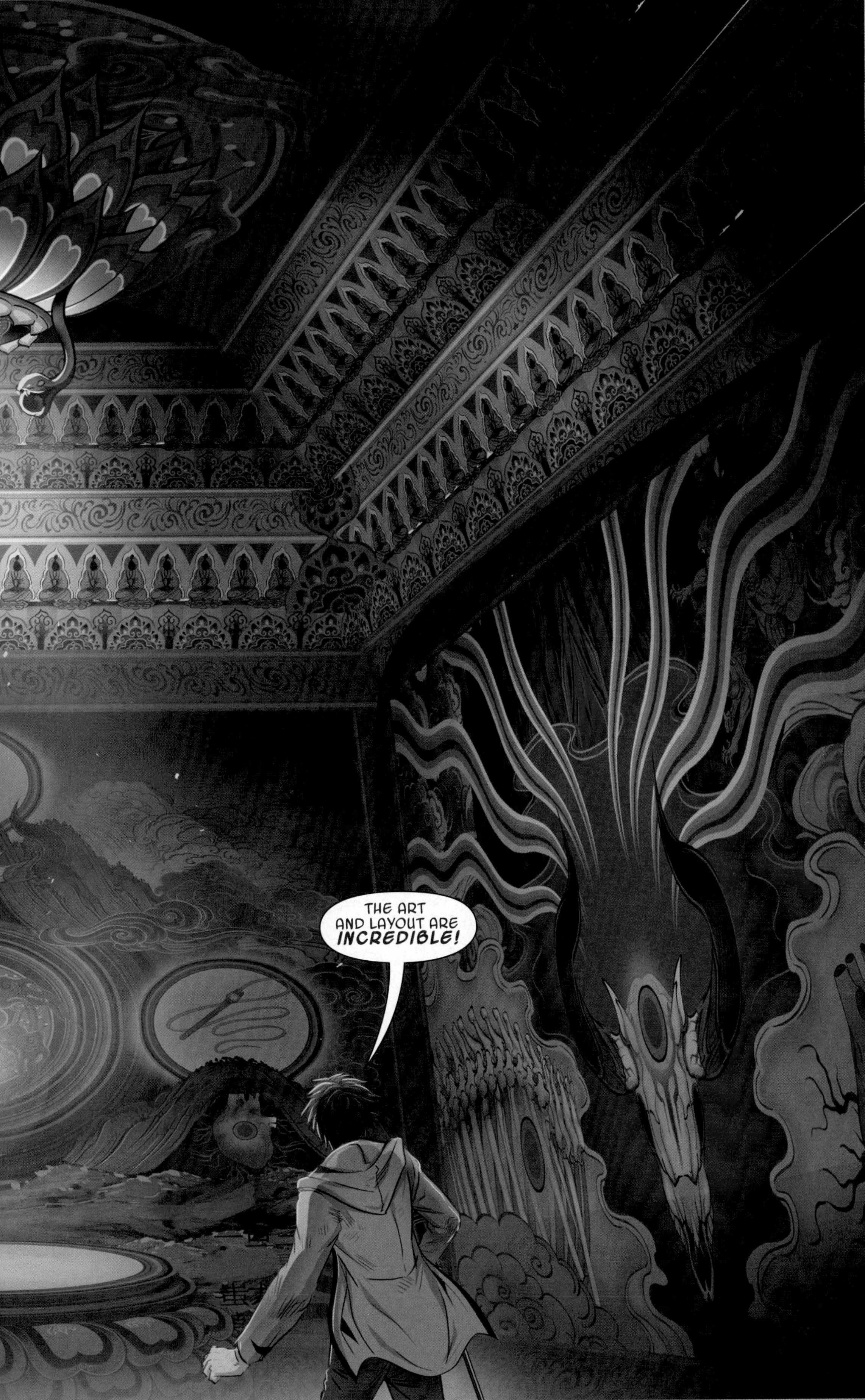
THE ART AND LAYOUT ARE INCREDIBLE!

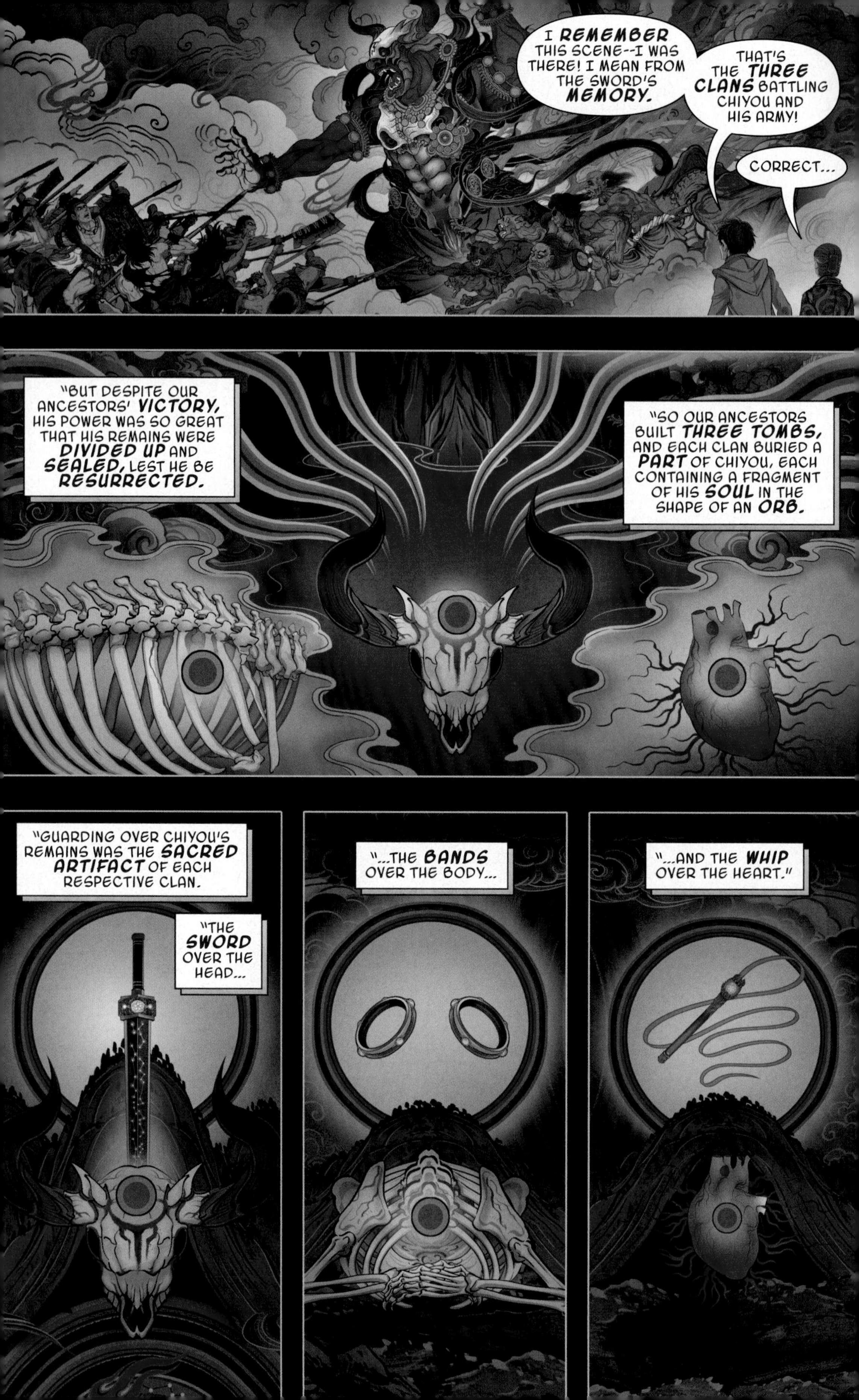
I REMEMBER THIS SCENE--I WAS THERE! I MEAN FROM THE SWORD'S MEMORY.
THAT'S THE THREE CLANS BATTLING CHIYOU AND HIS ARMY!
CORRECT...
"BUT DESPITE OUR ANCESTORS' VICTORY, HIS POWER WAS SO GREAT THAT HIS REMAINS WERE DIVIDED UP AND SEALED, LEST HE BE RESURRECTED.
"SO OUR ANCESTORS BUILT THREE TOMBS, AND EACH CLAN BURIED A PART OF CHIYOU, EACH CONTAINING A FRAGMENT OF HIS SOUL IN THE SHAPE OF AN ORB.
"GUARDING OVER CHIYOU'S REMAINS WAS THE SACRED ARTIFACT OF EACH RESPECTIVE CLAN.
"THE SWORD OVER THE HEAD...
"...THE BANDS OVER THE BODY...
"...AND THE WHIP OVER THE HEART."

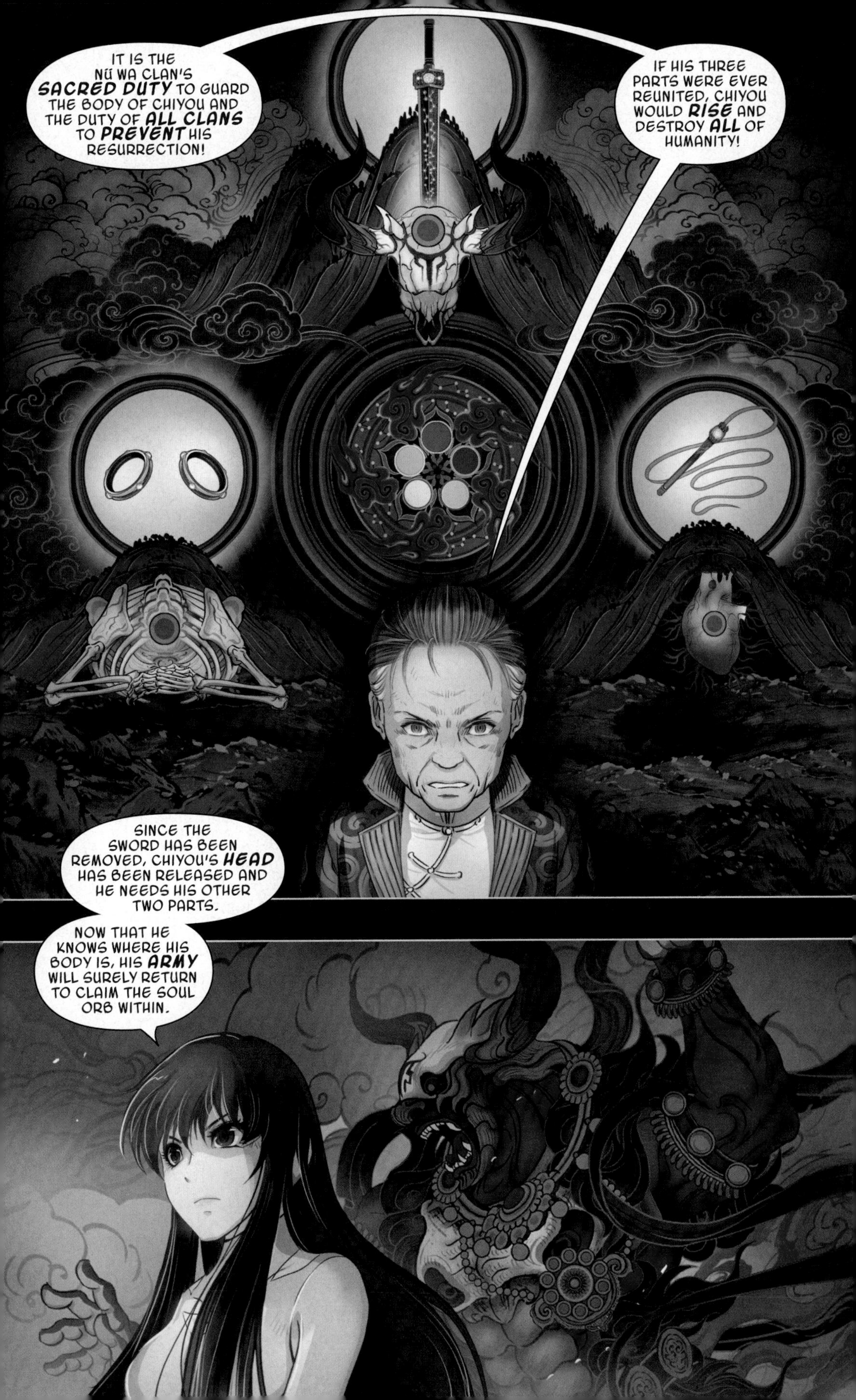
IT IS THE NŪ WA CLAN'S SACRED DUTY TO GUARD THE BODY OF CHIYOU AND THE DUTY OF ALL CLANS TO PREVENT HIS RESURRECTION!
IF HIS THREE PARTS WERE EVER REUNITED, CHIYOU WOULD RISE AND DESTROY ALL OF HUMANITY!
SINCE THE SWORD HAS BEEN REMOVED, CHIYOU'S HEAD HAS BEEN RELEASED AND HE NEEDS HIS OTHER TWO PARTS.
NOW THAT HE KNOWS WHERE HIS BODY IS, HIS ARMY WILL SURELY RETURN TO CLAIM THE SOUL ORB WITHIN.

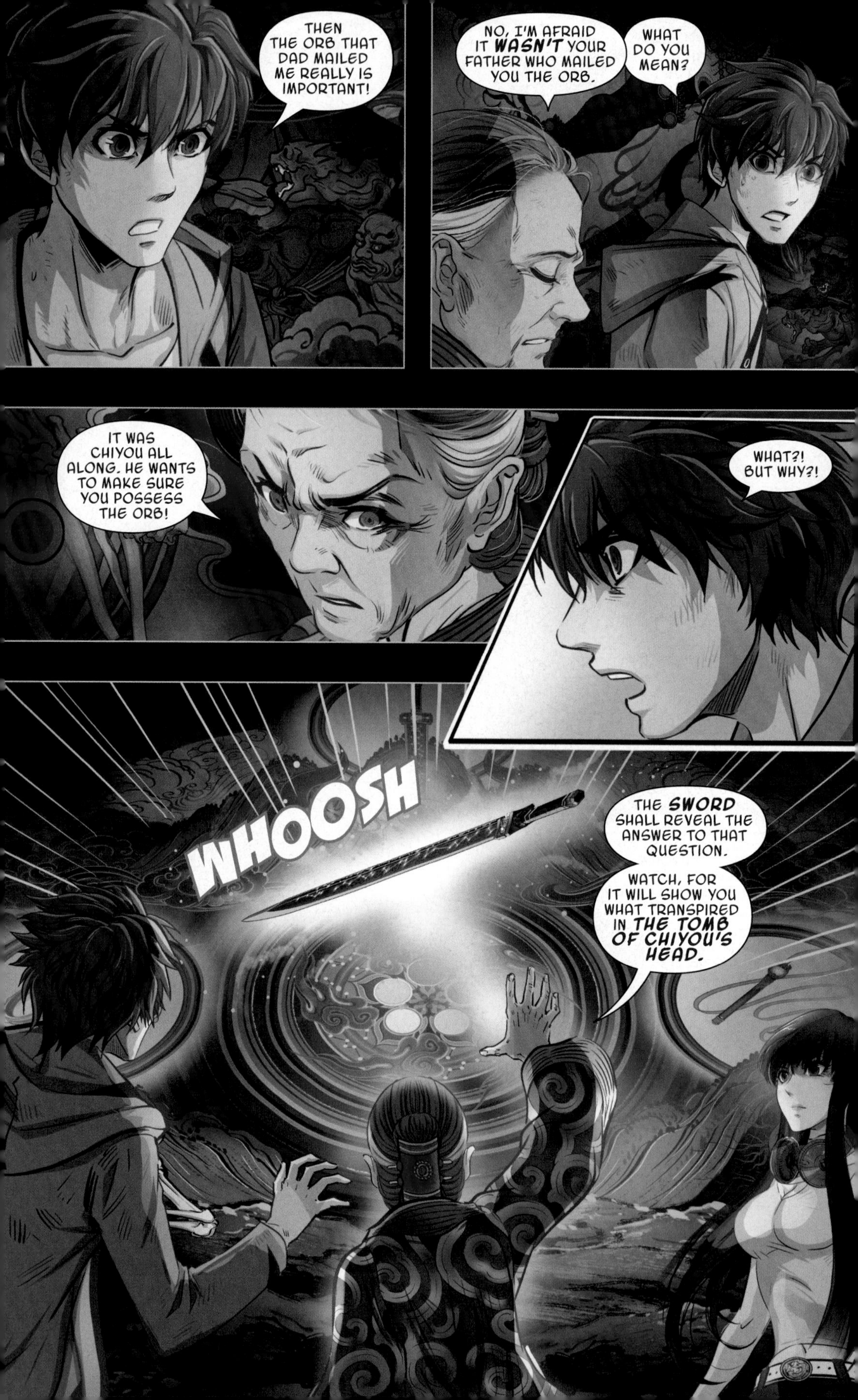
THEN THE ORB THAT DAD MAILED ME REALLY IS IMPORTANT!
NO, I'M AFRAID IT WASN'T YOUR FATHER WHO MAILED YOU THE ORB.
WHAT DO YOU MEAN?
IT WAS CHIYOU ALL ALONG. HE WANTS TO MAKE SURE YOU POSSESS THE ORB!
WHAT?! BUT WHY?!
WHOOSH
THE SWORD SHALL REVEAL THE ANSWER TO THAT QUESTION.
WATCH, FOR IT WILL SHOW YOU WHAT TRANSPIRED IN THE TOMB OF CHIYOU'S HEAD.

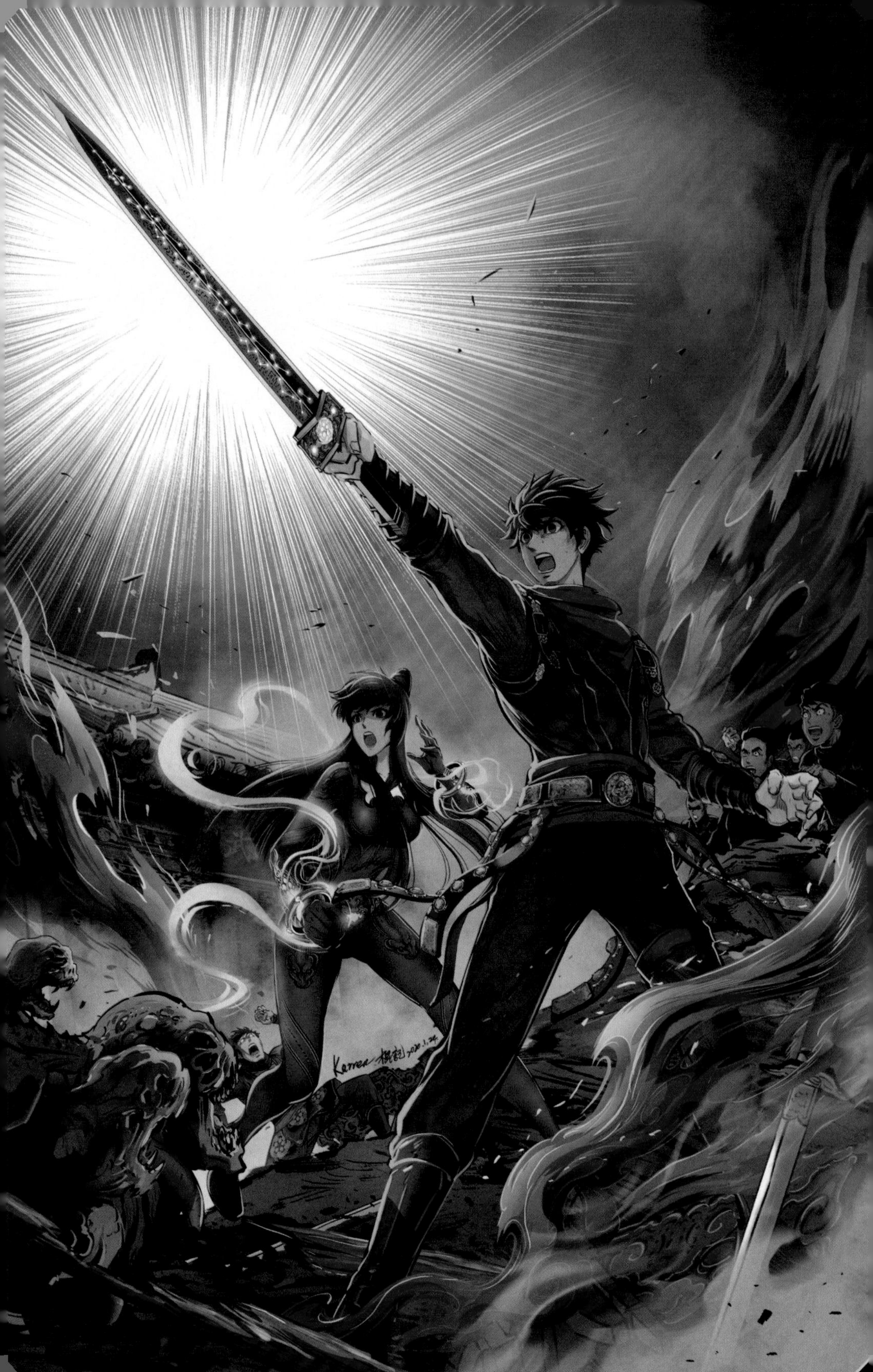

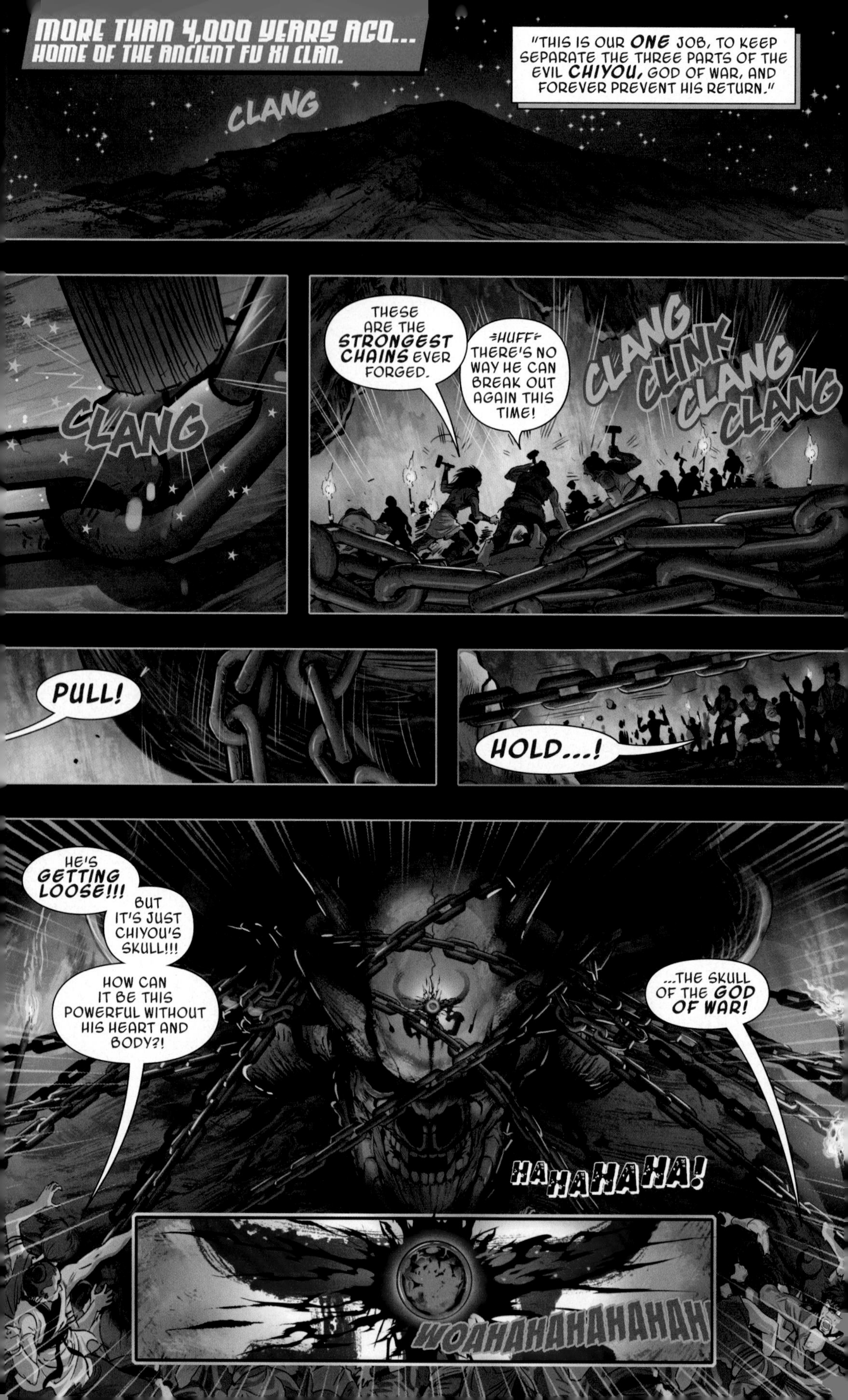
MORE THAN 4,000 YEARS AGO... HOME OF THE ANCIENT FU XI CLAN.
"THIS IS OUR ONE JOB, TO KEEP SEPARATE THE THREE PARTS OF THE EVIL CHIYOU, GOD OF WAR, AND FOREVER PREVENT HIS RETURN."
CLANG
CLANG
THESE ARE THE STRONGEST CHAINS EVER FORGED.
=HUFF= THERE'S NO WAY HE CAN BREAK OUT AGAIN THIS TIME!
CLANG CLINK CLANG CLANG
PULL!
HOLD...!
HE'S GETTING LOOSE!!!
BUT IT'S JUST CHIYOU'S SKULL!!!
HOW CAN IT BE THIS POWERFUL WITHOUT HIS HEART AND BODY?!
...THE SKULL OF THE GOD OF WAR!
HAHAHAHAHA!
WOAHAHAHAHAHAH

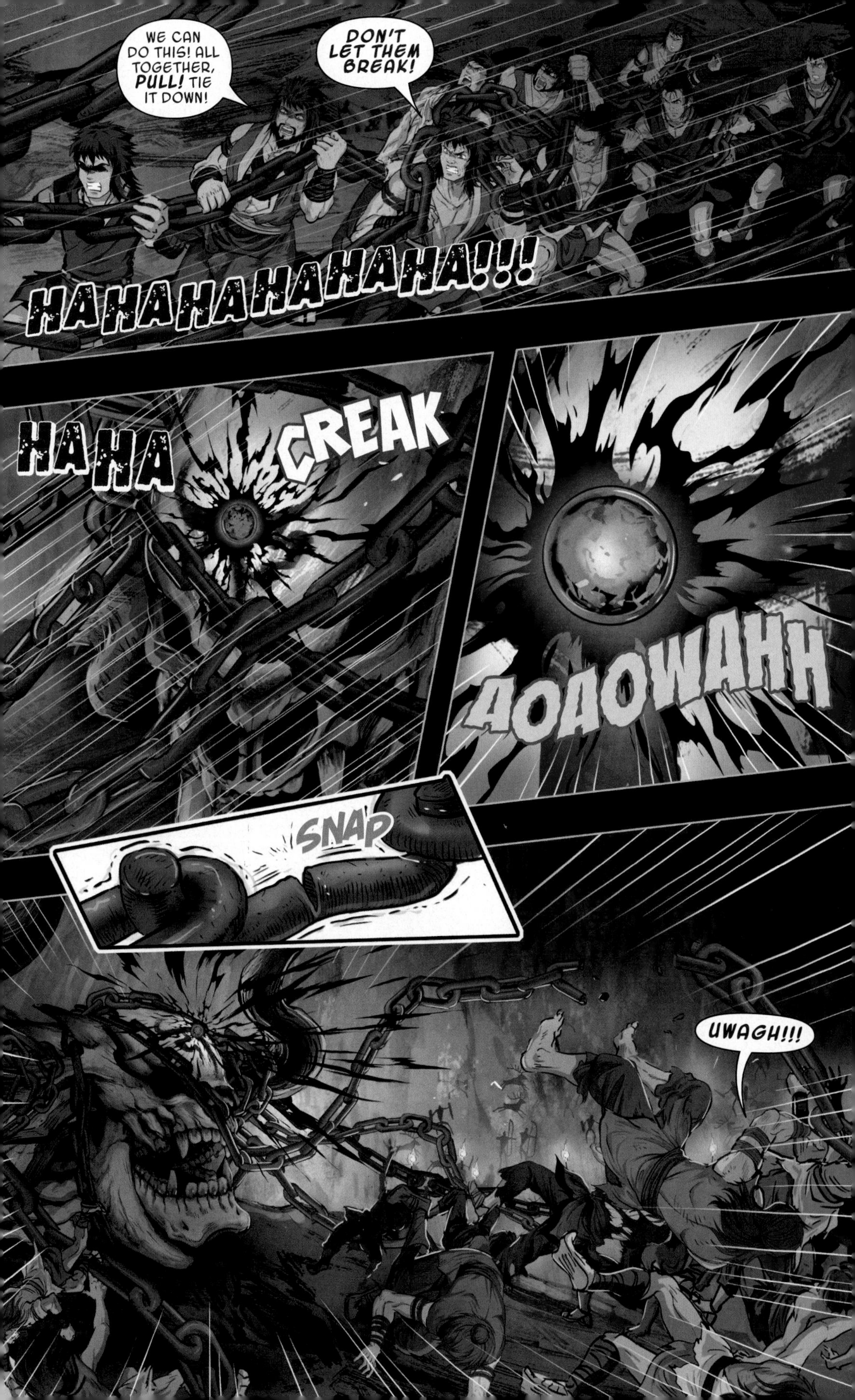
WE CAN DO THIS! ALL TOGETHER, PULL! TIE IT DOWN!
DON'T LET THEM BREAK!
HAHAHAHAHAHAHA!!!
HAHA
CREAK
AOAOWAHH
SNAP
UWAGH!!!

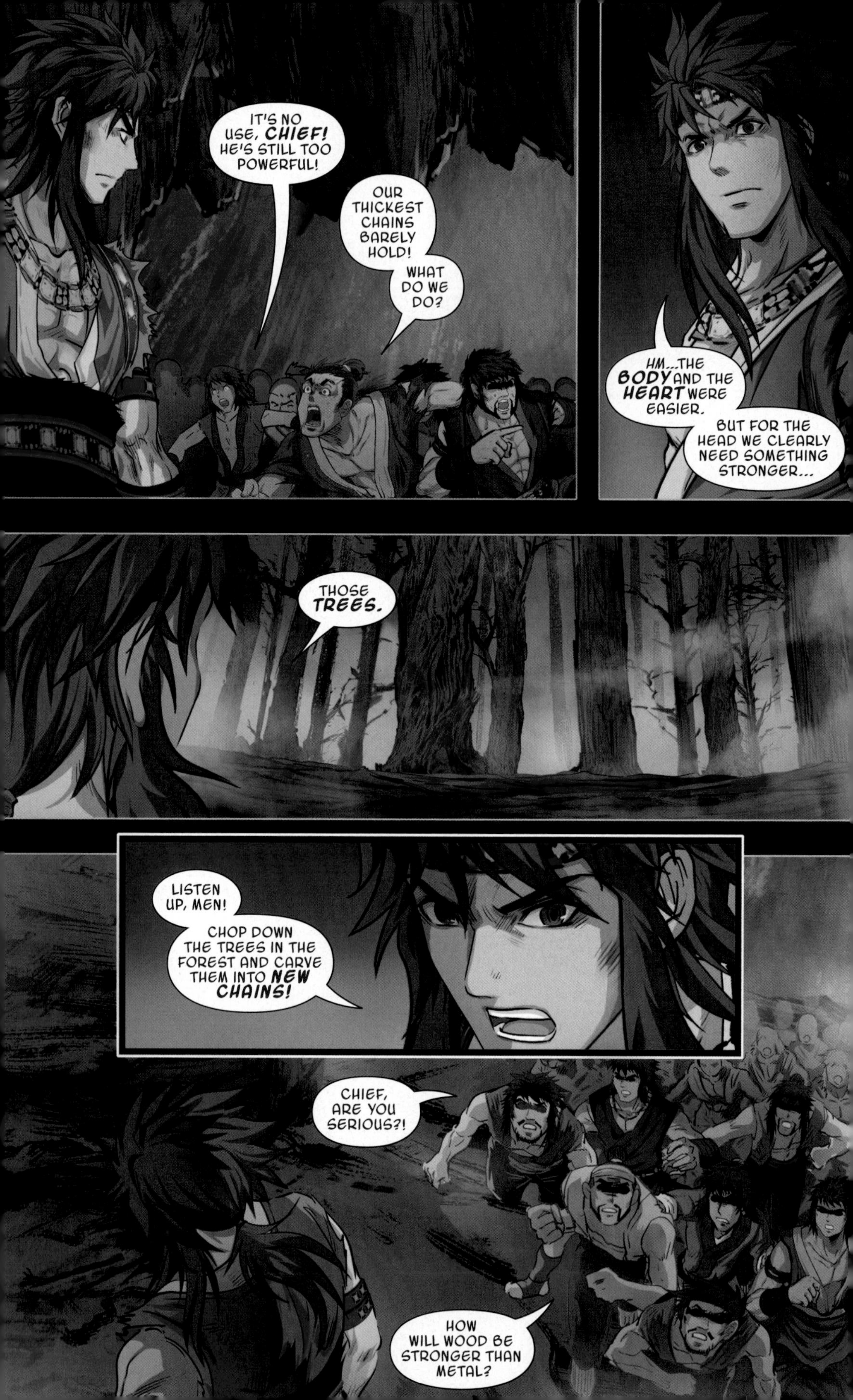
IT'S NO USE, CHIEF! HE'S STILL TOO POWERFUL!
OUR THICKEST CHAINS BARELY HOLD!
WHAT DO WE DO?
HM...THE BODY AND THE HEART WERE EASIER.
BUT FOR THE HEAD WE CLEARLY NEED SOMETHING STRONGER...
THOSE TREES.
LISTEN UP, MEN!
CHOP DOWN THE TREES IN THE FOREST AND CARVE THEM INTO NEW CHAINS!
CHIEF, ARE YOU SERIOUS?!
HOW WILL WOOD BE STRONGER THAN METAL?

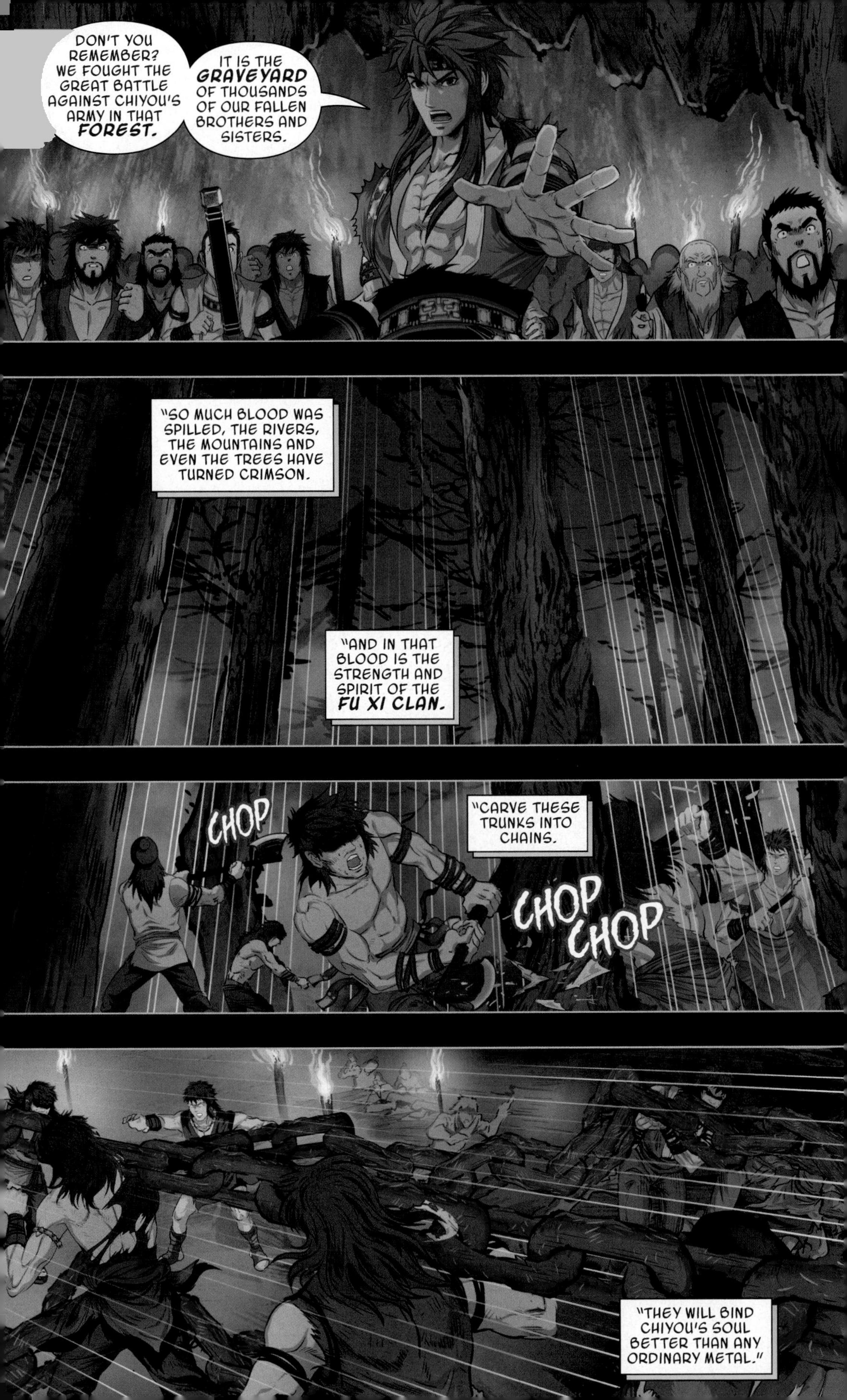
DON'T YOU REMEMBER? WE FOUGHT THE GREAT BATTLE AGAINST CHIYOU'S ARMY IN THAT FOREST.
IT IS THE GRAVEYARD OF THOUSANDS OF OUR FALLEN BROTHERS AND SISTERS.
"SO MUCH BLOOD WAS SPILLED, THE RIVERS, THE MOUNTAINS AND EVEN THE TREES HAVE TURNED CRIMSON.
"AND IN THAT BLOOD IS THE STRENGTH AND SPIRIT OF THE FU XI CLAN.
CHOP
"CARVE THESE TRUNKS INTO CHAINS.
CHOP CHOP
"THEY WILL BIND CHIYOU'S SOUL BETTER THAN ANY ORDINARY METAL."

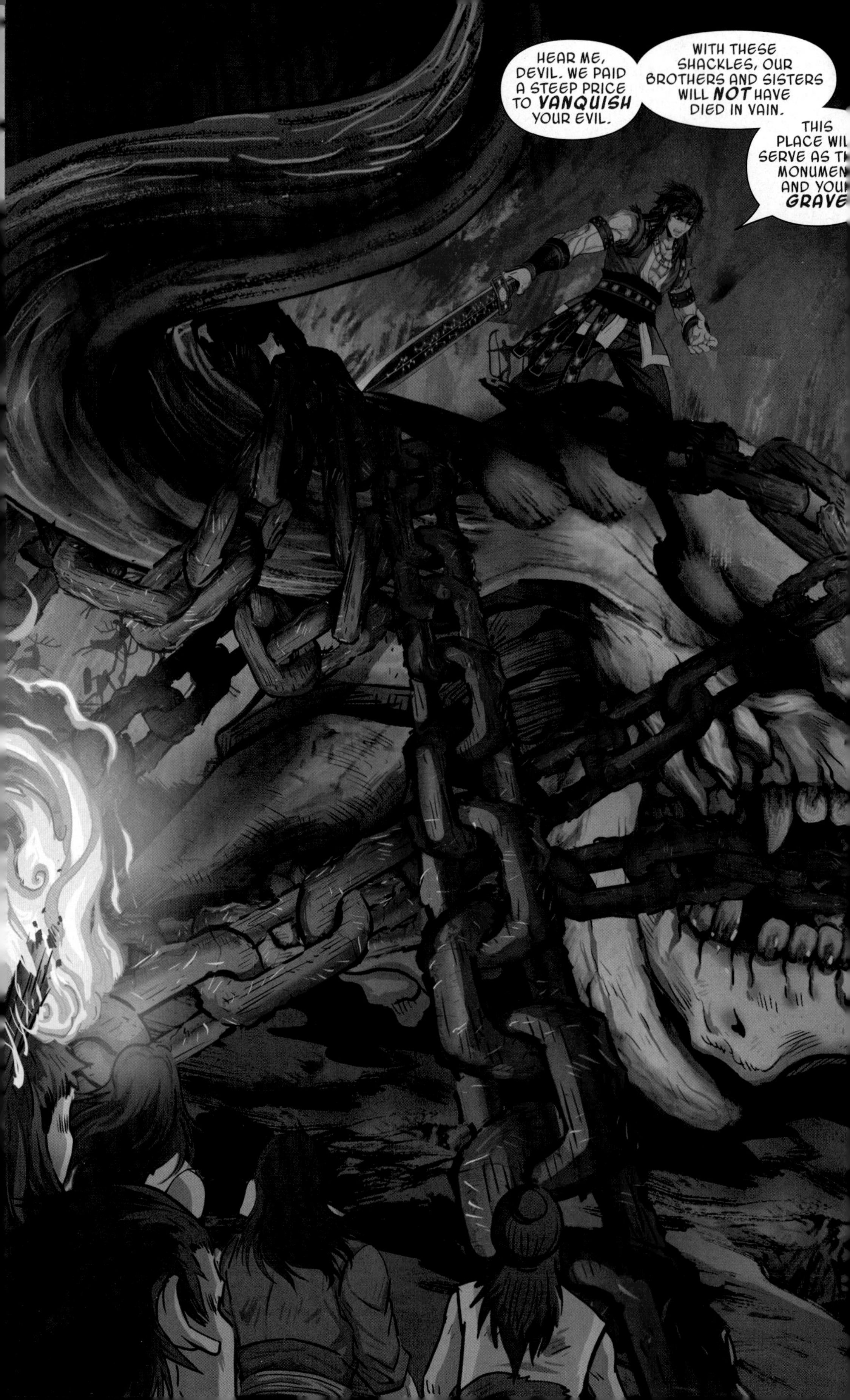
HEAR ME, DEVIL. WE PAID A STEEP PRICE TO VANQUISH YOUR EVIL.
WITH THESE SHACKLES, OUR BROTHERS AND SISTERS WILL NOT HAVE DIED IN VAIN.
THIS PLACE WIL SERVE AS TH MONUMEN AND YOU GRAVE

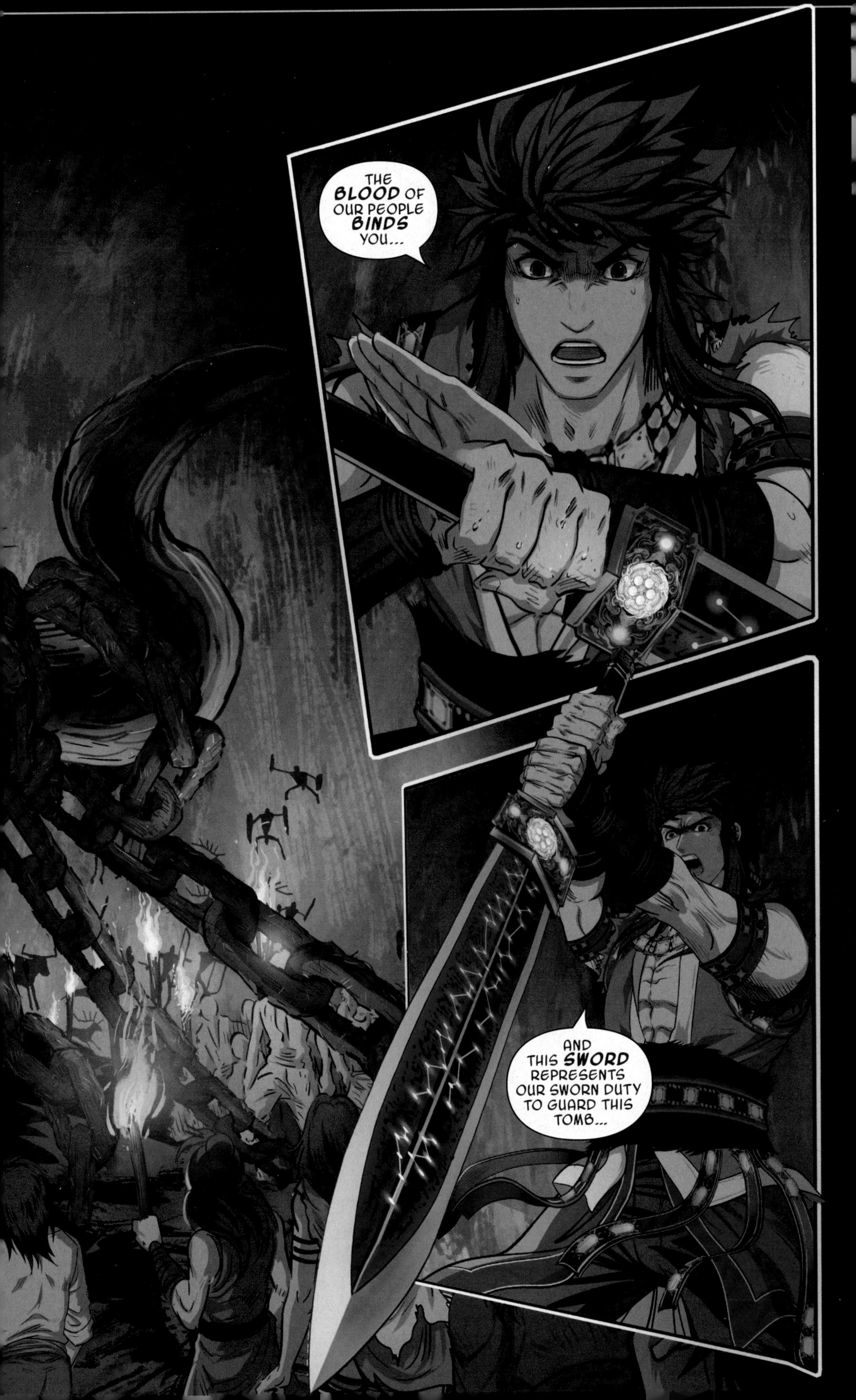
THE BLOOD OF OUR PEOPLE BINDS YOU...
AND THIS SWORD REPRESENTS OUR SWORN DUTY TO GUARD THIS TOMB...

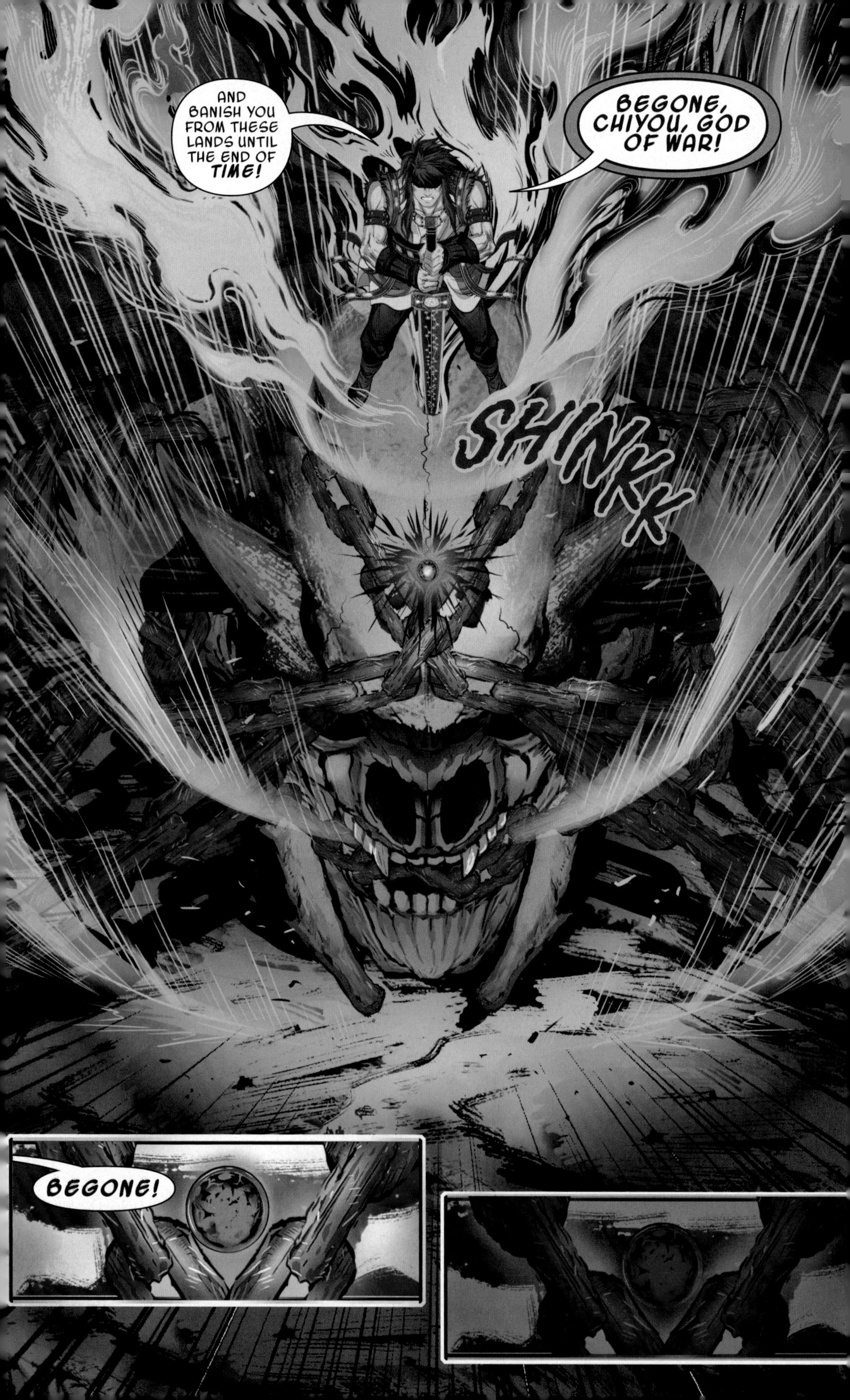
AND BANISH YOU FROM THESE LANDS UNTIL THE END OF TIME!
BEGONE, CHIYOU, GOD OF WAR!
SHINKK
BEGONE!

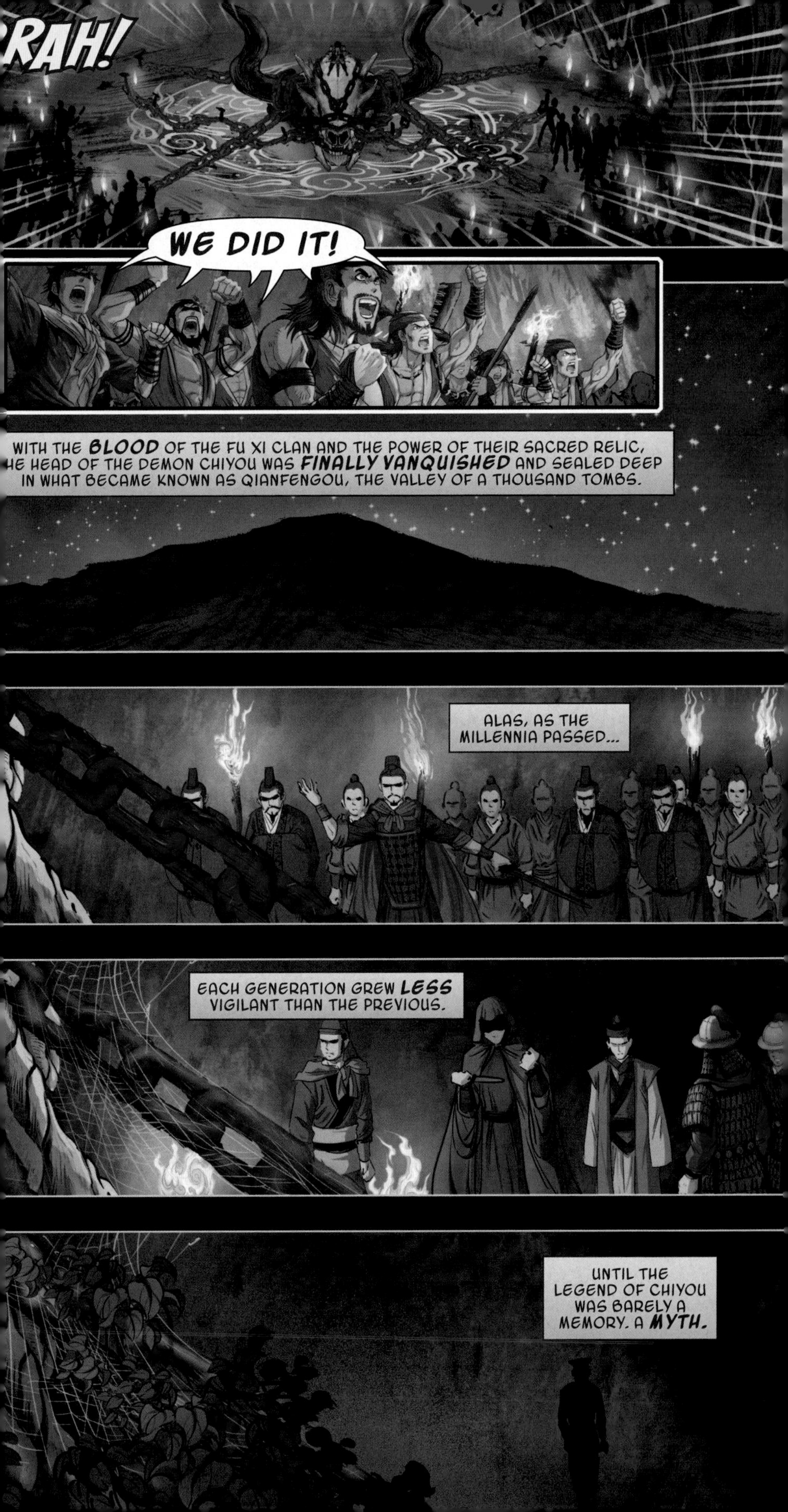

RAH!
WE DID IT!
WITH THE BLOOD OF THE FU XI CLAN AND THE POWER OF THEIR SACRED RELIC, HE HEAD OF THE DEMON CHIYOU WAS FINALLY VANQUISHED AND SEALED DEEP IN WHAT BECAME KNOWN AS QIANFENGOU, THE VALLEY OF A THOUSAND TOMBS.
ALAS, AS THE MILLENNIA PASSED...
EACH GENERATION GREW LESS VIGILANT THAN THE PREVIOUS.
UNTIL THE LEGEND OF CHIYOU WAS BARELY A MEMORY. A MYTH.

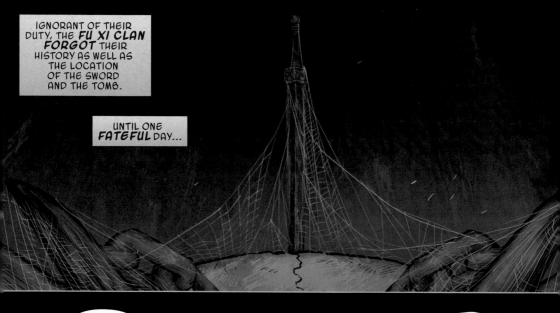

IGNORANT OF THEIR DUTY, THE **FU XI CLAN FORGOT** THEIR HISTORY AS WELL AS THE LOCATION OF THE SWORD AND THE TOMB.

UNTIL ONE **FATEFUL** DAY...

STOP! PLEASE, YOU CAN'T DO THIS!

SOMEONE SHUT THIS GUY UP...

WHACK

AAAAH! THIS IS A PLACE OF ARCHAEOLOGICAL SIGNIFICANCE. I HAVE GOVERNMENT PERMITS TO PROVE IT...

SORRY, OLD MAN...

SHKK

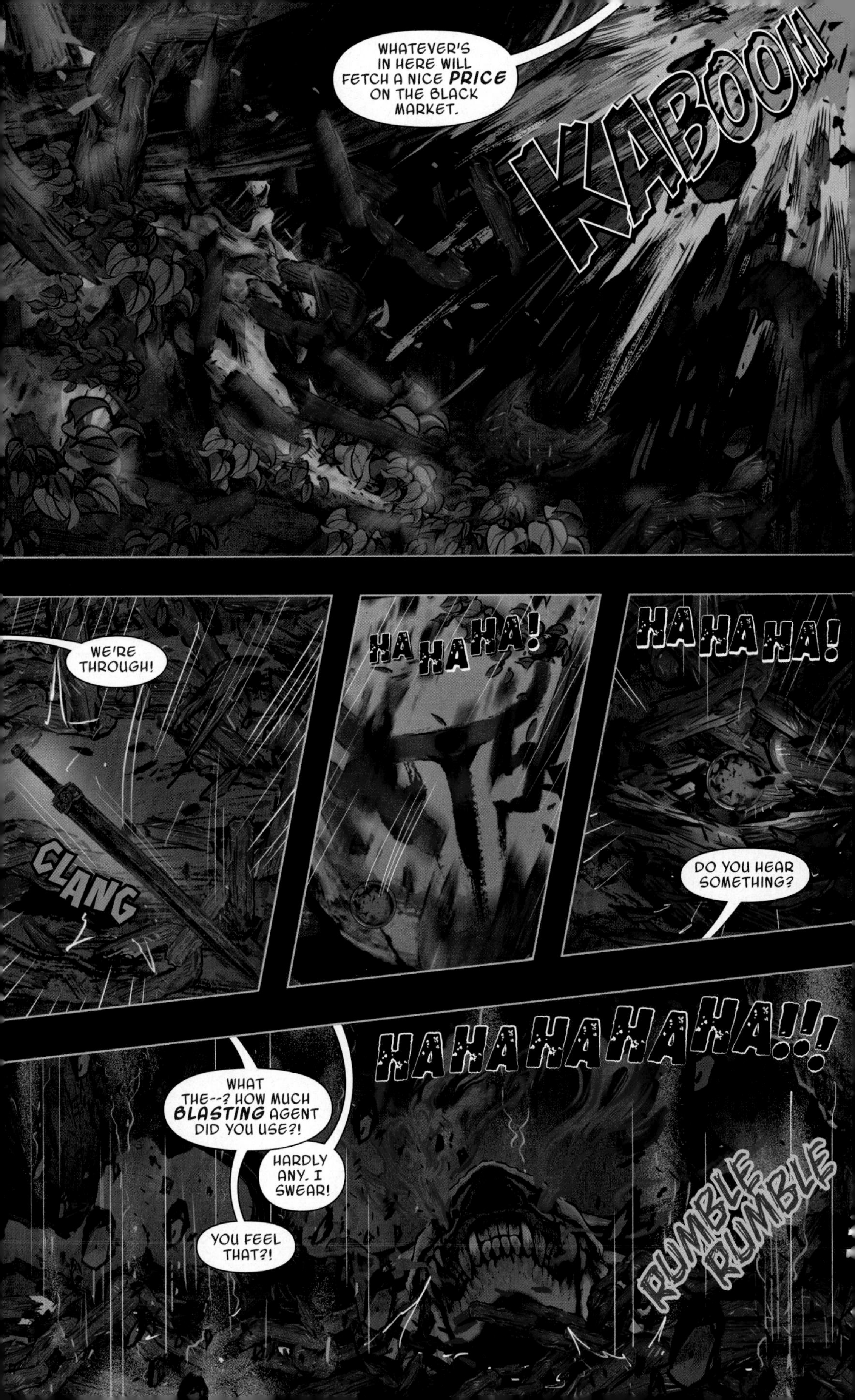
WHATEVER'S IN HERE WILL FETCH A NICE PRICE ON THE BLACK MARKET.
KABOOM
WE'RE THROUGH!
CLANG
HA HA HA HA!
HA HA HA HA!
DO YOU HEAR SOMETHING?
HA HA HA HA HA HA HA!!!
WHAT THE--? HOW MUCH BLASTING AGENT DID YOU USE?!
HARDLY ANY. I SWEAR!
YOU FEEL THAT?!
RUMBLE RUMBLE

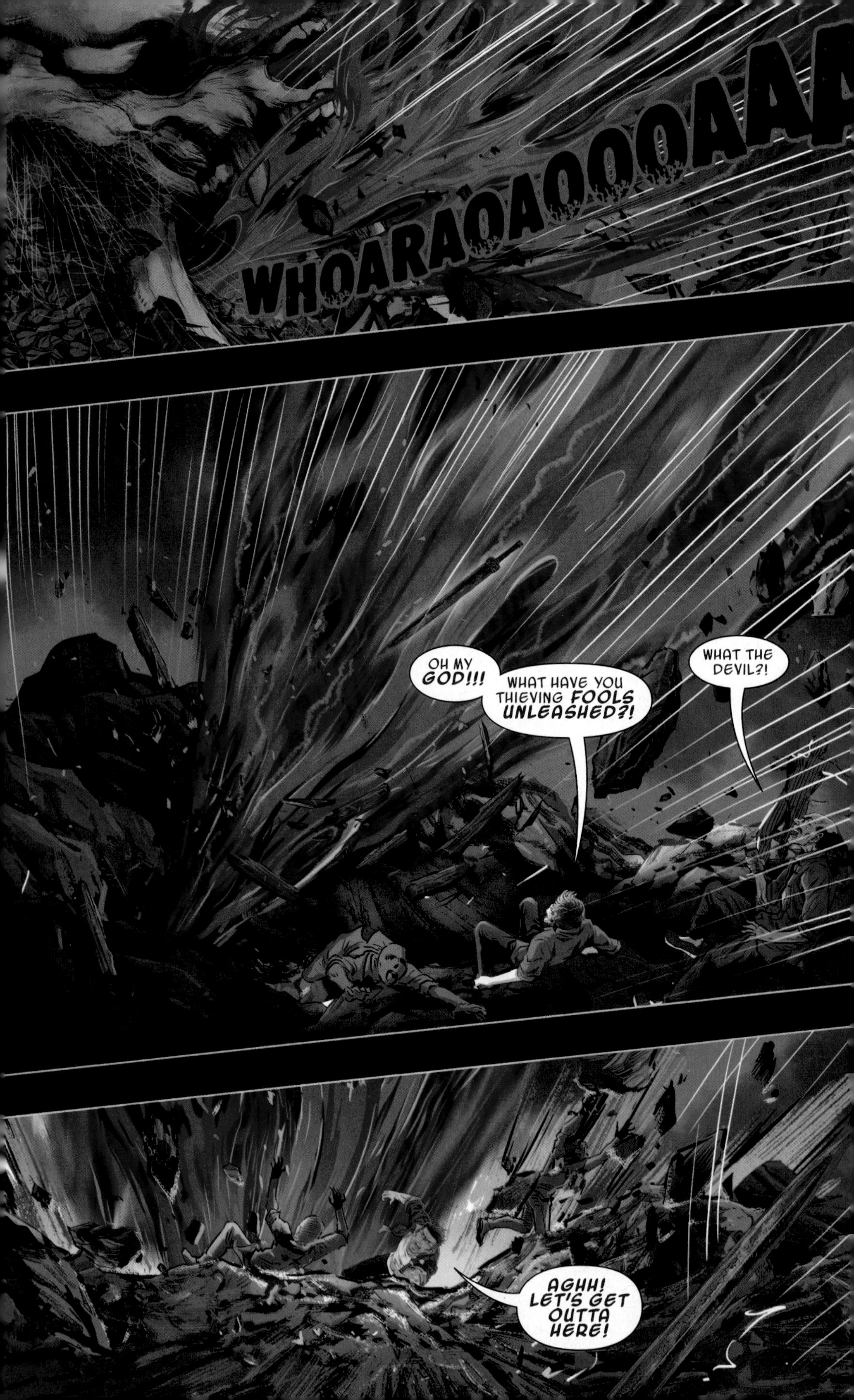
WHOARAOAOOOAAA
OH MY GOD!!!
WHAT HAVE YOU THIEVING FOOLS UNLEASHED?!
WHAT THE DEVIL?!
AGHH! LET'S GET OUTTA HERE!

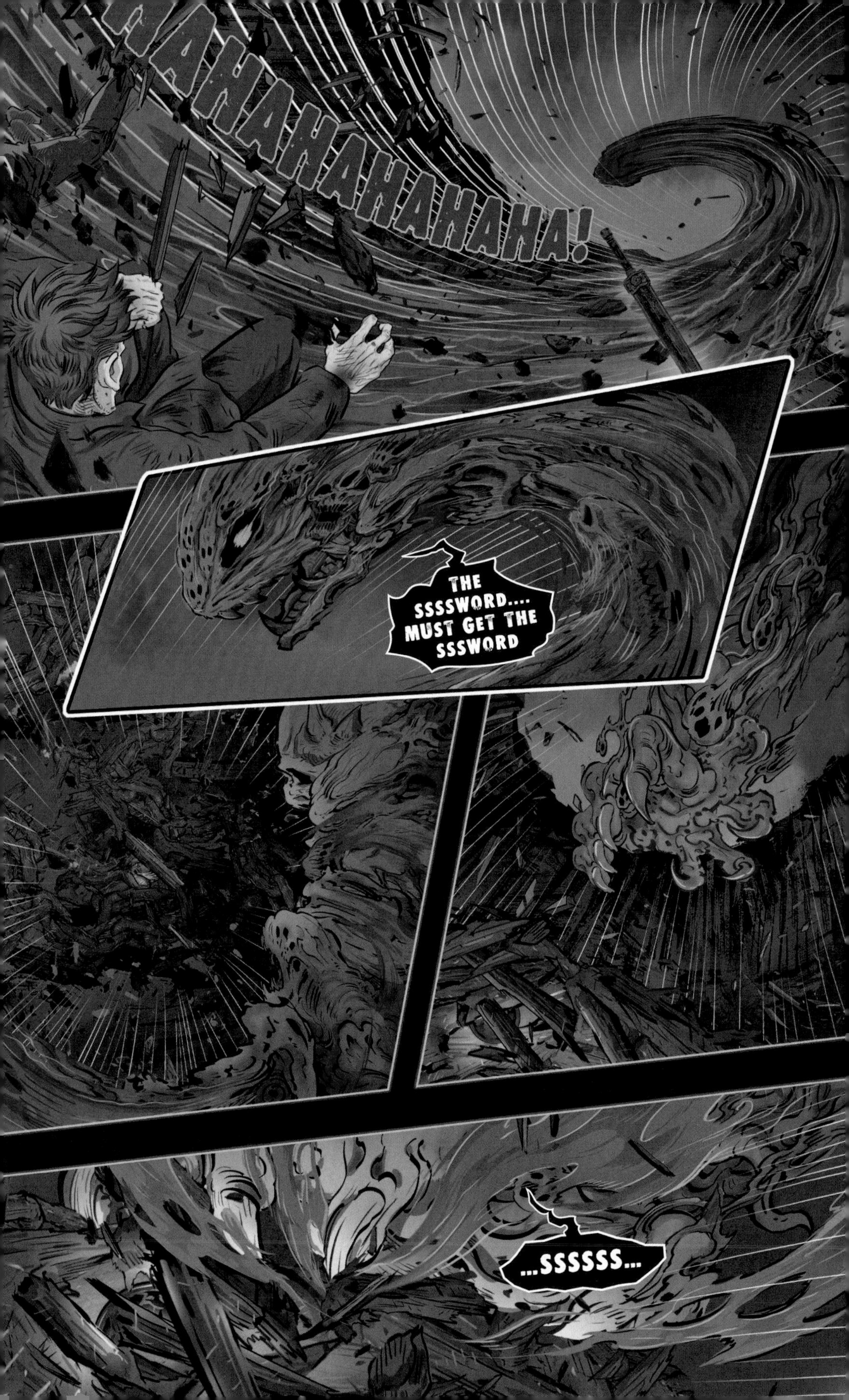
HAHAHAHAHAHAHAHAHA!
THE SSSSWORD.... MUST GET THE SSSWORD
...SSSSSS...

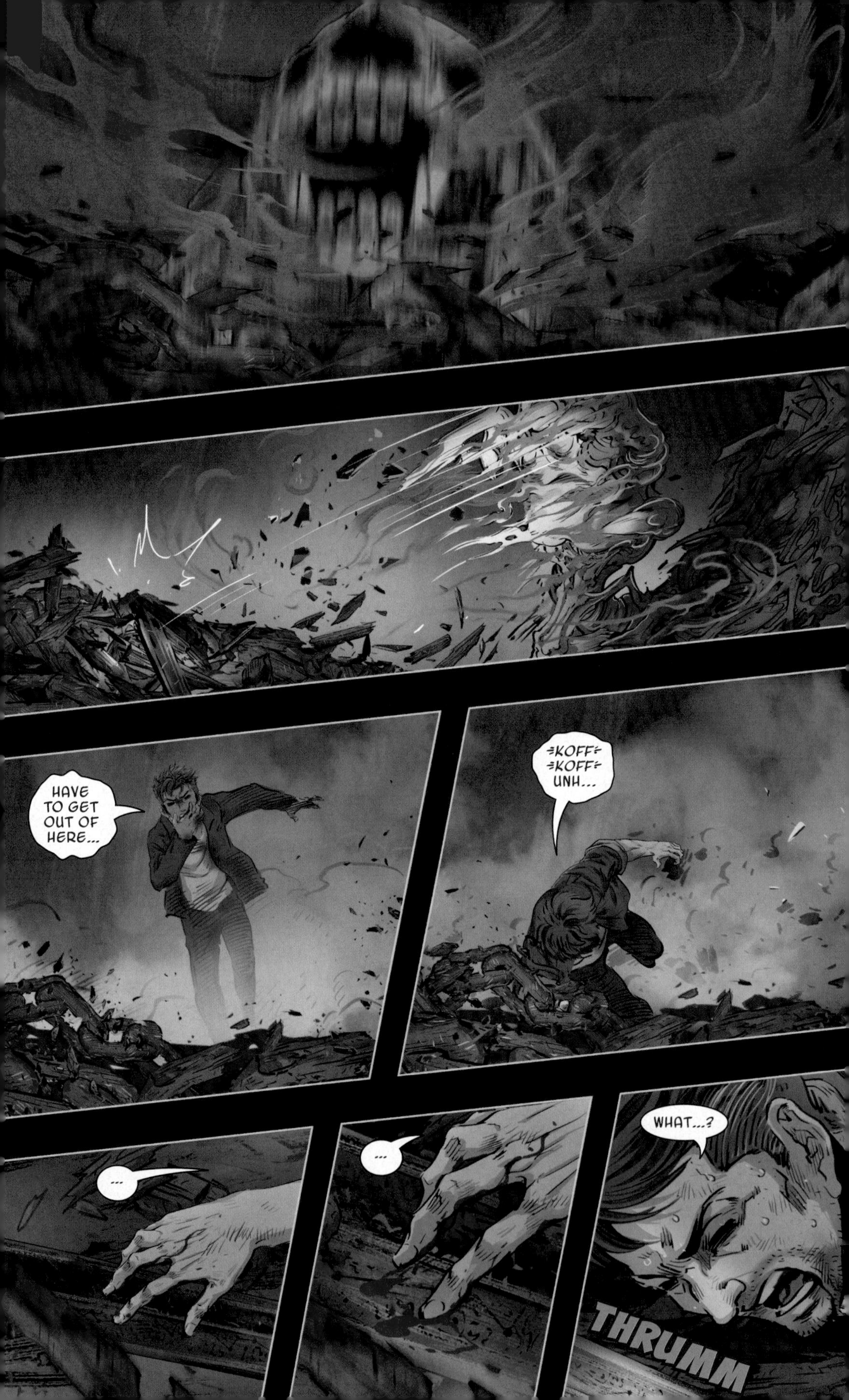
HAVE TO GET OUT OF HERE...
KOFF KOFF UNH...
...
...
WHAT...?
THRUMM

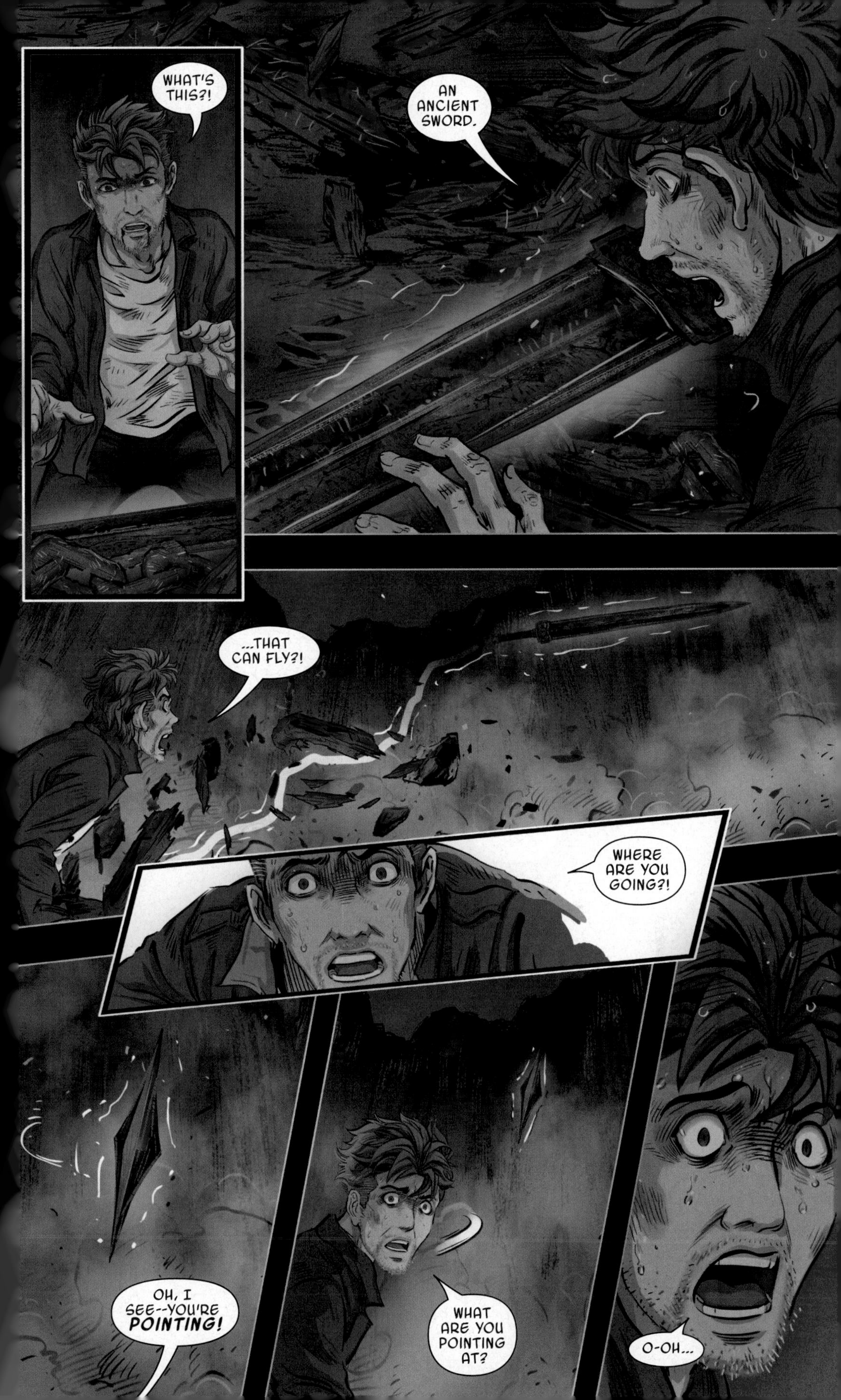
WHAT'S THIS?!
AN ANCIENT SWORD.
...THAT CAN FLY?!
WHERE ARE YOU GOING?!
OH, I SEE--YOU'RE **POINTING!**
WHAT ARE YOU POINTING AT?
O-OH...

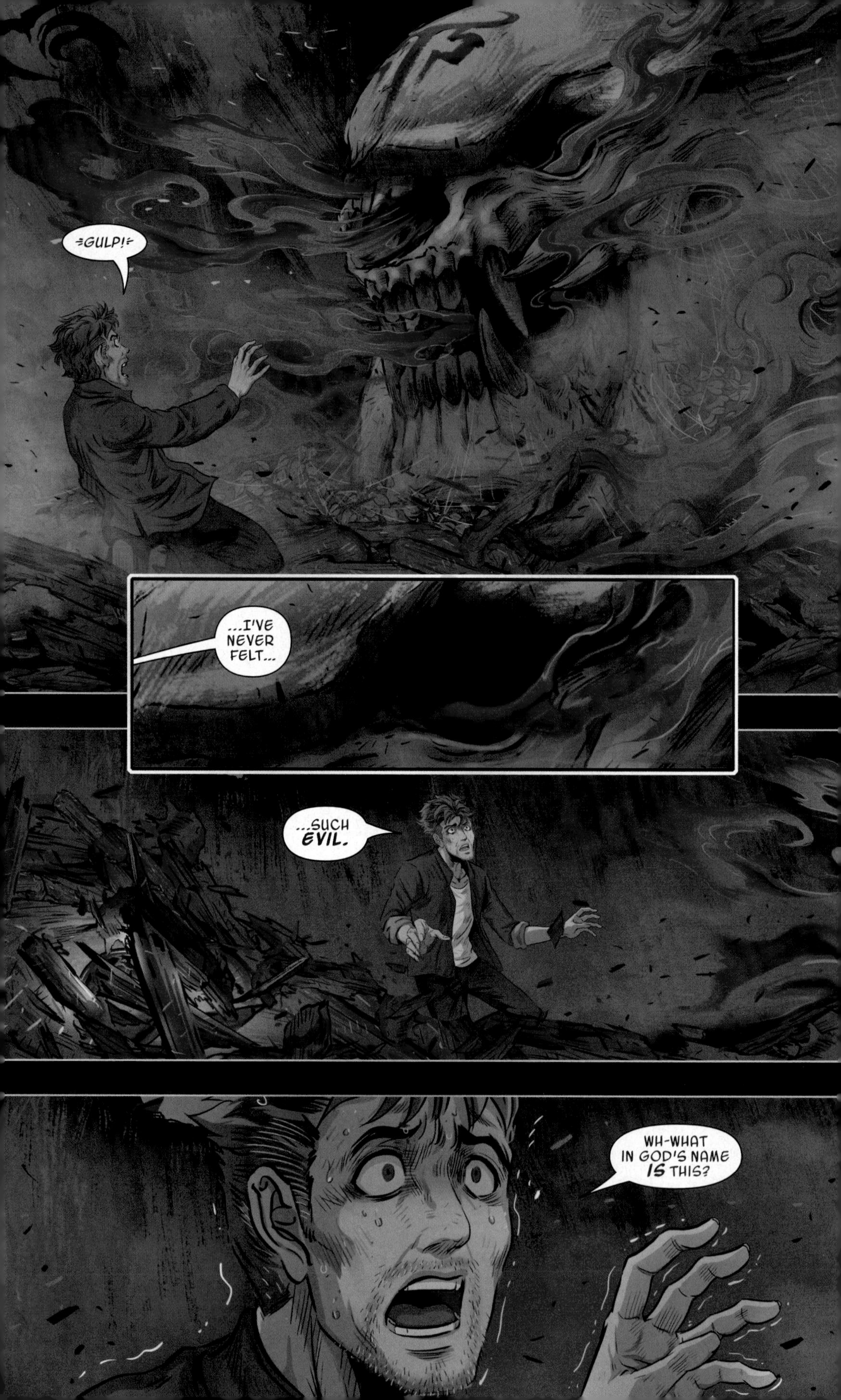

=GULP!=
...I'VE NEVER FELT...
...SUCH EVIL.
WH-WHAT IN GOD'S NAME IS THIS?

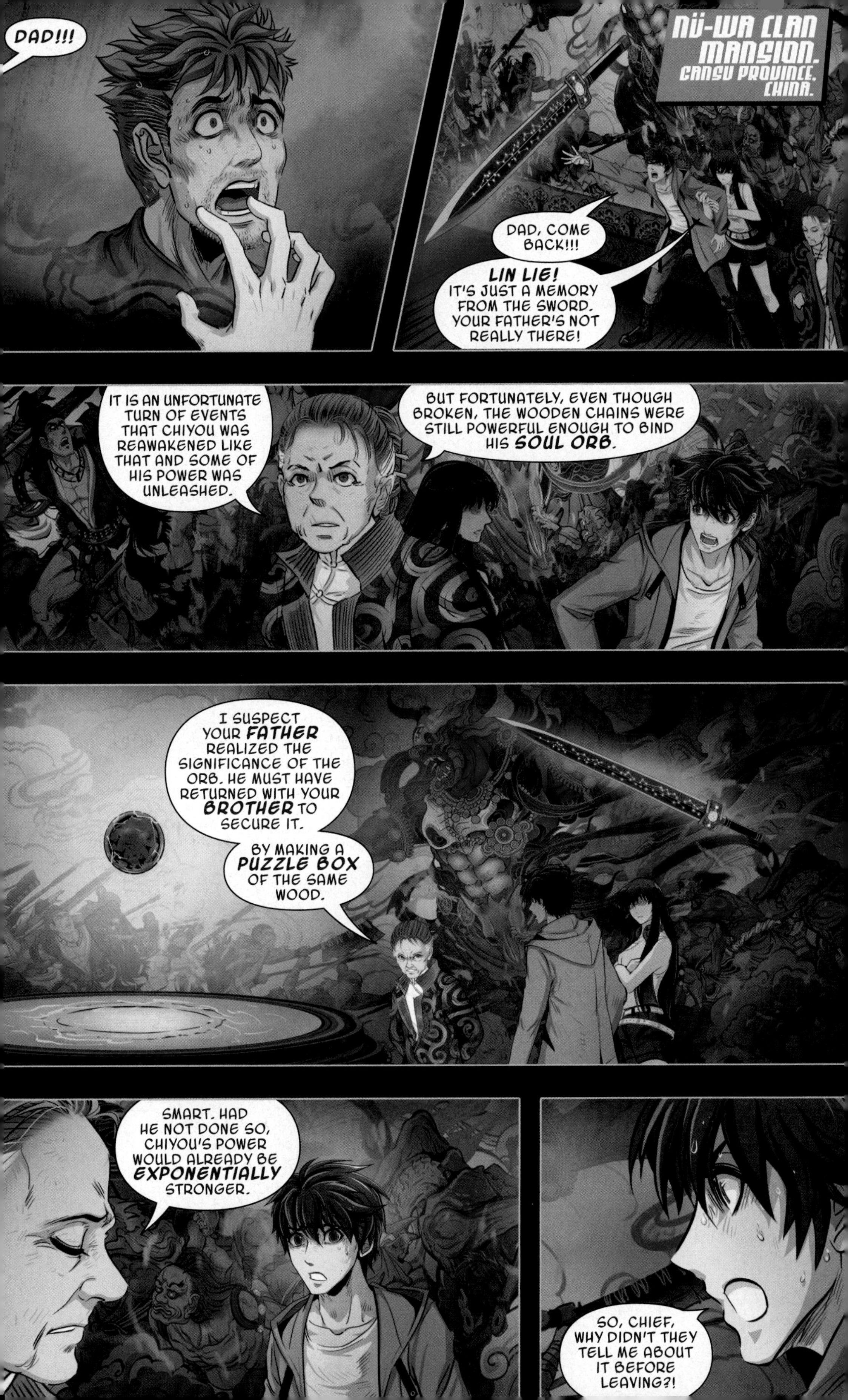
DAD!!!
NÜ-WA CLAN MANSION. GANSU PROVINCE. CHINA.
DAD, COME BACK!!!
LIN LIE! IT'S JUST A MEMORY FROM THE SWORD. YOUR FATHER'S NOT REALLY THERE!
IT IS AN UNFORTUNATE TURN OF EVENTS THAT CHIYOU WAS REAWAKENED LIKE THAT AND SOME OF HIS POWER WAS UNLEASHED.
BUT FORTUNATELY, EVEN THOUGH BROKEN, THE WOODEN CHAINS WERE STILL POWERFUL ENOUGH TO BIND HIS SOUL ORB.
I SUSPECT YOUR FATHER REALIZED THE SIGNIFICANCE OF THE ORB. HE MUST HAVE RETURNED WITH YOUR BROTHER TO SECURE IT.
BY MAKING A PUZZLE BOX OF THE SAME WOOD.
SMART. HAD HE NOT DONE SO, CHIYOU'S POWER WOULD ALREADY BE EXPONENTIALLY STRONGER.
SO, CHIEF, WHY DIDN'T THEY TELL ME ABOUT IT BEFORE LEAVING?!

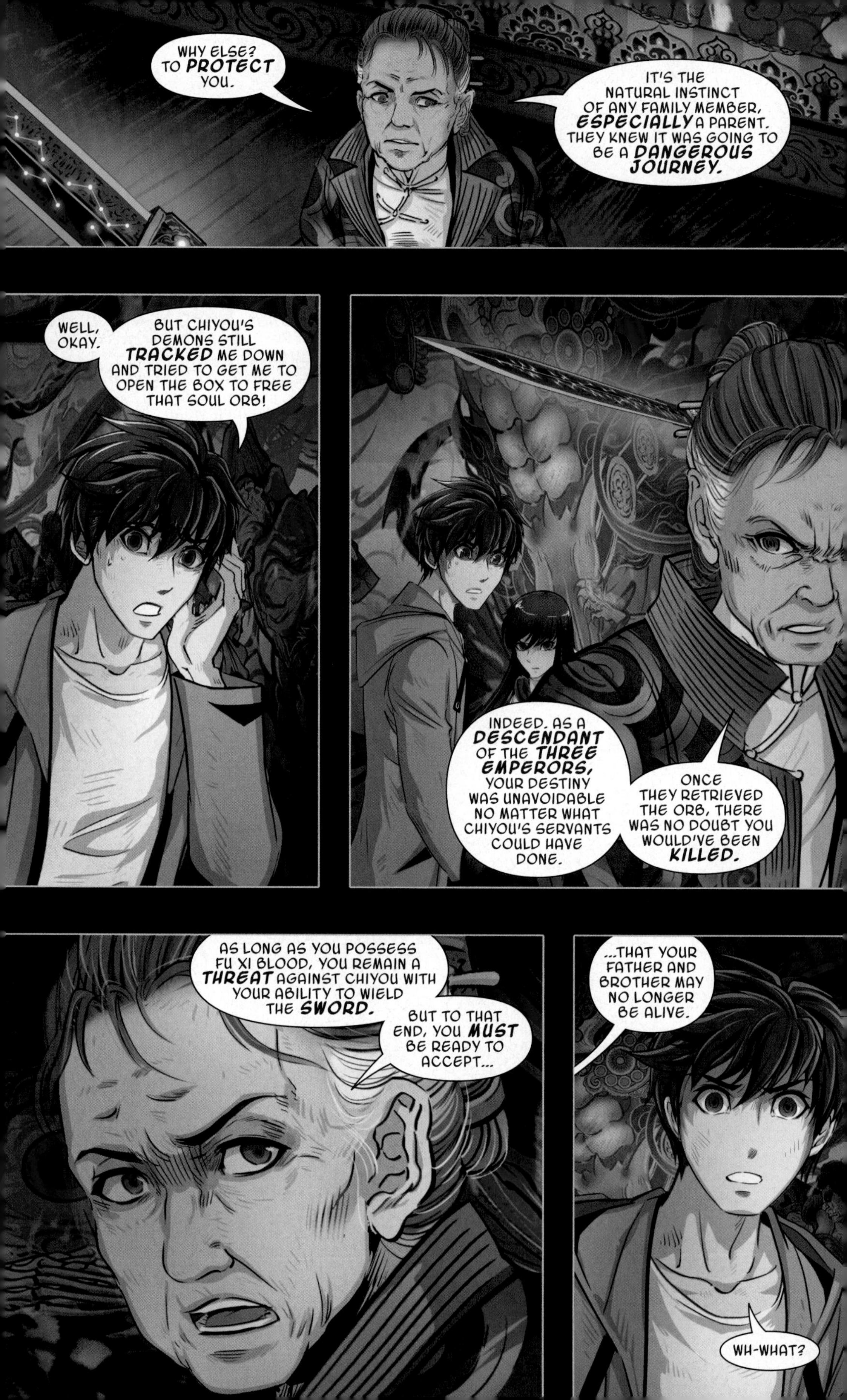
WHY ELSE? TO PROTECT YOU.
IT'S THE NATURAL INSTINCT OF ANY FAMILY MEMBER, ESPECIALLY A PARENT. THEY KNEW IT WAS GOING TO BE A DANGEROUS JOURNEY.
WELL, OKAY.
BUT CHIYOU'S DEMONS STILL TRACKED ME DOWN AND TRIED TO GET ME TO OPEN THE BOX TO FREE THAT SOUL ORB!
INDEED. AS A DESCENDANT OF THE THREE EMPERORS, YOUR DESTINY WAS UNAVOIDABLE NO MATTER WHAT CHIYOU'S SERVANTS COULD HAVE DONE.
ONCE THEY RETRIEVED THE ORB, THERE WAS NO DOUBT YOU WOULD'VE BEEN KILLED.
AS LONG AS YOU POSSESS FU XI BLOOD, YOU REMAIN A THREAT AGAINST CHIYOU WITH YOUR ABILITY TO WIELD THE SWORD.
BUT TO THAT END, YOU MUST BE READY TO ACCEPT...
...THAT YOUR FATHER AND BROTHER MAY NO LONGER BE ALIVE.
WH-WHAT?

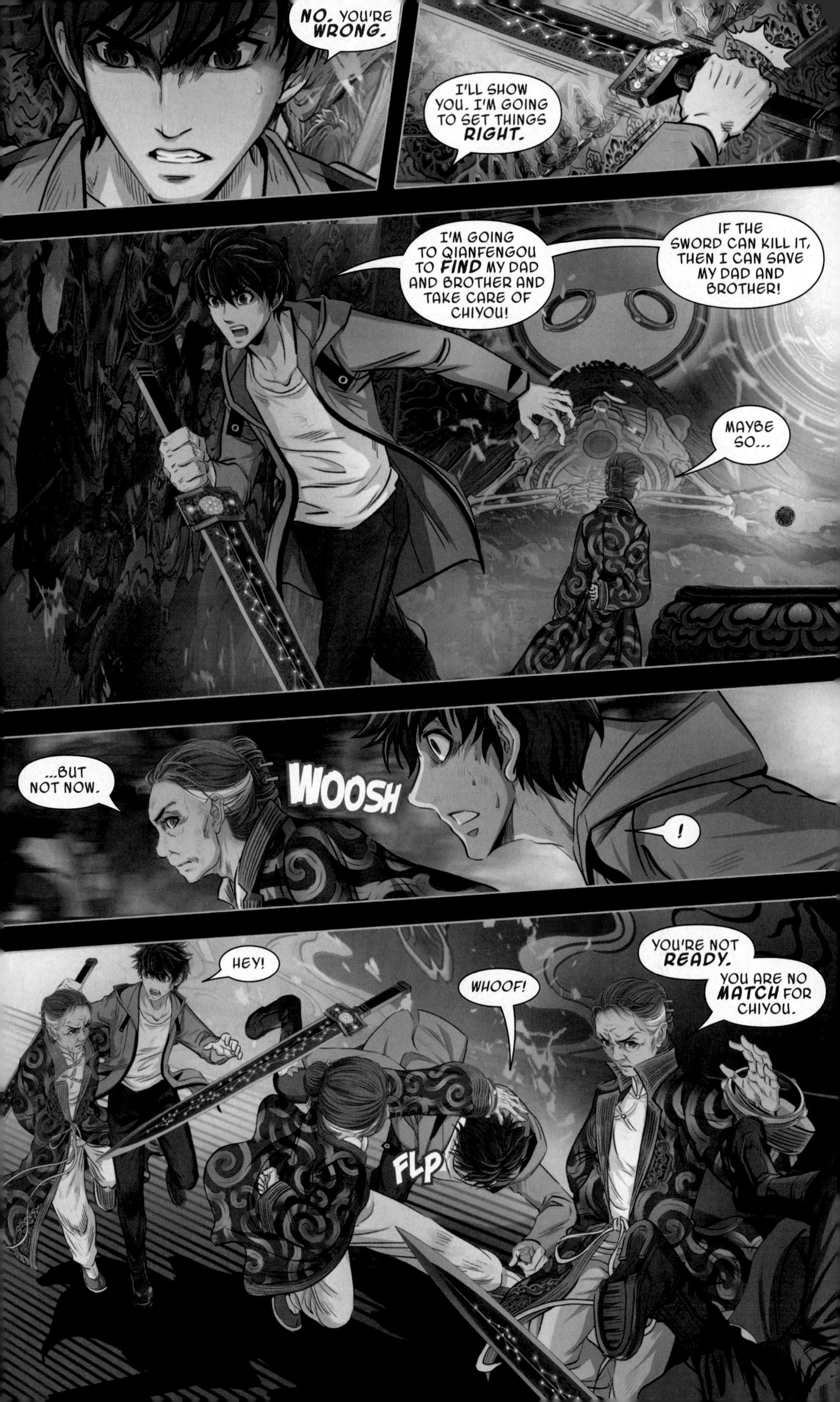
NO. YOU'RE WRONG.
I'LL SHOW YOU. I'M GOING TO SET THINGS RIGHT.
I'M GOING TO QIANFENGOU TO FIND MY DAD AND BROTHER AND TAKE CARE OF CHIYOU!
IF THE SWORD CAN KILL IT, THEN I CAN SAVE MY DAD AND BROTHER!
MAYBE SO...
...BUT NOT NOW.
WOOSH
!
HEY!
WHOOF!
YOU'RE NOT READY.
YOU ARE NO MATCH FOR CHIYOU.
FLP

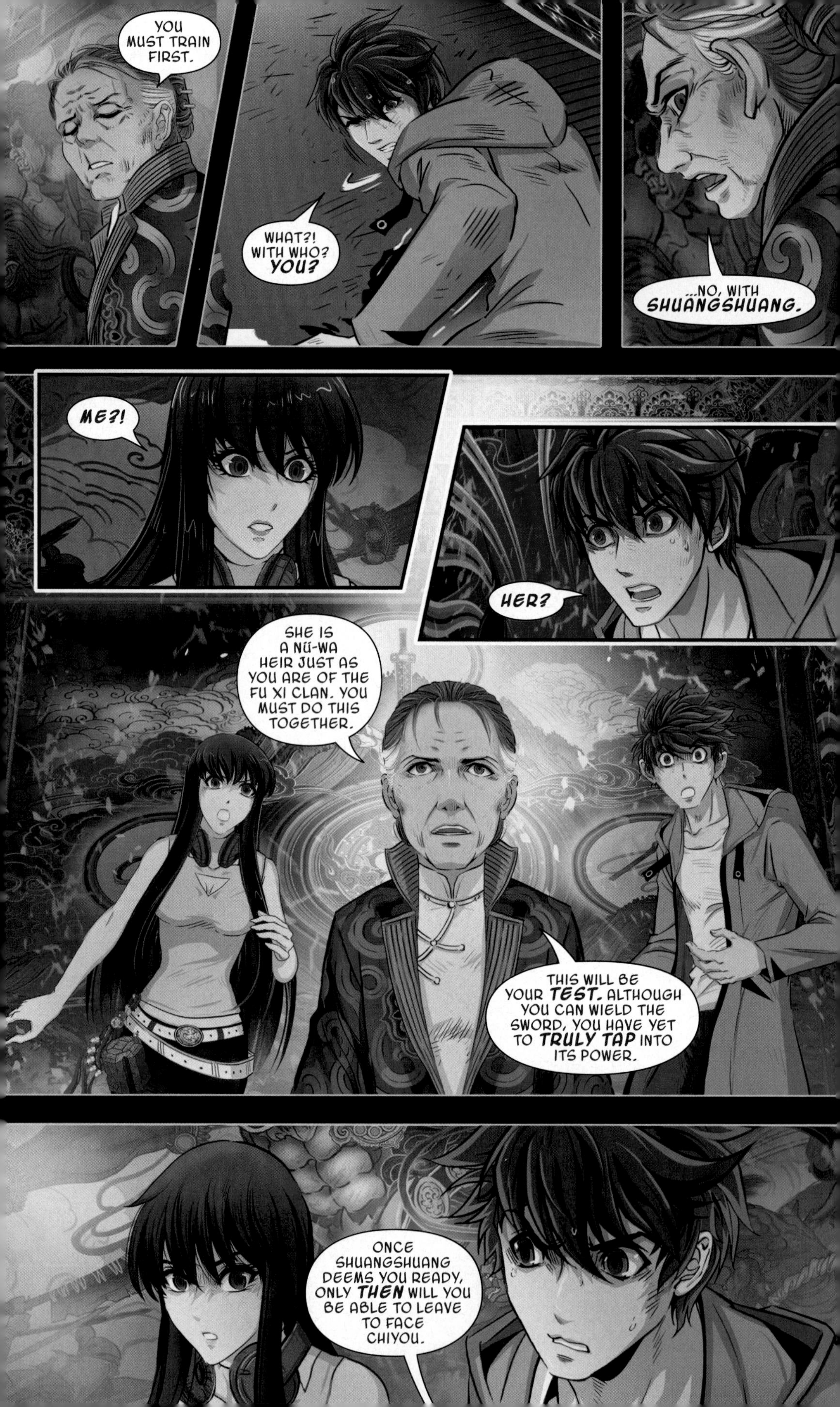
YOU MUST TRAIN FIRST.
WHAT?! WITH WHO? YOU?
...NO, WITH SHUANGSHUANG.
ME?!
HER?
SHE IS A NÜ-WA HEIR JUST AS YOU ARE OF THE FU XI CLAN. YOU MUST DO THIS TOGETHER.
THIS WILL BE YOUR TEST. ALTHOUGH YOU CAN WIELD THE SWORD, YOU HAVE YET TO TRULY TAP INTO ITS POWER.
ONCE SHUANGSHUANG DEEMS YOU READY, ONLY THEN WILL YOU BE ABLE TO LEAVE TO FACE CHIYOU.

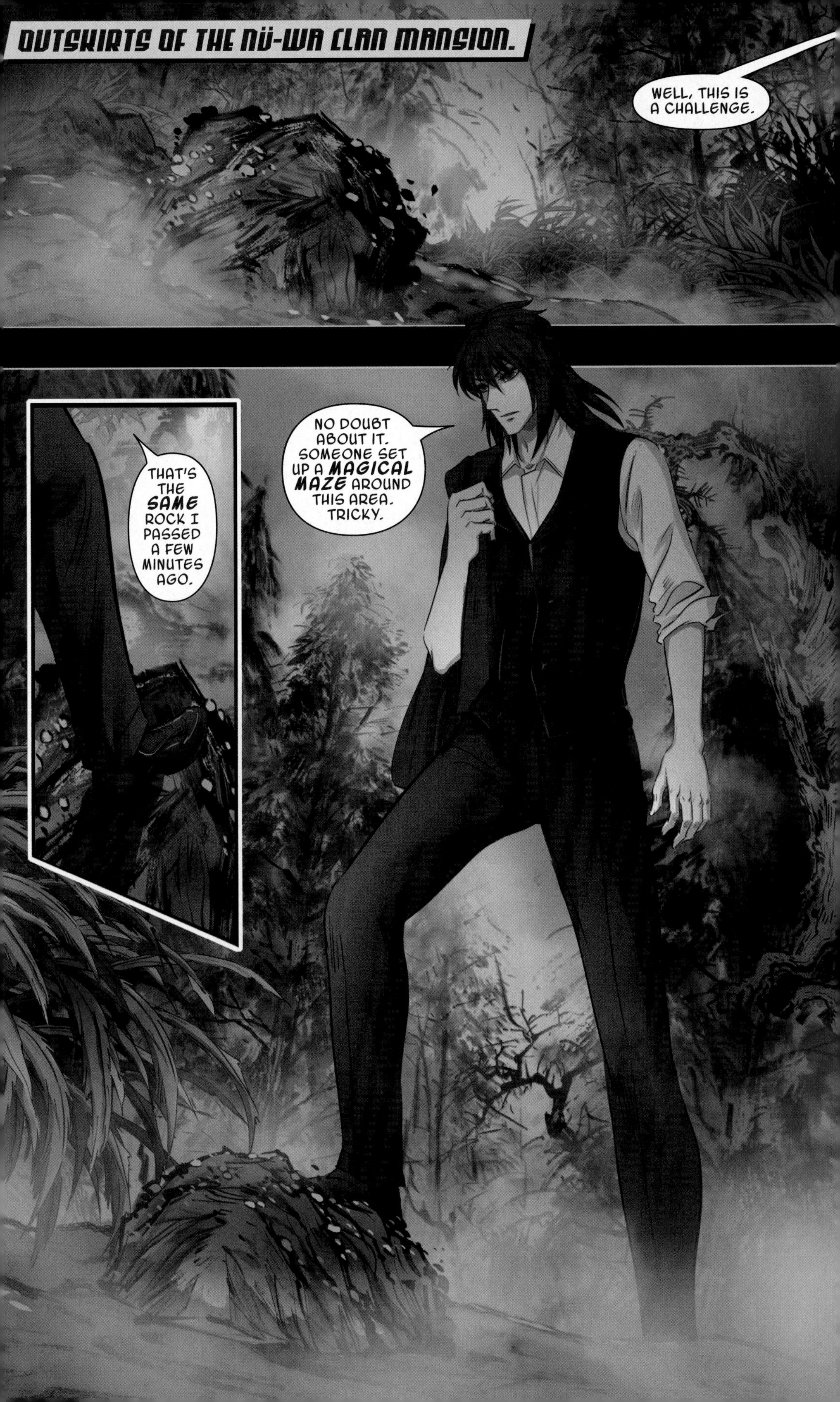

OUTSKIRTS OF THE NÜ-WA CLAN MANSION.
WELL, THIS IS A CHALLENGE.
THAT'S THE SAME ROCK I PASSED A FEW MINUTES AGO.
NO DOUBT ABOUT IT. SOMEONE SET UP A MAGICAL MAZE AROUND THIS AREA. TRICKY.

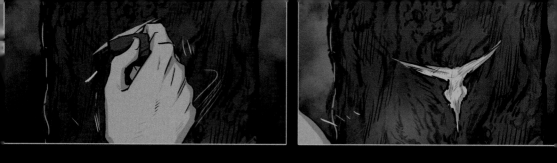

I SHOULD BE GETTING CLOSER TO THE END THOUGH.

AH, HERE IT IS.

I HOPE THEY DON'T MIND. I AM EAGER TO SEE MY LITTLE BROTHER, AFTER ALL.

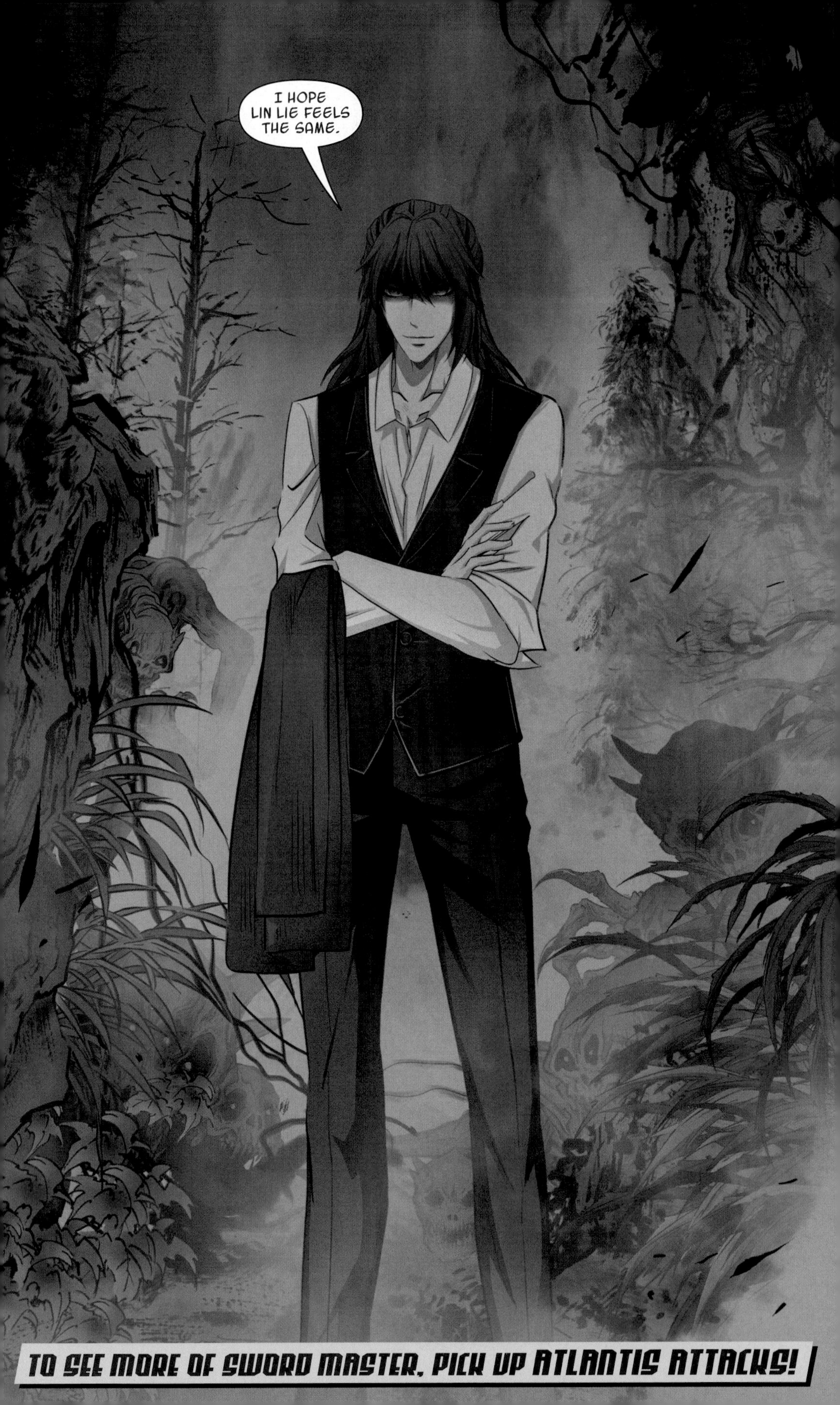
I HOPE LIN LIE FEELS THE SAME.
TO SEE MORE OF SWORD MASTER, PICK UP ATLANTIS ATTACKS!

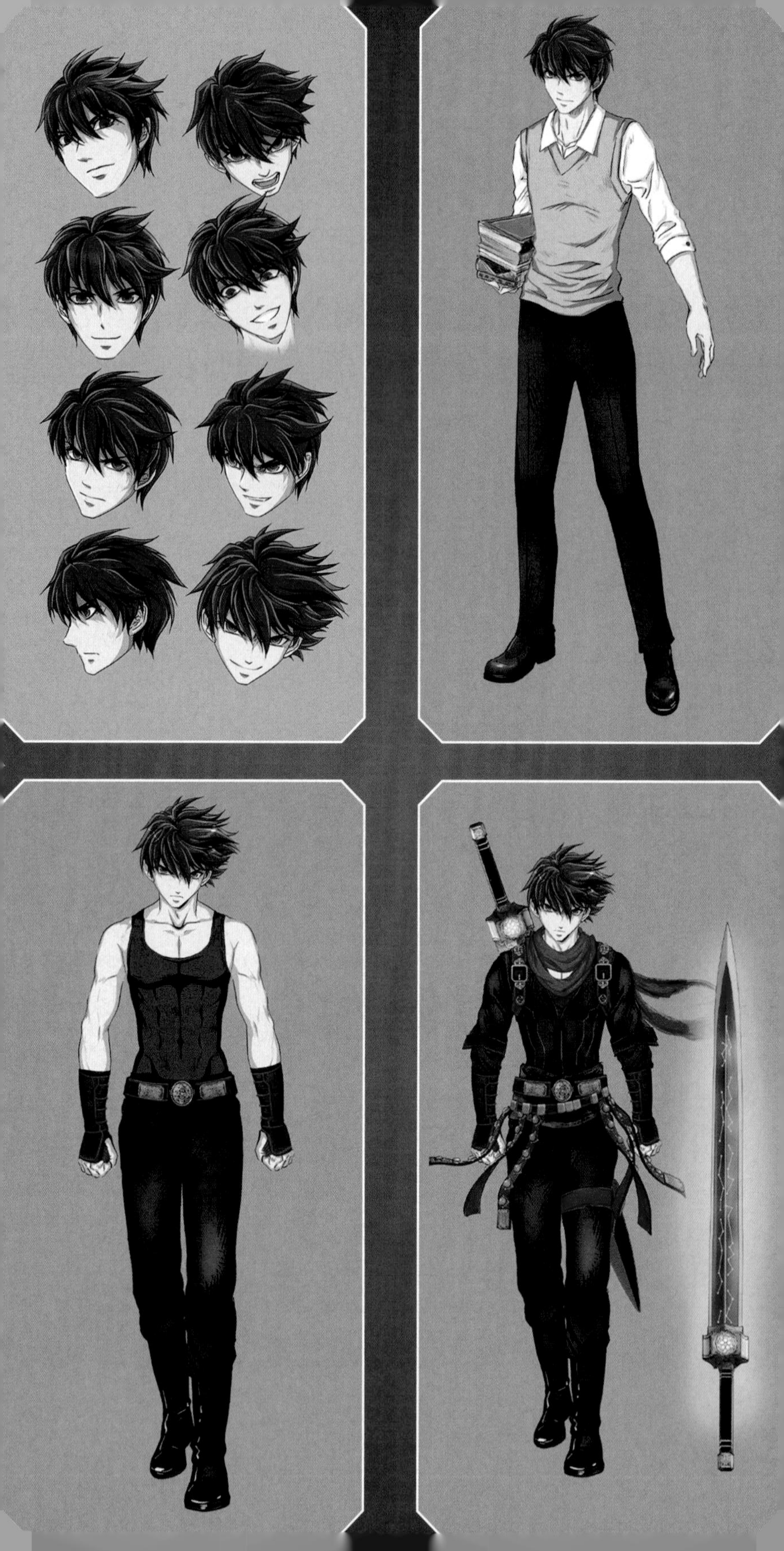

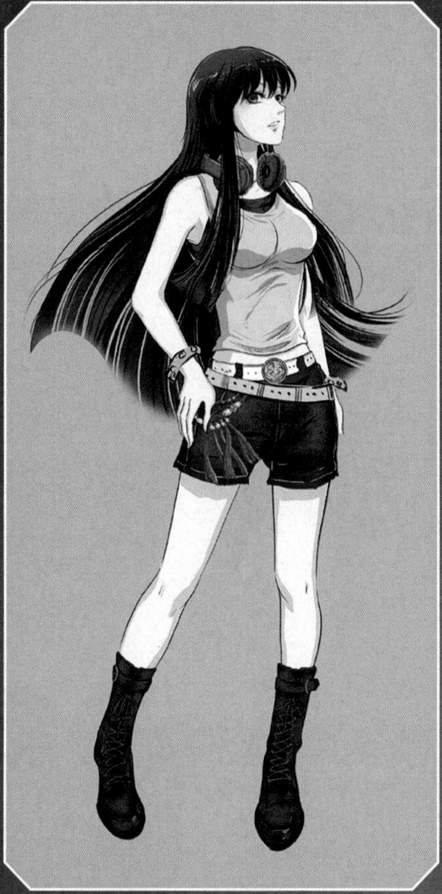

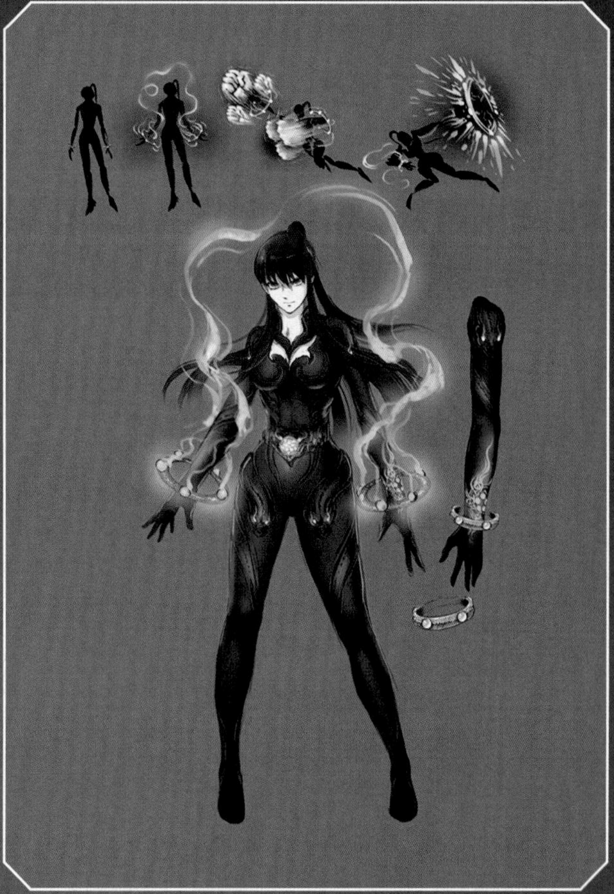

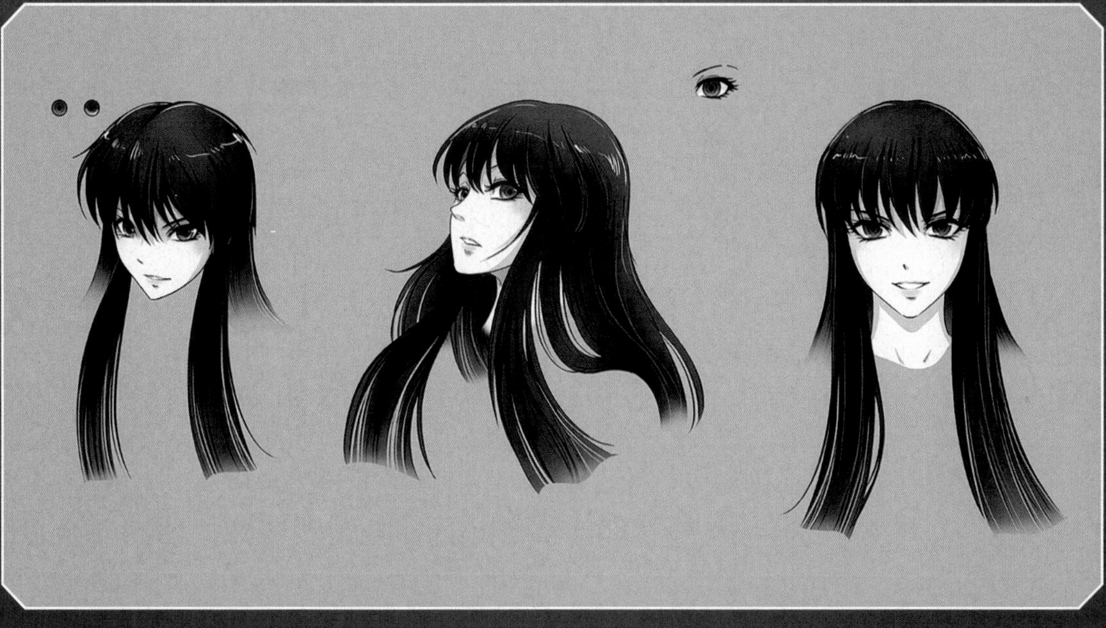

CHARACTER DESIGNS BY
GUNJI

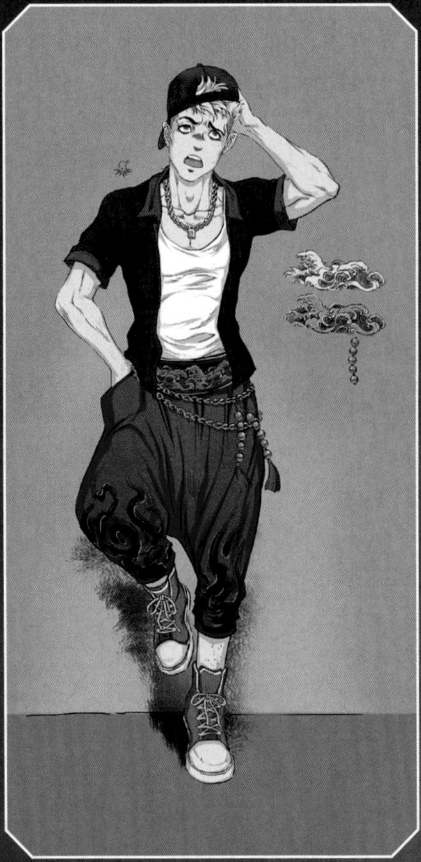
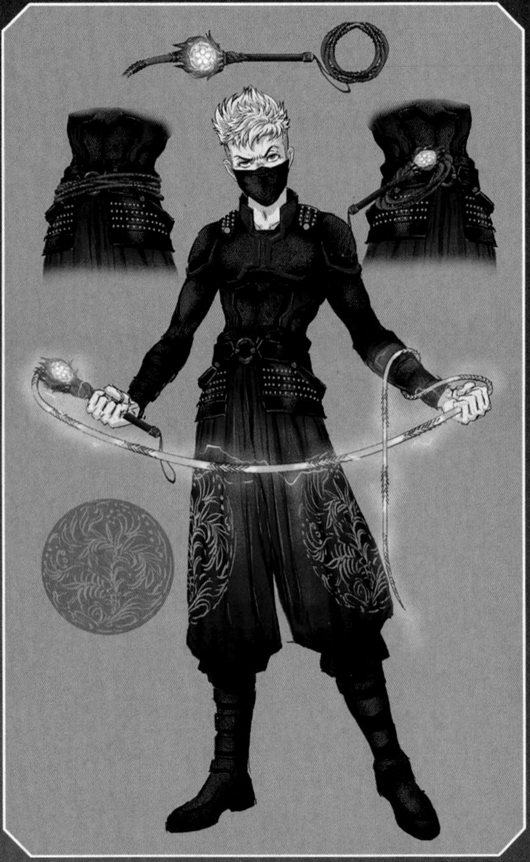
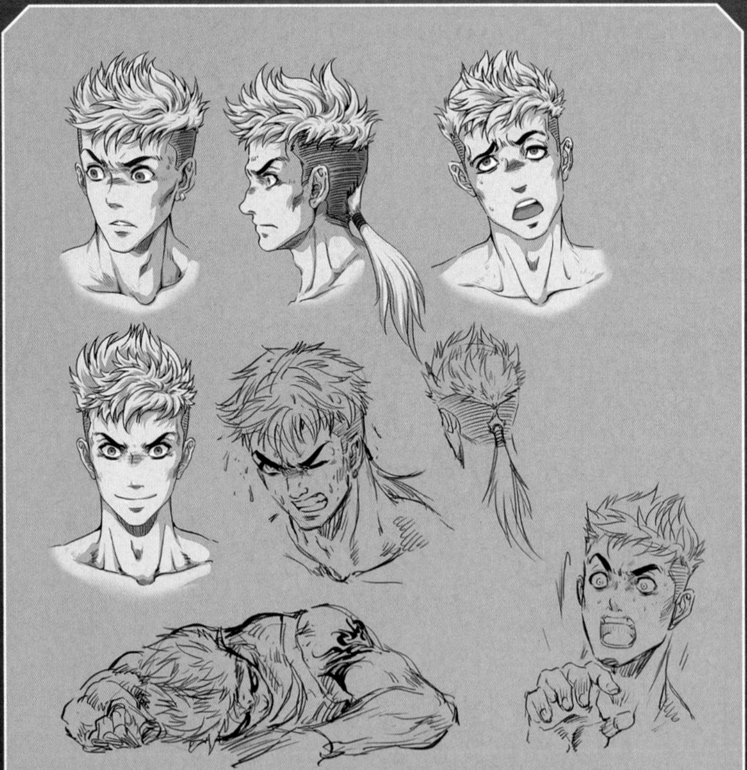

CHARACTER DESIGNS BY
GUNJI